Into the Wind

INTO THE WIND

Personal Reflections on the Early Years of
Golden Gate Baptist Theological Seminary

Harold K. Graves

BROADMAN PRESS
Nashville, Tennessee

© Copyright 1983 • BROADMAN PRESS
All rights reserved.
4265-74

ISBN: 0-8054-6574-X
Dewey Decimal Classification: 286.06
Subject Heading: GOLDEN GATE BAPTIST THEOLOGICAL
SEMINARY—HISTORY

Library of Congress Catalog Card Number: 82-74207
Printed in the United States of America

To my colleagues
trustees, faculty, staff, and students
whose dedication and labor made dreams
come true

Preface

During the last years of my tenure as president of Golden Gate Baptist Seminary, several trustees expressed interest in my writing an account of the beginning and development of the seminary through my period of service. As I neared retirement, the trustees took official action to commission me for the task. No time limit was set, so the pace has sometimes seemed slow as other activities claimed my time and attention. The task of gathering and recording the story has been most enjoyable. I was never bored, was usually stimulated, and was often exhausted as I relived some difficult times.

In the initial effort, I tried to put everything down as I found it in catalogs, minutes, and other publications. The memories of others and my own recollections were mined for unrecorded happenings. Anyone beginning to tell of the life of an institution is soon faced with the fact that he can only record *a* history and not *the* history. Objectivity is impossible in the selection of persons and events to be included. Choices have to be made that reflect the principal theme or emphasis the author has in mind. Another writer might well select characters and incidents that would present quite a different picture. The whole story can never be told. What is written here reflects my own viewpoint.

Many people have rendered invaluable service in providing material, clarifying details, and sharpening the end product. I knew well my two predecessors, Isam Hodges and B. O. Herring. Floyd Looney, who has known California Southern Baptists from the early forties, was most helpful in written and spoken word. Robert Hughes, as pastor, state convention executive director, and sometime seminary trustee since the late forties, was an interested contributor.

The late W. A. Carleton was invaluable in clarifying many happenings and issues from his long years in California. Only his untimely death prevented his being more heavily involved in the process.

Guy Rutland, Jr., and Floyd Golden gave valuable insights from the early fifties and the beginnings of the Southern Baptist Convention's operation of the seminary. Other colleagues among trustees, faculty, and staff have been most generous with suggestions and encouragement. President William Pinson, Jr., was supportive in every way. Mrs. Wanda Inglish's work in the preparation of this manuscript is greatly appreciated. The contributions of so many people have not been properly acknowledged, and many significant incidents have not been mentioned.

Stanton Nash's professionalism in so many areas was illustrated in part by the quality of materials that came from his office. Gene England's labors that kept him at his post after "quitting time" more nights than not held the operation together. Isma Martin built an integrity into the registrar's office that everyone came to rely upon. Paul Mason was so helpful in Berkeley and in the development of the new campus. Some capable and devoted women served as my secretaries when I was president of the seminary. Especially to be noted are Mary Jo (Lewis) Key, Sharon Nicholson, Hazel Mansfield, Wanda Inglish, and Bonnie Chappell. Other support staff across the years made contributions in labor and concern that cannot be measured.

Faculty members and their families have served far beyond the call of duty at the task for which the seminary exists. Books and denominational curriculum materials have been produced by almost every professor.

Many fine students have served in leadership roles in campus activities, in student government, in clubs, in conference promotion, and in musical organizations. Faculty and students alike have caused churches to begin and to grow.

To all these and dozens more who go unnamed, I say a hearty thank you! I am especially grateful to my wife, Frieda, for her patience, frank evaluations, and the needed encouragement which she offered in proper balance.

Golden Gate Seminary has a thrilling heritage, an exciting history, and a challenging future. I am grateful to have been a part of her story. May the product of this joint effort bring honor to God whom we serve, encouragement to those who now serve in the seminary we love, and advancement to the kingdom of our Lord whom we adore.

February 16, 1981   HAROLD K. GRAVES

Introduction

Some years ago there appeared in the press a story about courage on a Pacific isle. During a refueling stop for a plane on an international flight, a hurricane struck. The pilots are reported to have struggled through powerful winds to reboard their plane. Then throughout the storm they steadfastly kept the aircraft, though sitting on the ground, headed into the wind. Their heroics were credited with saving the plane.

Anyone acquainted with how an airplane flies is aware that it takes off *into the wind*. Force works against force to produce the lift necessary for the plane to fly. I see in this phenomenon an analogy to the beginning of Southern Baptists' seminary on the West Coast. The struggle seemed at times to be against almost impossible odds. This is reflected in its efforts to gain a place in the minds and hearts of Southern Baptists. It is seen in the development of an institutional and academic identity in higher and theological educational circles. It is shown in the growth of its status in its immediate community and environment.

Men and women of vision and dedication set the seminary on its course *into the wind*. Others have added fuel for the climb to proper altitude and direction.

Golden Gate graduates have labored in the churches, in denominational activities, and one third of them in mission service at home and abroad. God's infinite wisdom and power have made triumphs possible. The following pages recount a part of that story.

Contents

1
Baptist Beginnings in California

The earliest accounts of contact with the western shores of the American continent reveal a fascination with the land that became the state of California. When the government of Mexico formally ceded it to the United States by the Treaty of Guadalupe Hidalgo, February 2, 1848, interest increased throughout the nation.

It seems appropriate in recounting the story of Golden Gate Baptist Theological Seminary to start with a brief account of Baptist beginnings in that very fascinating period at the middle of the nineteenth century. Both the Board of Domestic Missions of the Southern Baptist Convention (SBC) and the American Baptist Home Mission Society of Northern Baptists considered sending missionaries to California. The first missionaries to California, the Reverend and Mrs. Osgood C. Wheeler (Northern Baptists), arrived in February, 1849. That was one year before California became a state.

Osgood C. Wheeler, pastor of the First Baptist Church of Jersey City, New Jersey, attended a Monday morning minister's meeting at the First Baptist Church of New York City on November 1, 1848. He was summoned to the office of Dr. Hill, secretary of the American Baptist Home Mission Society. Dr. Hill greeted Wheeler with, "We want you to go to California as our pioneer missionary."[1] Wheeler was contacted daily for the next sixteen days. Many prominent pastors and others urged his acceptance. S. H. Cone, pastor of First Baptist Church, New York City, and president of the society, pressed for an affirmative decision and then went on to say, "But do you know where you are going, my brother? I would rather go as a missionary to China or Cochin China than to San Francisco. Don't you stir a step, my brother, unless you are prepared to go to the darkest spot on earth"(12). On the seventeenth morning, after a sleepless night of prayer, Wheeler and his wife arose to acknowledge God's leadership in directing them to California.

When it was discovered that the steamer *Falcon* would sail on December first instead of the announced twentieth, Secretary Hill thought they could not make it, but Wheeler replied, "After what I have endured, to this point? I would rather go tomorrow morning than give it up, and have the Baptists fail to be as early in the field as the foremost." In fourteen days he resigned his pastorate, settled his business affairs, preached ten sermons, gave three addresses, and made such preparation so that he and his wife were on board the *Falcon* one hour before it sailed at noon December 1, 1848(13).

Their trip took ninety days. They were in New Orleans when they learned of the discovery of gold in California. Their travels were arduous both by sea and land. Many passengers died of cholera or other diseases. Mrs. Wheeler rode a mule across the Isthmus of Panama, the twenty-five miles in ten and one-half hours, "during which time (she) did not once dismount"(14). After thirty-four days they boarded the *California* which, with a capacity of only 210, carried 365. The captain, seeing the crowd desiring passage, said, "I hope to God you haven't any missionaries for me to take"(15). This feeling may have been reflected in the treatment they received during the twenty-eight day trip to San Francisco. They arrived February 28, 1849 on the first steamer ever to enter the harbor(16).

Years later Wheeler wrote a little booklet, "The Story of Early Baptist History in California," published in 1888. As he began to address the California Baptist Historical Society in April, 1889, he quoted a letter received from a lawyer friend in New York. Apparently Wheeler had sent a copy of his manuscript to the lawyer. In part the letter read:

In contemplating the account given . . . in this volume, the profoundest considerations are pressed upon the mind. Gold had slept in the bosom of those mountains, from time immemorial. Spanish occupants of the country had been there a century or more, apparently content with a few vines, and pastoral herds, never dreaming of the hidden gold, nor caring for the richer agricultural wealth of the soil. These pioneers evoked those elements, and transformed a barbarous wilderness into a highly civilized commonwealth; an achievement unparalleled in the annals of man.

. . . The "May-Flower" landed her "Pilgrims" on Plymouth Rock 200 years before these pioneers entered the "Golden Gate," and the results of that event have ever since been celebrated as a marvel of Civilization. But, excepting the promulgation of certain religious tenets, they can no more be compared with the work of these California pioneers, in celebrity of action, in breadth and scope of achievement, in the great march of human progress, than the state of Massachusetts can geographically compare with California. No more than the old mail stagecoach can compare with today's telegram(7,8).

Wheeler said that if his friend were right, then indeed it is a period worthy of consideration. Adding his own evaluation, he described it as "a time and place more full of inventive genius and energized activity, more rapid in commercial development, more diversified in population, more progressive in everything that constitutes national greatness than the world has elsewhere seen"(8).

California was a vast territory more barbaric than Christian. Wheeler stated it in dramatic fashion when he wrote:

In all the broad land there were no vestry meetings, no class meetings, no prayer-meetings, no organization of any kind for moral, social or literary improvement. There was no library, no infirmary, no "home" for the aged and the helpless. None of those institutions that spring up indigenous to a pure Christianity, for the amelioration of human suffering and the glory of God. Absolutely not one(17).

Wheeler described the scene that welcomed them in 1848, then hastened to write of the unfavorable situation for the gospel. The government was weak, "hence the gospel laborers found themselves as little sustained by legal influences and restraints as they would have been in the interior of Africa"(19). There were no helpers to assist the Wheelers for nearly two years. This was particularly disturbing to him as he wrote:

> Our want of laborers was not because they did not come to California, for between the 1st of April, 1849, and the 1st of August, 1850, I counted and registered forty-six men, all wearing the vestments and claiming the character of Baptist ministers in good standing, who arrived at San Francisco and passed through to the mines, not one of whom would stop for a single day to aid me in rolling to the top of the hill the ball that seemed ready to fall back upon and crush me—not an hour in the work of the Master(24).

Wheeler also wrote of a lack of harmony. People were independent, opinionated, and each sure in his own mind that no other opinion was worthy of consideration. (This characteristic continues to a significant degree until this day.) This was reflected in all walks of life, even in the churches as members came from all over the United States and the world bearing their customs and traditions.

From a positive standpoint, Wheeler listed many factors which contributed to the eventual success of his efforts. He acknowledged the presence of some dedicated laymen, among them C. L. Ross(25). Ross provided a place for the Wheelers to live, paid all their expenses, purchased a lot, and built a church building. George Inwood, a young man from England, was also most generous in support of the church. In addition, "Gentlemen of the army and navy on the coast, inferior to none in the service, received and treated us with every possible courtesy and attention"(27).

The first candidate for baptism was Colonel Thomas H.

Kellam of Accomac County, Virginia. He had sailed from Norfolk on the brig *Mariana* in March, 1849, arriving after a voyage of some six months. Wheeler reports that Kellam immediately sought out the missionary to report the change in his life and to request baptism and membership in the church. Apparently, Wheeler kept an accurate diary in which he recorded the activities relating to this experience for he included the account in his history:

At an appointed time he came before the church, related his experience, and was with unanimity and with deepest interest elected as a candidate for baptism and membership in the church. On the following Sabbath morning—it was the 21st of October, 1849, one of those lovely mornings that characterize San Francisco climate in autumn; clear, still warm and cheerful to the fullest extent, we assembled at our humble sanctuary, on the north side of Washington Street, one door east of Stockton. We had such a congregation as perhaps never assembled at any other time or place. The other churches in the city suspended their morning service. Their pastors with their officers and the body of their congregations were represented and joined in the procession. The mayor and other municipal officers of the city, and several of the officers of the State, and officials of the Government, resident on the coast or here temporarily on business, also Commodore Jones, commanding the Pacific squadron, U.S.N., and his naval staff, together with a large number of marines, all in full uniform, the chiefs of the medical staff of the Pacific division of both the army and navy, with their assistants, swelled our numbers and officially gave endorsement to our proceedings. We also had with us Dr. Judd, prime minister of the Hawaiian kingdom, then on his way as "Minister Plenipotentiary and Envoy Extra-ordinary" to the United States, England and France, having with him their heir-apparent and his cousin, who under Dr. Judd were receiving their royal education, and each of them afterward became king, preceding the present ruler of the nation. We had also with us large numbers of visitors from nearly every civilized nation on earth, who had been drawn here by the gold excitement, and hundreds of the citizens of San Francisco.

We formed with due deference to the rank and standing of our guests, and marched down Stockton street to Union, to Powell, to North Beach, where the water was shallow with sandy bottom. There was no wind that morning, and the water was clear and calm as a pond in the country. The whole train, from the church to the beach (about three-quarters of a mile), marched with all the decorum and precision you would expect to see in a platoon of the regular army or navy on dress parade. At the water each department of the long and numerous procession took its assigned position in silence, and gave to all the exercises the most undivided attention. Rev. S. H. Wiley, of the Presbyterian mission at Monterey, who had been a fellow passenger with me from New York to that place, was on my left and, at my request, read portions of Scripture and announced a hymn. He was deeply moved, having never before witnessed the ordinance of baptism in the Bible mode, though born, reared and educated in New England and New York. Rev. Mr. Hunt of the Congregational Church was on my right and offered the baptismal prayer. (I could not then, nor can I now see how he could have prayed more earnestly and appropriately if the exercises had been in and of his own church.) On his right was Commodore Jones and his staff, while all around us was the official and unofficial multitude of spectators, every one of whom seemed to be as fully interested as if a personal participant in the exercise.

When all was ready, the candidate, a noble specimen of man, 6 feet 2 inches tall and finely proportioned, took my hand, and we walked about 100 yards before reaching a depth of water sufficient for the ordinance. While we were thus going "down into the water," according to previous arrangement, the hymn was announced and the first two stanzas sung by the whole concourse; the last two as we were "coming up out of the water" (after the baptism in the scriptural form). And such singing I never elsewhere heard. It seemed as though every professional and every layman, every soldier and every marine, every officer and every subordinate, every citizen and every foreigner of that vast throng was suddenly and specially inspired by the holy grandeur and the spiritual significance of the divine ordinance which we were administering, to sing for that once, if never again this side of heaven, with the fullness of both his spirit and his voice. And as we neared the shore and the song rang out the mighty paean of the last stanza, it seemed to evoke responsive strains from before the "great white throne," which, as they rolled over the battlements of the New Jerusalem, came down to mingle with and sanctify our best efforts to "Magnify the Lord" in songs of praise to the Great Jehovah.

The hymn was that inimitable effusion, written by Adoniram Judson, to be sung at the first baptism in the Burman Empire, at the beautiful pond on the bank of the Irrawaddi, at Rangoon, June 27, 1819, "Come, Holy Spirit, Dove Divine."

As we reached the shore, Commodore Jones came forward and giving me his warm, earnest hand, expressed his extreme delight and gratitude for the privilege of attending that most solemn and interesting service of our denomination. We then reformed and returned, in the most perfect order, to the sanctuary, where the assembly was dismissed(27).

Colonel Kellam, the one baptized that day, wrote to a friend in Northampton, Virginia, sharing his experience. That friend gave the letter to the editor of the *Religious Herald*, the Virginia Baptist paper, who published it. It was perhaps that letter which inspired a Virginia lawyer, Edward J. Willis (a Baptist) to depart for California to offer his life in service. We are told that he pushed a two-wheeled cart, containing his law library, from Independence, Missouri, to Sacramento.

Some good ministers came, including Dr. Saxton of Vacaville.

Dr. Peneleton (a mere boy then) came, and with his voice

and organ rang sweet melodies through the congregation, cheering to the saints and inviting to sinners. He left his preparation for the bar, and turned to studies for the ministry. He was ordained here and served in the pastorate for a time. But our facilities for intellectual and theological training did not equal his desires, he went east(25).

Then there was Francis E. Prevaux (1851)—the first denominational teacher, well-schooled, and an effective leader—who died before the potential of his life could be reached(26). Others came, and churches were multiplied. In 1889 Wheeler could claim: "Moreover, you have 165 churches, and 10,290 members and a full set of the approved organizations for doing the work of the Lord"(37).

Workers were needed to maintain churches and to start others. Dr. Hill wrote Wheeler in 1853 of his futile efforts to enlist ministers for service in California. He said that the ministers were to blame, not the Society as suggested by Wheeler(19). Hill asked Wheeler to return East on a recruiting trip. He went in April, 1854, to spend four months traveling 5,000 miles visiting associations, conventions, and universities from Virginia to Maine. He enlisted only one man, his own brother. Others seemed willing to go if "a strong church in a pleasant town or city, and a good salary were guaranteed"(32).

The next year Osgood Wheeler developed a throat infection and was forced to retire from the ministry. For the remainder of his long life he participated as a layman in Baptist church and community affairs. Just as his star was setting as a ministerial leader, God raised up a Southern Baptist, J. Lewis Shuck.

While there had been much interest in California among Southern Baptists, financial considerations had prevented any action. A Domestic Mission Board report in 1849 said:

> Within the last few months many thousands of our fellow-men, of our own and other countries, have emigrated to that distant territory, and very many of them from the Southern states of the Union. . . . But it is not to send missionaries to

California, simply as it is now, that is important, but to California with its teeming millions of inhabitants that are destined to occupy it in a few years.[2]

In 1852 the Reverend Benjamin Brierly, for two years pastor of the church in Sacramento while a missionary of the Home Mission Society, sent a letter to *The Home and Foreign Journal* of the SBC, which said, in part:

> There are 150,000 or 200,000 Americans in California that need the gospel. It is a mistake that they will not hear preaching. . . . I have never found . . . more respectful or attentive audiences than I have met in California. They are ready to hear, but alas! there are but few ready to preach. . . . Sacramento, my late field, needs a man immediately. . . . There is a propriety in that church appealing to you; nearly all its members are from the south. Cannot your Board extend a helping hand?
>
> . . . So far as our denomination is concerned, the north has only one missionary there . . . the south has none. Is one Baptist missionary all that the great, growing, promising State of California needs—a state whose agricultural and commercial resources, even more than her mineral wealth, indicate, with unmistakable certainty, that in the lapse of a few years she will be the second in importance to no State in the Union?[3]

In 1852 Baptists in California learned that J. Lewis Shuck was returning to the United States from China and would pass through San Francisco. Hope was expressed that he could be persuaded to begin a work among Chinese. This sentiment was shared in the *Pacific Banner*, a paper edited by Osgood C. Wheeler and Edward J. Willis, the attorney and judge in whose home the Sacramento church was organized in 1850. *The Christian Index* of Georgia picked up this note from the *Pacific Banner* expressing the hope that Shuck might make California his field of operation. The *Index* added further: "For the sake then of Foreign as well as Home Missions, it behooves our churches to look out suitable men to send as missionaries to that vast state. Does not God himself by a remarkable manifestation of his providence call us to make a strong effort for California."[4]

Both lack of funds and the inability of the mission board to find men to go to California hindered the appointment. Many forces seemed to converge, however, in the search for ways to advance the cause of Christ there. The executive board of the Alabama convention petitioned the Southern Baptist Convention in 1853, resolving . . . that "the Chinese population in California presents an intensely interesting field . . . , and we respectfully suggest . . . Brother J. L. Shuck, as in our opinion pre-eminently qualified for that work."[5] The committee on California reported to the same Convention that they should occupy California at once because: "1. It is a very extensive field . . . will contain a population of about 20,000,000 . . . 2. It is a great jumping off place for the orient. 3. The fact that many Southern people have gone to California calls for missionaries."[6]

The next year the Foreign Mission Board reported:

> Rev. J. L. Shuck, who had labored as our missionary ever since our organization . . . tendered his resignation, having in view a series of labors on behalf of the Chinese in California. His resignation was accepted, with the expression of an earnest wish, that among the idolators who are peopling our Pacific shores, he might exercise an enduring influence for good.[7]

Shuck located in Sacramento, probably in part upon the advice of Judge Willis. He began at once to supply the pulpit of the First Baptist Church, pastorless since Brierly left. The church soon began to pay a large portion of his salary.[8] On August 15, 1854 he wrote to the *Religious Herald*:

> This whole country abounds with Baptists from just about every state in the Union, North and South; but vast numbers of them are positively opposed to uniting in a church capacity, because if they were connected with a church here, they would be expected to act like Baptists and Christians, and this they seem determined not to do in California.[9]

Southern California seems to have been affected little by the gold rush in the north. People came to the southern part of the state for the land. Here Baptist work was begun by Southerners. The first church was organized in El Monte in 1853—the only one there for another thirteen years. Its membership consisted of people largely from Texas, Arkansas, and Missouri. It was begun by two laymen, R. E. Fryer and John Fugua. Fryer arrived in 1852 and "soon began preaching wherever he could find a congregation, even though he was not at this time a minister."[10] He was ordained to the ministry after the arrival of an evangelist from Missouri, the Reverend J. A. Freeman, in 1857. Freeman is credited with having baptized over 700 converts in the state.[11]

Fugua also began preaching, perhaps as a lay evangelist. He was described as

> a man of peculiar temperament, of a rough exterior, with little education, a powerful frame, and capable of great endurance. He preached at El Monte and all over this part of the state, with little or no compensation, and no man could move an audience as he did when fully aroused.[12]

Thus the influence of Southern Baptists on the Baptist cause in southern California at this time was made by lay people who migrated to the state, not by missionaries sent by the mission boards. A similar action was to take place seventy-five years later to introduce the second wave of Southern Baptist influence.

Sandford Fleming, in his book *God's Gold*, mentions the part played by several other Southern Baptist ministers. Joseph Morris of Alabama started the church in Santa Clara. Stephen Riley of Missouri organized several churches, including the Napa River Church. Most of the settlers in Petaluma were from Missouri. James Oates of Florida began the work in Placerville.[13]

As early as 1850 interest in education was shown as revealed in the minutes of the San Francisco Baptist Association. A resolution adopted that year read: "That as Christians, as Baptists, we regard the cause of education with deep and prayerful interest; and that as a denomination we will do what we can to promote its interests."[14] In 1851 education claimed a central place in the annual meeting. A school founded by Francis E. Prevaux was taken under their direction.[15]

In 1853, following a sermon by Wheeler, the California Baptist Education Society was organized and charged with specific plans for an educational institution. It was reported in the *New York Recorder* in August under the title, "Our Educational Interests in California: A Literary and Theological Institution for California." One of the aims of the society was,

> to look out and assist such indigent, pious young men in their preparation for the work of the ministry as may give evidence that they have been called of God; and through its board of managers, to take early measures for the founding of a literary and theological institution, at some suitable place within the bounds of the State.[16]

The need for ministers was apparent to Baptist leaders in California and at both mission boards. In December, 1854 the Domestic Board (SBC) appointed Edward J. Willis as a missionary to Oakland. In reporting their actions to the SBC they said:

> Repeated efforts had been made to carry out the instructions of the Convention to send missionaries among the Americans in California, but all proved failures; no one would say, "Here am I, send me." Thousands on thousands of Southern people petitioned for Southern ministers, but the Board had none to send. There was, however, a young lawyer in that country—a man of fine talents and a Southern man by birth and education—him God converted and placed in the ministry.[17]

Willis served two years before visiting his home state of Virginia where circumstances prevented his returning to California.

Willis had commented in 1854 that Francis E. Prevaux had

Harvey Gilbert, a Southern Baptist home missionary, recognized the need to provide training for Christian workers in California as early as 1859. That year he founded the San Rafael Baptist Institute, a boarding school which taught academic subjects, about ten miles north of the present-day Golden Gate Seminary campus. After a few years the school closed.

broken his health by doing what the denomination as a whole should have done.[18] He agitated for ministers and doubtless affected Harvey Gilbert.

Harvey Gilbert was converted in Sacramento and became a charter member of the First Baptist Church there.[19] He later moved to San Francisco. In 1857 he was asked to care for the First Baptist Church of Oakland for three months. Beginning May 1, he served several months before he was ordained.[20]

The need for pastors continued to be overwhelming. In 1858 Shuck wrote, "There are feeble Baptist churches, most of them without pastors scattered throughout many portions of California."[21] Gilbert resigned the pastorate in Oakland December 25, 1858 and moved to San Rafael to establish the San Rafael Baptist Institute.[22]

The *Home and Foreign Journal* of August, 1860 printed a letter from Harvey Gilbert to J. Lewis Shuck dated April 27, 1860, in which he said, "the School is in a flourishing condition."[23]

The *Home and Foreign Journal* of February, 1861 printed a letter from Shuck in which he said a church was organized in

San Rafael with eight members. Shuck later wrote:

> This institution ought to be at once crowded with the sons and daughters of our California Baptist brotherhood. Board is reasonable, educational facilities abundant, and there is no healthier place in all the state than San Rafael. Here too is a fine beginning for a Baptist Theological School.[24]

It is interesting that during the year (1859) that The Southern Baptist Theological Seminary was opened in Greenville, South Carolina, an institution was begun on the West Coast with the same purpose. The War Between the States that almost ended the life of Southern Seminary did, indeed, snuff out this feeble beginning in California. One's imagination cannot refrain from pondering what might have been had the San Rafael Baptist Institute survived. It might be said that approximately a century later it was re-established as the Golden Gate Baptist Theological Seminary which occupied its new campus in Marin County, about ten miles away from the location of the earlier effort. That is another story to which we now turn.

Notes

1. Osgood C. Wheeler, *The Story of Early Baptist History in California*, California Baptist Historical Society, 1888, p. 11. Unless otherwise noted, references in this section are from this source with page noted in parentheses.
2. *Proceedings of the Southern Baptist Convention* (1849), p. 42.
3. *Home and Foreign Journal*, Vol. I, No. 8 (Feb. 1852), p. 1.
4. *The Christian Index*, Vol. XXXII, New Series Vol. 21, No. 6 (Feb. 10, 1853), p. 22.
5. *Proceedings of the Southern Baptist Convention* (1853), p. 7.
6. Ibid., pp. 14-16.
7. Ninth Annual Meeting, Foreign Mission Board (1854), p. 11.
8. Sam Harvey, *The Southern Baptist Contribution to the Baptist Cause in California prior to 1890*, (unpublished Th.M. thesis Golden Gate Baptist Theological Seminary, Berkeley, 1958), p. 17.
9. *The Christian Index*, Vol. XXXIII, New Series Vol. 22, No. 41 (October 12, 1854), p. 162.
10. Harvey, p. 3.
11. *Twentieth Century Baptist Conference*, First Baptist Church, Los Angeles, December 31, 1900-January 2, 1901, Souvenir, pp. 53-62.

12. Ibid.
13. Sandford Fleming, *God's Gold*, (Philadelphia: The Judson Press, 1949), p. 95-113.
14. Ibid., p. 200.
15. Ibid., p. 201.
16. Ibid.
17. *Proceedings of the Southern Baptist Convention* (1855), p. 331.
18. Fleming, p. 199.
19. Harvey, p. 4.
20. Ibid., p. 24.
21. *The Commission*, Vol. II, No. 12 (June 1858), p. 357.
22. Harvey, p. 26.
23. *Home and Foreign Journal*, Vol. X, No. 2 (Aug. 1860), p. 5.
24. *The Evangel* III: 14 (Oct. 18, 1860), p. 3.

2
Founding of the Seminary

The last recorded reference to support of SBC causes from these early California Baptist churches is in 1904.[1] Between 1904 and 1925 Baptist witness in California was left to Northern Baptists and other independent groups. In the first quarter of the twentieth century, many conservative-minded Baptists in California turned to Norris fundamentalism and later to the Conservative Baptist Convention. One pressure that encouraged such alignments was the widespread effort among Northern Baptists to favor comity agreements. These arrangements assigned territory (geographical areas) to the various denominations for religious influence and work.

The movement of Southern Baptists to California in this century began as early as 1925. Just before Christmas that year, the Marvin Mouser family from eastern Oklahoma arrived in Shafter. His brother Virgil came in 1927. Their father, George, who was a Baptist preacher, arrived in 1928. Henry, another brother, settled in the San Joaquin Valley in 1929. Almost simultaneously, the Mouser sisters and families joined their extended family in Shafter. The second wave of Southern Baptist migration to California had begun.

Some of the Mousers joined the Northern Baptist church in Shafter, but they could not accept the practices of alien immersion and open communion. They began holding services for worship and fellowship, meeting regularly in the Mouser homes. By 1933 a Sunday School was begun.

A Southern Baptist church was organized in the Seventh Day Adventist church building May 10, 1936. The covenant and declaration of faith found in *Pendleton's Church Manual* was adopted. The Kern County Land Company gave them a building site in June, and a church building (purchased from another denomination) was soon moved to the site. The first mission offering was taken in December that year.

Other churches soon appeared: Delano, Oildale, and Lamont in 1938, followed by Arvin and Porterville. In April, 1939 the San Joaquin Valley Missionary Baptist Association was organized. By the time the second annual meeting of this association was held in September, 1940, there were fourteen churches in cooperation. During the year the association voted to include the entire state in their territory, repudiating the comity arrangement that other denominations operated under. Churches were located from Bakersfield in the south to Port Chicago in the San Francisco Bay area. This kind of thinking and work led to the inevitable action of organizing the Southern Baptist General Convention of California.

Elmer Gray wrote in *Heirs of Promise*:

> The members of the 14 churches were primarily Baptists who had come from churches in the South. They wanted curriculum materials that were strongly biblical. They wanted organization and methods that promoted evangelism and missions. . . .
>
> The organization of a convention resulted from the desire of the people in the California churches and not from plans of leaders of the Southern Baptist Convention.
>
> The growing desire for a state convention prompted R. W. Lackey, half-time association missionary and half-time pastor of Bakersfield, First Southern Baptist Church to write a proposed constitution for a State convention. . . .
>
> Lackey took this constitution with him to the association meeting in Shafter. More than a hundred were present and everyone expected something more to happen than just an association meeting.
>
> Thirteen of the churches had messengers at the 1940 meeting . . .
>
> On the afternoon of September 13, 1940, . . . Silas Hill,

pastor of the Salinas church moved that the association be adjourned long enough to consider the organization of a state convention. Those present moved from the auditorium to an upstairs Sunday School room.

Silas Hill was elected temporary chairman. The Southern Baptist General Convention of California was organized and the following officers were elected: president, Sam Wilcoxon of Shafter; recording secretary, Vester E. Wolber of Taft; corresponding secretary-treasurer, R. W. Lackey. Lackey's title was later changed to executive secretary-treasurer.

. . . Those assembled voted to organize; adopted the constitution Lackey had written; elected officers including Lackey as their executive officer; and named the nine men who composed the first board of directors.

Lackey wrote later in an editorial in *The California Southern Baptist*: "Some cried, some shouted for joy, all were happy. The long looked for day had come. Southern Baptists now face the future with a zeal and determination, the like of which we had never seen before."[2]

At the second meeting of the convention in 1941, Dr. W. W. Hamilton, president of Baptist Bible Institute (later New Orleans Baptist Seminary) and president of the SBC, was a speaker. On November 27 following the second convention, the board of directors for the convention adopted the *Southern Baptist Stamina* as the official California Baptist publication and elected Dallas Faulkner as editor. By April, 1942 they became dissatisfied with Faulkner and terminated him, but he refused to release the printing plates. They asked Secretary R. W. Lackey to assume editorship of the convention paper under a new name, *The California Southern Baptist*.

The first plea for a Baptist school in California was heard in a report on Christian education during the 1942 convention. The following resolution was adopted: "We recommend that Southern Baptists in California pray, labor, and pay, that these institutions which we now have may continue in their work and that we may soon have schools of our own in

California to prepare our young people for greater service in the Kingdom."[3] The convention then had forty cooperating churches and sixty-six ordained ministers listed in its membership.

At the 1943 meeting of the convention, held November 3-4 in Fresno, Isam B. Hodges, pastor of the Golden Gate Baptist Church in Oakland, was elected to succeed Sam Wilcoxson as president. The Golden Gate Church had not yet officially sought membership in the Golden Gate Baptist Association and the Southern Baptist General Convention of California but was to do so on November 17.

Before his first year as president was half over, Hodges found himself in an awkward position. He was presiding over a meeting of the state executive board when the matter of his newly organized seminary was being discussed. Dr. Faulkner had brought copies of his latest edition of the *Stamina* to Oildale where he was attending the state Sunday School convention. In this issue he told of the organization of the Golden Gate Baptist Theological Seminary, stating that probably one day it would become an institution of the state Baptist convention.

The board was meeting in connection with the Sunday School convention. Floyd Looney wrote:

> Secretary Lackey and all the board members, save Hodges, took exception to what they regarded as a presumptuous statement on Faulkner's part. Then, too, there was objection to the seminary because of one or two other persons who had become associated with it. Faulkner had referred to it as a Southern Baptist institution.[4]

They called Faulkner out of the convention for an explanation. He stated that *Southern Baptist* was a general term and that the board of directors had no monopoly on the use of it. To quote Looney further:

> The result of the whole matter was that the board instructed Looney, who was serving as recording secretary in the absence of F. W. Carter, to draw up a resolution stating

that California Southern Baptists would not be responsible for any statement other than statements made in *The California Southern Baptist* itself. Looney wrote the resolution which all but consigned the seminary to the regions of despair and it was adopted by the board and read before the Sunday School convention.[5]

Looney went on to write:

Little did Looney know that within less than one year he would be editor of *The California Southern Baptist* and that one of his first editorials would be in support of the seminary. Nor did he know that he was destined to serve as its vice-president and field representative and fly 28,000 miles while serving on a committee upon whose recommendation the Southern Baptist Convention accepted the seminary. Of course [O. Dean] Johnson, who supported the resolution, didn't know that he was destined to serve as president of the seminary's board of trustees for three or four years and later serve as its business manager.[6]

One can only imagine what must have been going through the mind of Isam B. Hodges, whose dream was bound up in that seminary. That dream is another story. We turn back the calendar to the early part of this century and to a farm in the northern Arkansas hill country. In Hodges's own words we read:

When I was about five years old three men came to our home one day and asked for my dad. He was across the field making the ground ready for spring planting. I watched these men as they went across the field, stopped and talked with my dad for some time. They had a small briefcase from which they took some papers. Dad signed some and they went on their way, and Dad went on plowing. He was laying off rows for planting corn.

When Dad came to the house for dinner, the one question uppermost in our minds was what did these men want? Dad took time to relate what they wanted. The Baptists in Arkansas were building several mountain schools in the

Ozark Mountains of North Arkansas and they were placing one at Mountain Home, Arkansas, some 24 miles away. Mountain Home Junior College, it was to be called. "Some of you children may go there when you go off to school." He furthermore said, "I am going to give enough money this fall when I gather my crop to pay for 100 bricks to go into the walls when this building is built." I never forgot this story of the three men.[7]

Isam Hodges was converted when he was sixteen while attending a revival meeting held in their small village in the mountains. Sometime later he had a dramatic experience with the Lord as he walked along the road returning home from the village. It left him with joy in his heart and a conviction that God was calling him to preach. He knew that he must have more schooling to prepare for such a calling.

Mountain Home College had been unable to keep its doors open. Hodges knew about Ouachita Baptist College, but it was too far away. There seemed no likelihood that the junior college would reopen soon, yet open it did that fall. H. F. Vermillian was a mountain boy from near Hodges's home who had gained prominence as a Baptist preacher. At the May, 1916 meeting of the SBC, he told the Convention about Mountain Home College. He made a motion that the Home Mission Board (HMB) reopen the college and the motion carried. In another action, Vermillian was asked to serve as its president.

News about the reopening of the college spread rapidly in the mountains of northern Arkansas. When Hodges heard of it, he felt it was being opened for him. He was "keeping company with a mountain girl," and she agreed to go with him to school so they were married September 18, 1916. They spent four years at Mountain Home, earning the equivalent of a high school diploma and one year of college.

Wayne Swindall recounts many influences on Hodges's life from his schooling and the men who affected him most:

> While enrolled in Mountain Home College, the young couple was considerably involved in the life of the small, close academic community. . . . He was active in the

Athenian Literary Society, the Ministerial Association, the Glee Club, and a mission study group called the Volunteer Band. He received his high school diploma in 1920.

Swindall goes on to say:

In view of the direction of Hodges' career, it is worth noting the personal friendship and close contact he had with H. F. Vermillian, who served as president the first two years Hodges was a student of Mountain Home College. . . . Undoubtedly, this powerful personality with his strong emphasis on missions, the local church, and impatience with the restrictions of comity agreements impressed the young Hodges.

Moreover, Hodges was deeply affected by the sacrifice and vision of the men who brought a school to the mountain people to enrich and edify their lives, and he sought to identify with their spirit. Such an environment could have easily created in him a susceptibility for the experience at Mountain Home that further directed his course.[8]

While at the junior college, Hodges counted bricks in the building to determine the size of the space occupied by the hundred bricks paid for by his father. He concluded that it would be a rather large hole if they were torn out. He saw how important even a small number was. Even then another thought came that turned his mind and imagination to the far West, to California. It was as if an inner voice were asking, *How would you like to go to California, pastor a church, and start a school there that would do for the young men there what this is doing for the young ministerial men here?*

As he completed his work at Mountain Home College, Hodges wanted to go to California at once and complete his college work at Redlands University. He wrote the president but received a discouraging letter, suggesting that unless he had support he had better not plan to go so far. Hodges entered Ouachita Baptist College at Arkadelphia, Arkansas, in the fall of 1920. During his three years there, he threw himself into the many opportunities that were offered him. His activities included membership in an organization formed to train in parlimentary law and in the ministerial association, of which he was president in 1923.

His interest in California continued during those years. Automobiles bearing California license plates caught his eye and he sought out the owners to discuss their state. Surely the magic of California as the land of opportunity was affecting the life of Isam Hodges through these formative years.

After Ouachita he entered Southwestern Baptist Theological Seminary at Fort Worth. President L. R. Scarborough spoke in chapel one day, having just returned from a long trip over the Convention territory. He mentioned Southwestern, Southern Seminary in Louisville, Kentucky, and the New Orleans school, and then raised a question, "Who will open the western seminary on the Pacific Coast?" With California in his thoughts, it is not surprising that Hodges quietly vowed in his heart that he would.

Upon receipt of his Master of Theology degree in 1926, Hodges was again rebuffed in his effort to work in California. He was told by a Baptist leader he had written in San Francisco that churches were few and most didn't pay a living wage. He returned to Arkansas and became pastor of the Hazel Street Baptist Church in Pine Bluff.

Hodges maintained a vigorous program in his church and community, as well as in associational and state Baptist work. The Hazel Street Church maintained five preaching stations and often led the association in baptisms. He served as a member of the executive board of the Arkansas Baptist Convention. His sermon notebook reveals a continued interest in the social issues of the day as well. With all this effective ministry, however, he was unable to free himself from the longing to go to California.

A crisis point was reached in 1935 when Hodges was called as pastor of the First Baptist Church of Harrisburg, Arkansas. He accepted the call but continued to be distressed and unsettled about the decision. *Is now the time to go to California? Will another pastorate in Arkansas close that door to the West?* If he were ever to go, it had to be soon. Yet he wondered how could he take his wife and five children to California with no assurance of a place of service or a source of livelihood? He was, indeed, at the fork of the road. He decided that perhaps a visit to his mother in northern Arkansas, the place where so much had been revealed to him, would help. As he drove through the hills that day, the answer came and with it a calmness of spirit. He followed through with his decision by writing the Harrisburg church declining their call. He told them that he was going to California in answer to the call he had felt for years.

Hodges traded his car for a ton-and-a-half truck, loaded his family and belongings into it, and headed for California. Thus he entered California in 1935, one year before the organization of the first Southern Baptist church in this century in California. As Hodges crossed the California border, everything he saw and heard seemed to be saying, "California for Christ! California for Christ!" They established their home in Berkeley, where they were to live for the next sixteen years. Seeking the center of Baptist life in the San Francisco area, he entered the Berkeley Baptist Divinity School.

Hodges preached in several Baptist churches and some expressed interest in him, but he did not encourage them until he had earned his Master of Arts degree in May, 1937. He accepted the call as pastor of the Golden Gate Baptist Church in Oakland in June. It had been organized in 1892 and cooperated with the Northern Baptist Convention.

Mission minded as he was, he began gathering facts about surrounding communities that needed churches. Hodges found cities with 35,000 to 70,000 people that had no more than 1 or 2 Baptist churches. Berkeley, with a population of more than 125,000, had only 1 Baptist church. Albany, a city of 16,000, had none. He began agitating for an aggressive program of evangelism and missions, but there was no ready response from fellow pastors. He became especially distressed over comity agreements that prevented work in an area assigned to another denomination.

Hodges's frustration with the situation did not keep him

Isam B. Hodges, pastor of Golden Gate Baptist Church in Oakland, led the movement to establish Golden Gate Seminary. He served as its first president in 1944. During that year he also served as president of the four-year-old Southern Baptist General Convention of California.

from opening his heart to his own people. His sermons were filled with Baptist history and missionary information. He challenged them with descriptions of sacrifice and determination by those who had spread the gospel in other areas. He sought in every way he could to spur their evangelistic concern.

As Southern Baptist churches began to be organized nearby, Hodges and his people became aware of their work and growth. He suggested to his Northern brethren that this was the kind of work they should be doing. This only antagonized them. They saw only the danger of a Southern Baptist invasion of their territory. His repeated efforts to get his fellow pastors to go afield to enlist the Baptists moving to California were fruitless. He finally came to the conclusion that the only way to get an effective expansion program going was to join Southern Baptists. He saw no alternative but to give his church a choice.

On November 17, 1943 the Golden Gate Baptist Church voted thirty-six to six to seek affiliation with the Southern Baptist Convention. Hodges had been their pastor for more than six years. No one could possibly believe that he joined that fellowship to turn it toward Southern Baptist alignment. Those six years of evangelistic and missionary promotion, however, must have made a difference in the life of the congregation. One gets the feeling that Hodges might have left the Golden Gate Church had they not decided to change.

The church had been using some Southern Baptist Sunday School materials and had been cooperating with many Southern Baptist activities. Hodges had established sufficient reputation among Southern Baptists to be elected president of their state convention. This happened about two weeks before his church officially sought Southern Baptist affiliation.

As president of the Southern Baptist General Convention of California, Hodges gave aggressive leadership to the propagation and defense of Southern Baptist work in California. He wrote scores of letters. One took the form of a news release in 1944, "A Letter from a Southern Baptist Pastor in California to a Brother Pastor Back East." In it he listed city after city with little or no Baptist witness and then described what Southern Baptists were trying to do. He urged the HMB and The Sunday School Board of the Southern Baptist Convention (Baptist Sunday School Board) to enlarge their support.

Hodges told the Southern Baptist story in other areas as well. One exchange of letters was between him and W. B. Lippard, editor of *Missions*, an international Baptist magazine (Northern), following an article in the issue of November, 1944. Hodges replied to a charge by Lippard of an illegal invasion by Southern Baptists. He described the effort as due to the lack of any effort for a Baptist witness in California. Lippard at one point in the *Missions* article mentioned that "quite likely also a Southern Baptist theological seminary will eventually be established."[9] Hodges had not referred to this possibility in his letters, even though Golden Gate Seminary was already in operation.

Hodges served his denomination in many ways, including being the California member of the executive committee of the SBC. In less than a decade in California, he had risen from the ranks of an unemployed Baptist preacher to the president of a new Southern Baptist General Convention of

California. In addition he was the representative of that group in the highest circles of SBC life. These were exciting and fulfilling days for the mountain preacher from Arkansas. His vision of ministering to the millions in California was being realized.

Wayne Swindall said that Hodges's

> romantic inclinations enabled him to grasp intuitively a vaster significance in the surge of Southern Baptists in California than just the right of the local church to choose its affiliation and program of work. He saw the hand of God in the manipulation of his people. He had been imbued with the boldness of great men who allied themselves with the providence of God, and became willing instruments in his hands. Hodges identified with such men.[10]

As Hodges looked about him in early 1944, he knew that his hour had come. He was caught up in the vast movement of people to California. They were people with a history of determination and spirit. He once described those who had come to California:

> Some of the cream of the earth are among those people who have been driven out of that central section of our country. They are the children of the people who came to this country to escape the terrible persecution of the old world. . . . These people were prosperous back there before the dust began to blow. . . . But alas, all changed. They saw their lands blow away. . . . As they faced the future there was no other solution to their outlook than to move to other realms and start life anew.
>
> We never know all there is behind a movement. God may have caused this dust bowl in order to scatter these people over the western country and evangelize it for Him. This country is the greatest mission in all our nation. These people will build churches wherever they go. They will become leaders for God in every community where they reside. God may be getting ready for the great revival that he knows ought to sweep this western country.[11]

Hodges knew that only a great network of churches in every city, town, and village could accomplish what God would do in the West. New missions and churches had to be started. He prayed and worked to this end. The Hodgeses invited the six deacons of their church and their wives to their home for fellowship and prayer on the evening of March 23, 1944. One of those attending, caught up in the spirit of the meeting, said, "This will go down in history as a great prayer meeting."

Hodges reported that, as he arose the next morning, a familiar voice was saying, "This is the time to begin that school." Yet this realization seemed to frustrate him. Like Moses of old he began to argue with the inner urge disclaiming his being a school man. He sat at his typewriter and wrote these words: "God has given us a vision of a Western Baptist theological seminary. There shall be a theological seminary here in the Bay Area which shall be called the Golden Gate Baptist Theological Seminary."[12]

He might not have been an educator, but God was laying on him the responsibility to begin a school. How could there be more missions and churches without preachers? One of his friends did have school experience, Dallas Faulkner, pastor of the First Southern Baptist Church in San Francisco.

Hodges wrote that, on his trip to Faulkner's home, every one of the seventeen traffic lights turned green. However, Faulkner was not home; and after a long wait, Hodges left a note urging a visit the next morning. Hodges described their conference and the subsequent action:

> Dr. Faulkner came to my home the next morning. I laid before him my feelings and leadings for these several years past. And there in my home that Saturday we talked, prayed, planned, and then and there took definite steps to organize the Golden Gate Baptist Theological Seminary. The next morning, March 26, 1944, at the morning worship hour in the Golden Gate Baptist Church, I asked that the six ordained deacons be recognized as a committee from the church to meet with a like committee from the First Southern Baptist Church of San Francisco to formulate plans in an orderly and

Golden Gate Seminary was founded in Golden Gate Baptist Church in Oakland. This building housed the seminary from 1944 through 1947.

legal manner for the purpose of establishing an educational institution to be known as the Golden Gate Baptist Theological Seminary. The church unanimously adopted this and these deacons with the pastor met with a like committee from the First Southern Baptist Church, San Francisco, [the] following Friday night, March 31, 1944, and orderly and legally organized the Golden Gate Baptist Theological Seminary.[13]

Like Hodges, Faulkner was a native of Arkansas and a graduate of Ouachita Baptist College and Southwestern Seminary. He had continued his studies and earned the Doctor of Theology degree from Southern Seminary. He came to California in the thirties, settled in the Bakersfield area, and was first associated with the church in Oildale.

Members of the first board of trustees for Golden Gate Seminary were laymen, six each from the two churches. From Golden Gate Baptist Church in Oakland came Wade Pearce, Lee Armstrong, G. C. Evans, H. Hanley, J. D. Rowsee, and Perry Van Tuyl; and from First Southern San

Francisco, Sam Ashley, Henry Cash, G. F. Hendrickson, Edwin McCracken, Darwin O. Phillips, and C. W. Russell. Wade Pearce was elected chairman, and Edwin McCrackin was secretary.

Hodges and Faulkner set about organizing the seminary immediately following the action of the trustees. A charter from the state was applied for on July 12 and obtained, bearing the date July 24, 1944. The official name on the charter was Golden Gate Southern Baptist Theological Seminary. A curriculum and outline of courses had to be arranged and sufficient faculty enlisted to teach the first year. A catalog announcing these decisions had to be prepared and distributed.

The curriculum they prepared was similar to that of other seminaries. The grand design is reflected in the terms used. Under the heading "The Several Departments or Chairs of the Seminary," they cited twelve:

1. Chair of Bible
2. Chair of Missions
3. Chair of Evangelism
4. Chair of Church History
5. Chair of Christian Education
6. Chair of Homiletics
7. Chair of Theology
8. Chair of New Testament Greek
9. Chair of Old Testament Hebrew
10. Chair of Christian Psychology & Christian Sociology
11. Chair of Sacred Music
12. Apologetic & Polemics
    Department of Literary Improvement[14]

The word *chair* is usually reserved to describe an endowed professorship. Hodges and Faulkner were either hoping to have chairs endowed or giving dignity to the program. One wonders why number 12 is not listed as a Chair of Apologetics & Polemics, since Hodges himself provided instruction in these areas. The listing of such a discipline emphasizes the stance sometimes taken by Hodges. He and others often presented their Southern Baptist positions over against other

Christian groups, even Northern Baptists. This is illustrated by the continuing debate over who should be admitted to church membership. So-called alien immersion and open communion have been areas of discussion throughout the life of the Southern Baptist General Convention of California. (Note that an offending constitution stipulation about such practices in a church having to do with its membership in the convention remained until 1978.)

The Department of Literary Improvement was concerned with grammar and other rules of good speech. It may also reflect Hodges's interest in literature, history, and dramatics throughout his own school experience.

The catalog proclaimed that

Our Board of Trustees, in their first sitting as an organized body, and at which sitting the Golden Gate Southern Baptist Theological Seminary was established, adopted the articles of faith as given in Dr. J. R. Hobbs' manual. The Board also adopted the articles of faith found in Pendleton's Church Manual.

Why both sources are listed is not known.

A list of statements set forth "The Purpose of This Institution." Those listed were:

1. To help educate preachers, missionaries and other religious workers for more effective Kingdom service;

2. To answer the urge and call of God deep down in the hearts of those who originated this institution;

3. To more effectively and more rapidly evangelize the great mission field found in this state and throughout this wide west territory;

4. To help make the best possible contribution of true New Testament spirituality and religious fervor to this present day need; of the lost world of human souls steeped in sin;

[Number 5 seems to have gotten lost.]

6. To do as thorough seminary training as there is done anywhere in any institution;

7. To grant creditable degrees of as high standard of requirements as granted elsewhere;

8. To answer the hungering call of large numbers of our Southern Baptist constituency for such a Kingdom and denominational institution;

9. To answer the loud and wide open call to do our best at this hour for the ministry, for the spread of the gospel and for the salvation of lost souls.

10. The degrees already provided for are the degrees of Bachelor of Theology, Bachelor of Divinity, also Bachelor of Bible and Religious Education.

The faculty listing and qualifications are interesting. President Hodges's academic credentials were listed, and then the catalog says, "later he did one-and-one-half years post graduate work for which he received his master of arts degree with extra credits." (It does not mention that this was from Berkeley Baptist Divinity School, a Northern Baptist institution.) After reporting his sixteen years pastoral experience, the statement continues: "He knows well the teaching work. His initiative and his insight for institutional ministry will easily measure up to par, and is ample for the place he fills."

J. V. Dawes was listed for missions, with a Bachelor of Science degree and a Doctor of Divinity degree. He is described as having spent forty years as a missionary to China. "He lives, dreams, talks and teaches missions. As a teacher he is a 'natural.'" (Dawes appeared on a California State Convention program in 1949.) "Rev. Louis R. Adams is a B. A. [Bachelor of Arts] graduate from Howard Payne College with extensive graduate credits. . . . He will teach New Testament, Greek, Christian Sociology and will, perhaps, have some work in Religious Education."

Stockwell B. Sears was listed to teach "largely in Religious Education with, perhaps, some work in Missions and Evangelism." Sears was in the San Francisco area studying Chinese in preparation for mission service in China. Conversations with him in 1978 reveal that he never actually taught.

G. Dallas Faulkner was listed as teacher of Bible and theology. He had a Bachelor of Arts degree from Ouachita

College with graduation credits in Expression, Bachelor of Theology and Master of Theology degrees from Southwestern Seminary and his Doctor of Theology degree from Southern Seminary. He is further described as having "extensive credits in English, in History, in Psychology, in Education and School Management from Arkansas University, Arkansas State Teachers College, Jonesboro College and Southwestern University, Jackson, Tenn." In the more than half page about Faulkner, Hodges reports his having ten years teaching experience with six being on the college level.

Under the heading "Other Teachers to be Provided," the catalog states:

> Rev. E. K. Daugherty, graduate of Howard Payne and Southwestern Seminary, will likely be placed for Homiletics and to help in Religious Education. Contacts are being made by President Hodges toward securing a most capable teacher for the Chair of Sacred Music. . . . A full faculty of teachers will be had within a reasonable time.

No mention is made of George Kendall and H. H. Stagg, who worked in the Golden Gate Baptist Association. However, they are shown and listed as teachers under a picture taken at the closing exercises in May, 1945.

Several courses of study are described in the catalog. Under the "Chair of Evangelism," President Hodges is listed as the one who would supervise the department with "able evangelists covering a wide range of speakers . . . being selected to direct this class . . . also, provision will be made for extensive service in revival, evangelistic and soul-winning ministry."

Under finances the catalog states: "Golden Gate Church is furnishing her church plant for the Seminary's use indefinitely, and probably, the utilities largely. Several teachers will draw no salary directly from the Seminary the first year. Within the next twelve months this Seminary will likely be placed in the budget of a number of our churches in the West. . . . In due time our State and Southwide budgets will accord this institution ample financial consideration."

One paragraph describes the library:

Steps are already being taken toward building a usable, practical library. Books will be added for each department as rapidly as possible. Prospects are to the effect that we will have several hundred books by the time the Seminary opens, September 4. Continued efforts will be made to secure valuable books until the Seminary will have one of the best libraries to be found.

Thus was the seminary described to its public before it opened. During the seminary's first year, a total of sixty-two students enrolled. Only sixteen were ministerial students. Others were church members taking music or other helpful courses. Several classes were offered at night. As the first year drew near the end, few of the ministerial students remained. Six are so identified in a listing below the picture taken at the closing exercises. Many had left for college.

Recognition outside the seminary came first from the Golden Gate Baptist Association. On September 22, 1944 it voted to give their "prayerful and moral support." At Hodges's request, they also elected six trustees to sit with the twelve original members from the two churches. Among these were the first ministers on the board: A. T. Douglas, G. E. Armstrong, A. F. Byrd, H. L. Wyatt, and George B. Kendall. There was one layman, A. F. Burns.

Following the meeting of the state executive board in April, 1944, no action concerning the seminary was taken for several months. It is perhaps fair to say that the April action may have been directed more at Faulkner than at Hodges. There was, however, the feeling expressed that they wanted no responsibility for a "doorstep baby." One cannot help wondering what might have been had Hodges consulted state leaders before the seminary was begun. It appears that none of them knew anything about the school before the *Stamina* article.

Almost from the day the seminary was founded, President Hodges wrote people over the SBC territory telling the story and asking for support. A letter of April 21, 1944 to J. B.

Rounds in Oklahoma City, retired executive secretary of the Oklahoma Baptist Convention, reads:

> This school is an adventure of the Golden Gate [Oakland] and the First Southern Baptist Church, in San Francisco. . . . These two churches had in mind in operating the school to attract men to this area who would help us to evangelize this great area. . . . Forty miles from Golden Gate . . . in every direction there are three million people, and just a scattering number of Baptist churches.

On October 16, 1944 Hodges wrote M. E. Dodd of Shreveport, Louisiana, and former president of the SBC:

> Some of us have seen the need for organizing and building an institution where our young men on this coast could get their training in an evangelistic atmosphere, and go out from these walls to preach the eternal riches in Christ Jesus.
>
> We sure need your prayers, and you may be able to enlist some of our good financially able Southern Baptists to come to our aid in the building of our seminary. . . . We are laying broad plans for this institution and are to undertake great tasks for it. Our plans for it reach into the far distance and call for a program which shall be for today, tomorrow and for all time.

In light of these letters directed outside the state, it is interesting to read Hodges's letter answering a word from Pastor C. O. Watts of Sanger, California. Hodges wrote on February 16, 1945:

> I have wished from the beginning of the conception of this institution that it would not only become statewide but also southwide in its scope and interest and have thanked God for the interest, love, and adoration which has come from the good brethren both here in the state and out of the state, everywhere it became known.
>
> The blessings of God [have] already been demonstrated to be on the institution.

Hodges went on to enumerate God's blessings, including library additions and

other blessings which have come to us in a material way. . . . Our boys are going out here and there in this bay area, starting missions, organizing these into churches, which make our hearts to rejoice and thank God. We have been on the mountain top ever since the day of our opening.

He ended his letter with:

I would rather wait for some time before the state organization begins to help us financially. We are weak, and not well organized. . . . We have great things before us and we must proceed with caution. Let us have more time to demonstrate our interest, love, and faith in our good brethren here in this state, and in due time we will have an institution which the brethren everywhere throughout the state will take pride in and will then be accepted with deep gratitude unanimously. I think this will be the better way.

In the May, 1945 issue of the *Southern Baptist Stamina*, Faulkner reported on the seminary's first year. On the front page is a picture of trustees, faculty, and students. Mrs. Frances Ibsen wrote an article in which she spoke of a growing spirit and genuine friendship as the year progressed. "As the various new churches were started by the students, our prayers and interest increased. . . . There is a bond between students and faculty that is real."[15]

Mrs. Ibsen also reported on the closing exercises which began with a dinner. It was at this gathering the picture was taken. George Kendall was in charge of the program. Among the speakers she listed were President Hodges, Faulkner, and Floyd Looney, editor of *The California Southern Baptist*, "who gave us an inspiring glimpse of his idea of the need for the seminary and assured us of his support for our library." The Reverend E. K. Daugherty gave the principal address. Mrs. Ibsen closed her report by stating: "Each of us left the building with the impression of work well begun and the vision of much more work yet to be done and with a mighty vision of the seminary's possibilities and opportunities through the coming year."[16]

President Hodges's message at the seminary's closing exercises included words of thanks for those who shared in "this new adventure of faith." "Our men took charge with an enthusiasm, with a devotion, with a sense of responsibility that is not found in any other institution," were his strong words of praise for the faculty.

> They have served with their time, talents, energies, with but even the slightest thought of remuneration from any source. . . . They have volunteered their services for another year, and they are looking forward for a better time, a greater number of students, and a greater opportunity for service. There will likely be another faculty member, or perhaps two added to the present force of teachers.[17]

Hodges was proud of the fact that the seminary students were engaged in mission service. He said, "Some eleven churches have been the result of the program fostered by the Seminary. This is enough to cause rejoicing and thanksgiving and a conquest to cause us to take courage and lead us to put our hands to the task for greater things for the Christ who died to save."[18]

He expressed appreciation for the Golden Gate Church and for Southern Baptist military chaplains in the area. The chaplains had given books and cash for the library. Listed among these contributions was one for $55.90 from R. F. Royal, an army chaplain, later to become a member of the faculty.

In that same issue of the *Stamina*, there were spot fillers pointing to areas of need for new churches. "Chico is calling. Marin City wants work. Sausalito is open. Daley [sic] City is open. Biggs and East Biggs should be seen after." Marin County was frequently in their thoughts. San Rafael and Novato had new churches organized that year. Two of the needy places mentioned, Marin City and Sausalito, were near the campus to be occupied by the seminary fourteen years later.

The catalog produced in preparation for the second year reveals some notable changes. The word *Southern* was dropped from the seminary name. Number 5 in the list of elements in the purpose of the institution, apparently left out by accident from the first catalog, was present and read, "To help increase the number of much needed preachers thoroughly equipped for a richer ministry."[19]

E. K. Daugherty was listed to teach, in addition to homiletics, church and denominational history. Perry M. Johnson, pastor at Rodeo, was listed as "head of New Testament Greek." He was described as an all "A" student in his university, with "teaching experience and is accomplished in the Ministry." A native of Oregon, Johnson left the seminary after the 1946-1947 year to become pastor of the Calvary Baptist Church of Klamath Falls, Oregon.

Course offerings were more detailed in the second catalog. "Diploma in Theology" and "Master of Theology" were added to the degrees offered. An interesting note read: "A woman student may pursue and finish for any degree offered if she so desires."

Concerning seminary finances, two paragraphs in the catalog indicate progress in hope:

> Furthermore, the Seminary is needed and our people denominationally are coming favorably to recognize the need for the Seminary to the point of deserving their support in the same way that our older institutions are receiving denominational support. The turn in this direction seems quite favorable.
>
> Special efforts are being put forth to provide at least part pay for some three or four of the teachers during the next session and that without interfering with our denominational cooperative funds and contributions.

The quality of work at Golden Gate was a concern according to the catalog. "Credits earned in the Golden Gate

Seminary are as thorough and deserving of recognition and acceptableness as credits earned elsewhere. Real merit will always be held high in this school and will be required of the students."

Under the title of "Literary Courses" the catalog says, "High School and College courses with acceptable credits, will be offered both during the regular session and during Summer School." Did that mean that a college was envisioned as a part of the institution or was this simply remedial work? Perhaps it was the latter in light of the fact that many students left during the first two years to complete their college work.

The mission impact of the seminary was reflected in the catalog by words concerning "Provisions for Students":

> The Seminary with the students and pastors in this area make surveys of needy and neglected fields, organize Sunday Schools and churches. Many of the new churches call our Seminary students. These churches are generally self-supporting in a few months, paying a good salary. A number were organized the last year and now the salary ranges from $30.00 to $75.00 per week. More ministerial students in the Seminary means more churches. With more than fifty towns and cities in the bay area alone with a total population of more than 2,500,000 and with a large percent of these towns with no Baptist church makes the opportunity for organizing churches unequaled anywhere. The people are here, the money is here, but the ministers are few.

Speaking of the library, the catalog makes amazing claims:

> The Sunday School Board has permitted one of their workers to assemble material as a suggestive library. This compilation has been completed and these volumes are being purchased as fast as the funds are sent in for this. These books, valued at $5,000, are the best, most up-to-date and essential books for library facilities. When all these books are in, our library will be the most up-to-date library found in these parts.

The first statewide notice of the school came at the close of the first year when an editorial appeared in *The California Southern Baptist*. Floyd Looney had been elected as its editor in November, 1944. He served part-time while continuing as pastor at Tulare. In May, 1945 Looney visited Golden Gate Seminary and was present for the closing exercises. Looney said he went because he was interested in it, was a friend of Hodges, and knew that California Southern Baptists were divided over supporting it. Many fine people whom he respected were anxious to see that support enlarged. As editor he felt compelled to see for himself.

Looney reported that he heard some fine teaching being done. He found students anxious to learn and studying hard. He said he felt the state board had acted wisely the year before but they needed to take another look at their support of the seminary. He returned to Fresno and, as a reporter, wrote of the facts he had observed.

In his editorial in *The California Southern Baptist* in June, 1945, he outlined the brief history of the school along with a rather specific description of its relationship to Southern Baptists and the state convention. He then detailed what he found on his visit:

FIRST, I found that some sixty-five young preachers and their wives along with others interested in better equipping themselves were enrolled in the Seminary.

SECOND, I found that since the school opened that the ministerial students and the faculty together with others interested have led in the organization of six additional cooperating Southern Baptist churches.

THIRD, I found that both the faculty and students were constantly engaged in missionary activity.

FOURTH, I discovered that they are incorporated under the laws of our state, with the right to hold property and grant degrees, etc.

FIFTH, I found them studying such books as *The Preparation and Delivery of Sermons* by Dr. John A. Broadus.

SIXTH, I saw their needs. They need our prayers above all else. . . . Then they need material equipment, especially books. Many preachers and a few laymen could spare a good book. . . . I am persuaded that they need some money to employ the needed professors whose scholarship is second to none in California. The pastors and others have done their best, but the time has come when they need a faculty who can give of their best to the training of our workers. These young preachers are needed in California while they are getting their training. . . .

SEVENTH, I discovered that it presents a great missionary challenge. There is room for no less than 100 Southern Baptist churches within convenient reach of the present location of the school. . . .

These are simply observations of my own. I am dealing in the first person singular. I cannot speak for the State Board of Directors nor for any other Southern Baptist in California on the matter. I have felt impressed to speak for myself and then pass it on to you for whatever it may be worth.

This editorial appeared just as a new state executive secretary was being installed as leader of Southern Baptist work in California. He was A. F. Crittendon of Oklahoma. It soon became apparent that he did not support the new seminary at that time. Crittendon felt a college was preferable but that the economics of the situation did not warrant any effort in education. The state convention needed to apply its energies in other significant programs.

Crittendon met with the board of directors of the state convention after assuming office. The meeting was held at Camp Sierra in August. A news story in the September issue of *The California Southern Baptist* reported a number of actions taken. Among these was one concerning Golden Gate Seminary which Looney described in his book, *History of California Southern Baptists*:

Among the matters brought to the attention of the board that day was a proposition by O. Dean Johnson to appoint a committee to investigate Golden Gate Baptist Theological Seminary and to report to the board concerning the advisability of recommending to the state convention at its next meeting that the seminary be taken over by the state convention.[20]

The official records of the state board contain a reference to this meeting under the date of August 16. The committee chosen to investigate the seminary consisted of O. Dean Johnson, G. E. Armstrong (also a seminary trustee), Thomas Blair, Ed. F. Harness, and J. L. Brantley.[21]

At the state convention held in San Bernardino in November, 1945, the feature of the Tuesday afternoon session was described by Looney. It was "a report on Christian education by I. B. Hodges, President, Golden Gate Seminary, followed by an address by Dr. Jesse Northcutt, at that time a member of the faculty of Southwestern Baptist Theological Seminary. Northcutt was representing the three Southern Baptist seminaries."[22]

Looney stated that without a doubt the highlight of the Wednesday evening session was "the adoption of one single recommendation included in Dr. A. F. Crittendon's first annual report of the board of directors."[23] That report, read by O. Dean Johnson, chairman, said in part:

> Your committee found that some very good work has been done by Reverend I. B. Hodges and his co-workers. We wanted to commend Reverend Hodges and his workers for pioneering in this education field.
>
> Your committee is unanimous in its conviction that California Baptists need this Seminary; that the time is here when the Southern Baptist General Convention of California should take the responsibility of providing such an institution.
>
> In order to bring this matter direct and to give the Convention complete right-of-way—Your committee hereby recommends to the State Board of Directors and to the Southern Baptist General Convention of California, that you take over the Golden Gate Baptist Theological Seminary. That you elect all members of the Board of Trustees, instructing them to call a meeting at once to organize and do all

things necessary to take over and conduct said Seminary; and to set up proper constitution and by-laws for controlling said institution.[24]

Surely, much had happened to cause President Hodges to share in this action in light of his letter to Pastor Watts the previous February. The convention approved the recommendation of the board of directors and Golden Gate Seminary became an institution of the state convention.

Elected to serve on the seminary board of trustees were J. L. Brantley, A. H. Center, W. B. Huntsberry, H. H. Stagg, Thomas E. Blair, R. E. Cure, Ed. F. Harness, C. B. Maxwell, John O. Scott, Hollis A. Burge, O. Dean Johnson, and G. E. Armstrong (the only carry-over from the old board).[25] Their first meeting was held at the seminary in Oakland, November 20, 1945.

State board minutes record the actions taken by the trustees on that significant day:

> All members of the Board were present except Brantley, Scott, and Armstrong. O. Dean Johnson was elected permanent chairman and Thomas E. Blair, secretary. President Hodges turned over the Seminary file of documents and instruments for the Board to examine. C. B. Maxwell brought a financial report which indicated that there was no indebtedness and that there was a cash balance of $219.99.
>
> Hollis A. Burge was elected Vice-Chairman. Isam Hodges was elected President of the Seminary and Floyd Looney, Vice-president and Field Representative. C. B. Maxwell was elected Secretary-Treasurer. A motion was made, seconded and carried unanimously, that the President and the Secretary-Treasurer of the Seminary be elected to serve until the end of the current school year.
>
> The following were elected to the faculty:
>
> | | |
> |---|---|
> | I. B. Hodges | P. M. Johnson |
> | E. K. Daugherty | H. P. Ibsen |
> | W. E. Langford | H. H. Stagg, Supply Teacher[26] |

Faculty members were asked to serve until the end of the

current school term or until paid workers could be secured. The officers of the board were to constitute the executive committee. The minutes continue:

> Motion carried that $10,000 be the financial goal set for the general work of the Seminary and that the Sunday School Board and Home Mission Board each be asked to give the salary for one paid teacher in the approximate amount of $5,000 each.
>
> The following Special President and Faculty Committee was elected and asked to be prepared to report to the next annual meeting of the Board of Trustees, meeting during commencement week of 1946:
>
> W. B. Huntsberry, chairman
> R. E. Cure
> Hollis A. Burge
> John O. Scott
> J. L. Brantley
>
> The finance committee was asked to work out with the State Board of Directors the matter of a salary for Looney as a full time worker with his time divided between the Editorship of *The California Southern Baptist* and Field Man for the Seminary.
>
> They asked the chairmen of the various committees to serve as Catalog and Advertising Committee for the next year. They voted for the Seminary to pay W. E. Langford $10 per month for bridge toll and car expense in coming to teach Seminary classes.

When O. Dean Johnson gave a report of that trustee meeting to the state board of directors in December, he elaborated on some of their actions as well as indicated further developments. His report read in part:

> A committee was appointed to draw up [a] constitution and by-laws. Application was made to the Home Mission Board that they provide salary for an instructor, but this type of appropriation has been discontinued. The same appeal was made to [the] Sunday School Board, but they do not make such appropriations. The Board of Trustees requests

that the Field Man be given their approval to go on the field and present the Seminary needs with the endorsement of the Board [of Directors] and the approval under the constitution.[27]

The minutes also record the reaction to this report and the subsequent recommendations:

> Dr. Crittendon recommended that the Board set Christian Education Day in June as Seminary Day in all the churches and that special offerings be taken on that day for the seminary. The request was made that the Board pay the Seminary's half of the Field Man's salary. Dr. Crittendon stated that this was the business of the Board of Trustees, and not the matter of the Board of Directors. John Scott suggested that the State Board advance the money for his salary and that if the Seminary is not paying for itself by June that the offering taken on Seminary Day be used to reimburse the convention for whatever it might have advanced to the Seminary. O. Dean Johnson stated he will [be] willing to pay the salary himself for the first two months the Field Man was on the field.

Floyd Looney reported that at both the August and pre-convention meetings of the state board, Crittendon made strong pleas to proceed with caution. In the recommendation of acceptance of the seminary by the convention, no provision was made in the state budget for its support. The trustees, as well as the convention's board of directors, were trying to find other ways to secure funds for the seminary's operation. In spite of Crittendon's concern, *The California Southern Baptist* kept carrying comments about the seminary and the problem of "adopting a child and not providing clothes for it." The convention's board of directors took action in December, setting a June date for a Christian education offering in the churches for the seminary.

Thus, the initial working relationship between the convention and the seminary was established. Looney went to work as field man at once. With a salary of $150 per month from the seminary, plus $25 for travel, he seems to have been the first paid employee. With a like arrangement as editor of the Baptist state paper, his total salary was $300 plus $50 expense.

Looney believed that the first $10,000 the seminary received would be the most important it would ever have. He said that many thought he was punch-drunk to think he could raise that much from a little handful of churches. Crittendon did not want Looney to go to the churches directly. He began building a list of individuals he might approach, thinking in terms of asking for a minimum of $100 from each person visited.

One of his early experiences is worthy of reporting. Myrtle Scarborough Smith, a niece of L. R. Scarborough, president of Southwestern Seminary, lived in Pasadena. Looney thought that, if he could see her, she would give $100. The fuel tank of his car was almost empty, and he didn't have money for gasoline. As he drove toward Bakersfield, he saw many pop bottles discarded along the road and began gathering them. By the time he arrived in Bakersfield he had enough pop bottles to trade for money for gasoline to go on to Pasadena. He reported, "I went to see Mrs. Smith, gracious, sweet woman she was, very forthright. She listened for a while, reached over and picked up her purse, pulled her checkbook out and wrote me that check for $100."[28]

That was not the end of the story. Looney drove on to Bell Gardens to spend the night with Pastor D. A. Dalby and preach for him the next morning (Sunday).

It was a little 'shotgun' building and not very inviting. The church gave me $200 for the Seminary and promised to put it in their budget to send some more each month.

And that isn't all. As I gave the invitation following my sermon, a fine looking man came weeping down the aisle and his wife, as pretty as a store doll, was up in the choir. She cleared that choir loft's modesty curtain with the grace of a doe deer and landed right in the altar, grabbed Brother Dalby with one arm and her husband with the other. The man was saved and joined the church. That family became the backbone of that church for a time and then moved to the Trinity Baptist Church in Downey and were pillars there. They were Dutch and Juanita Douthett. They lent a Christian culture and refinement to the work that Baptists didn't have many places. After his retirement they had planned to spend time overseas in volunteer work. He became ill but insisted that she go, which she did and remained a year in that service.[29]

Many people gave. Often he had no idea they had it to give. Several were most generous. Among the first who shared was Professor Ribble, a school teacher living in Bakersfield. He had come from Texas and later headed up the Baptist Foundation in New Mexico. Several members of the First Southern Baptist Church of Fresno gave $100 each. Of these, John Herring gave more than $1,000. Looney said:

> I began to go down the state to find these Baptists, many on their jobs. It may not have been the best way but it was the only way I knew to do it. I drove that new automobile 63,000 miles and talked to most of the leaders of the Southern Baptist churches in California. . . . I got the leadership and got the money from them and then by the time Seminary Day rolled around I just about had the $10,000 in sight.

As all of this was being done, the second year of the seminary's operation was in progress. Some students from the first year had left to enter college; and as the level of requirements was lifted, others did not continue. Looney reported that the seminary almost died during that year. He went to Oakland to see what he had been elected to and says he could find only two students. When asked over the state how many students there were, he would often reply, "Well, we don't have as many as we had last year but we think the situation is going to improve. Some of them went away to school. Others will be coming during the spring semester."[30] And they did. Total enrollment for the year was thirty-two students from eleven states with eight colleges represented. Apparently class work was greatly improved over the first year. Requirements for degrees had been spelled out and several students planned to earn one of those degrees. Mission days had been set for the last Friday of each month for inspiration and to provide time for work on needy fields. The records show that they were successful in this endeavor.

Looney, in the meantime, was busy on two fronts seeking support for the institution. He was on the field raising money for it and writing about it in *The California Southern Baptist*. In the January 24, 1946 issue, he praised the volunteer faculty and the students for their missionary efforts. He emphasized that, while the seminary had been adopted by the state convention, they had made little provision for its support. He expressed confidence that the Lord had led in its founding and in its acceptance by the convention. He expressed belief that wider support would come when Baptists in California had demonstrated their faith in the venture.

The trustees of the seminary were busy also. Faculty members had been elected for the school term or "until their places will be taken by paid instructors." The president was elected to serve to the end of the current school year. Within three months, the trustees had met and elected a new president. Trustee minutes are not available but a report to the state convention's board of directors on April 3, 1946 records their action: "1. Dr. B. O. Herring of Waco, Texas, be extended an invitation to become president of the Seminary; Rev. I. B. Hodges, Vice-President and Instructor; Floyd Looney, Field Representative."[31]

Looney had been serving as vice-president and field representative. The trustees needed a place for Hodges since they had elected a new president. H. H. Stagg suggested that Hodges be named vice-president, stating that it would make no difference to Looney what he was called. Trustee chairman O. Dean Johnson sent a letter to Hodges, reporting the trustee action. Johnson was very careful to let Hodges know of the trustees' regard for him. Looney thought Hodges was encouraged to believe he could plan to continue teaching even before Herring came.

Hodges replied to Johnson's letter on May 4, 1946, stating that he had heard some news of the meeting before receiving Johnson's letter. No explanation was given for his failure to attend the meeting, but it was known he was back East raising money. He referred to a letter he had written B. O. Herring, stating that "whatever I can do to make your work a success here on the coast I will be delighted to do. And will look forward to the time when I can give you an active, personal cooperative effort for a greater seminary here where it is so desperately needed." Hodges went on to tell Johnson:

> I feel sure that Dr. Herring should be a great asset to our work and also to the Seminary. It is always a joy when trained men hear the call to come to this great and grand state to plant their lives here for the Lord, and I am sure with his training and ability will give a strong appeal to the brethren in other sections of the convention and cause them to feel that we sure are doing our best. Maybe they will take note of the things we are trying to do and will feel a need of making some sacrifices in aiding this western land and our work here to get on its feet and become established once and for all time.

Hodges told Johnson of the efforts to attract more students for the next school year. He and Perry Johnson had written to more than one hundred ministers who were graduating from college and universities, asking that they give Golden Gate Seminary due consideration. Hodges continued, "We feel sure that out of this number there will be a few who will cast their eyes and the longings of their hearts to this western land, and also to our school."

Further actions of that April meeting of the seminary trustees related to the budget and support of the school:

> 2. That the budget be set for the year at a total expenditure of $9,600. The following amounts were allocated: President's salary, $4,200 per year; travelling expense, etc., $300; and $300 moving expense for the President; salary for Vice-President, $1800; a like salary for the field representative,

with travel expense of $300; and for secretarial work, $900.

3. That the Board of Trustees give wide publicity to the Seminary and the special offering to be taken in June on Christian Education Day and that we go to the various associations and urge them to adopt similar resolutions and project the Seminary in the minds of our people.[32]

O. Dean Johnson reported to the state board that Hodges would be permitted to supplement his salary by evangelistic campaigns. He also said that support of the seminary would not entail any financial responsibility on the part of the state board other than that already assumed by it. The budget adopted for the operation of the seminary was the first ever. Only the field man had received compensation previously. In the first annual report of the seminary to the state convention in November, 1946, there was a summary of all collections and expenses of the school from its founding.

That report reveals some rather interesting facts. Some money had been spent on the faculty the first two years, perhaps for travel. There seems to have been a financial agent but we do not know who he was, what he did, or where he worked. In the second year of operation, the seminary received only $426.08 from all sources. Also during that year, someone who had given $500 the year before wanted it back, and the money was returned. There was a balance of $92.58 in the bank when Dr. Herring began service.

In the partial report for the first five months of the new year 1946-1947, nearly $7,500 of their anticipated $9,600 budget had been received. Just over $6,000 of this was from the Seminary Day offering in June.[32] Some money was paid to Golden Gate Church for the use of its property. In the first trustee meeting after the state convention assumed control, the finance committee was asked to look after "the matter of the Seminary assuming its part of utility and janitor's expense in connection with the work of the Seminary."

Minutes of the next several meetings of the seminary trustees are not extant but other sources reveal some actions.

In a letter to Hodges June 27, 1946, O. Dean Johnson wrote:

At Asilomar, we are calling a meeting of the Seminary Board of Trustees as per copy of letter herewith and are looking forward to having you with us at that time.

It now looks as though your dream is really coming true and that more rapidly than any of us anticipated. Everyone up and down the State appreciates the pioneering and foundation work that you so sacrificially put in to the movement. Come and make this meeting at Asilomar one of the greatest meetings of the year and one that will set and mold for the future of the Seminary.

Since several men were members of both the state board of directors and the board of trustees of the seminary, they often held their meetings at the same place. The minutes of the state board record recommendations from the trustees at that Asilomar meeting July 25, 1946:

O. Dean Johnson reported the action of the Seminary Board. The following recommendations were presented:

1. That the Seminary and the Board be authorized to draw annuity contracts with prospective donors which will revert to the benefit of the Seminary.

2. That we be permitted to go afield and organize $1000 a month clubs with a view of getting a thousand people up and down the state who will send $1 per month through their church, to the state office, and then to the Seminary treasurer.

3. That in connection with their library campaign the Seminary be permitted to go through the Training Union Department and the young people of the Training Union organizations with an appeal to each for enough money to buy a book. . . . H. H. Stagg suggested that people and churches back South be contacted by friends here in an appeal for gifts to the Seminary. Dr. Herring announced Sept. 2 as the opening of the Seminary. The inauguration of Dr. Herring as President is to be the evening of the 2nd. One hundred students are expected to enroll in September.[33]

Thus Golden Gate Seminary moved into a new era under the leadership of a new president, Dr. B. O. Herring. Hodges had realized his dream of founding a school. He continued to be a vital part of the instructional program and expected to remain with the school through the rest of his productive years.

Notes

1. Sam Harvey, *The Southern Baptist Contribution to the Baptist Cause in California Prior to 1890* (unpublished Th.M. thesis, Golden Gate Baptist Theological Seminary, Berkeley, 1958). Appendix I.
2. Elmer Gray, *Heirs of Promise* (The Executive Board of the Southern Baptist Convention of California, 1978), pp. 22,23.
3. Floyd Looney, *History of Southern Baptists, 13 Golden Years*, pp. 37-38.
4. Ibid., p. 53.
5. Ibid., p. 54.
6. Ibid.
7. Isam Hodges, private papers.
8. Wayne Swindall, *Isam Bradley Hodges: Founder and First President of Golden Gate Seminary.* (Unpublished Th.M. Thesis, GGBTS, Mill Valley, 1972), pp. 38,39.
9. Hodges.
10. Swindall, p. 55.
11. Hodges.
12. Ibid.
13. Ibid.
14. Golden Gate Southern Baptist Theological Seminary, *First Catalog*, 1944, p. 5.
15. Frances Ibsen, "Seminary Impressions," *Southern Baptist Stamina*, Vol. III, No. 9, (May Issue 1945), p.5.
16. Ibsen, "Seminary Exercises," Ibid., p. 7.
17. Hodges, p. 7.
18. Ibid., p. 9.
19. The Golden Gate Baptist Theological Seminary (A Western Seminary at the Golden Gate), Second Annual Catalog (1945-1946), p. 6.
20. Looney, p. 76.
21. Board of Directors, Southern Baptist General Convention of California, Minutes, August 16, 1945.
22. Looney, p. 79.
23. Ibid., p. 80.
24. Southern Baptist General Convention of California, *Annual* (1945), pp. 24,25.
25. Ibid., p. 41.
26. Board of Directors, SBGCC, Minutes, December 18, 1945.
27. Ibid.
28. Looney, Tape of conversations, November 8, 1978.

29. Ibid.
30. Ibid.
31. Board of Directors, SBGCC, Minutes (April 3, 1946).
32. Southern Baptist General Convention of California, *Annual* (1946), pp. 19,20.
33. Board of Directors, SBGCC, (July 25, 1946).

3

Toward National Recognition
and Support

B. O. Herring had been a popular and effective teacher of Bible at Baylor University for twenty years. As J. B. Tidwell approached retirement as chairman of the department of religion at Baylor, it was logical for Herring to anticipate succeeding him. Since that did not happen, he was approachable for service elsewhere. The offer from Golden Gate Seminary perhaps provided a challenge he was anxious to accept.

Exchanging the security of faculty membership at Baylor for the insecurity of heading the administration at a struggling infant seminary must have been a truly traumatic experience. The very existence of the seminary was being tested almost daily. Though owned by the Southern Baptist General Convention of California, it had no guaranteed support from the state convention. Even the convention's executive secretary was less than sympathetic toward the seminary's existence. One has to wonder how much of the true circumstances of the school were known to Herring. It could be that he knew enough but was still anxious to get away from Baylor.

Whatever may have been the case, Herring assumed a new role in his career with his administrative skills untried. All of these circumstances could cause a man to be sensitive to any criticism or potential challenge to his leadership. Herring may have been uneasy with the founder and former president of the seminary still at the seminary. Herring was better qualified by training and experience as a teacher than Hodges. He would obviously seek teachers with similar

Benjamin O. Herring, professor of Bible at Baylor University for twenty years, became the second president of Golden Gate Seminary in 1946. He served in that capacity until 1952.

qualifications as resources became available.

With the high level operation of Baylor in his mind, perhaps Herring reacted automatically at times to the many phases of the operation at the seminary that failed to measure up. On the other hand, the seminary was Hodges's dream and he would have natural tendencies to react to comments or actions by Herring that emphasized this contrast. Both men were in difficult positions, yet both were anxious to see the school live and succeed.

This was the setting as Herring planned for his first year as president of Golden Gate Seminary. He had to enlist additional faculty members in the hopes of raising the level of instruction. He had to give attention to the outlining and clarification of course requirements. A new catalog had to be prepared that presented the seminary in the best possible light. The 1946-1947 catalog Herring produced lists Hodges as vice-president and professor of theology and apologetics. R. F. Royal and Mrs. Claudia Royal are listed in religious education.[1] The catalog states that application had been made to qualify the seminary for attendance by veterans of the armed forces; approval was expected by September.[2]

The fall semester opened September 2, and that evening B. O. Herring was inaugurated as president. His address was entitled "The Wheel of Progress." The text was 2 Timothy 2:2, "The things which thou hast heard of me among many witnesses, the same commit thou to faithful men, who shall be able to teach others also." The message was basically an exposition of the text. Herring committed the institution to continue its emphasis on sound theology and missionary zeal.

Herring's address appeared on the front page of *The California Southern Baptist*, September 26, 1946. Spirits were high, and the future of the seminary claimed the attention of many Southern Baptists in California. Early concerns of the new administration are revealed in a report to the board of directors of the California convention. At the preconvention meeting of the board in November, O. Dean Johnson, chairman of the seminary trustees, reported:

> Your Golden Gate Baptist Theological Seminary [GGBTS] faces imperative need caring for normal growth and development and future growth; therefore, we request authority of the Board of Directors and of the Convention to permit the Seminary Trustees to negotiate for the purchase of suitable housing for the purposes of the Seminary and to purchase same.[3]

It was moved that "insofar as this Board has authority and in keeping with our constitution, that the Board approve the request."[4] The motion carried seven to one.

Herring reported that thirty-one students enrolled in September. Of these, eighteen were ministerial students coming from twelve states, with Texas providing ten, Oklahoma four, and California only three. Eleven were college graduates.

In his address to the convention, Herring said,

> The chief assets of this institution are to be found in the interest, love, prayers, and co-operative support of those who compose the constituency of our churches. The devotion of those who founded her and of those who nourish her with their manhood and money will preclude all possibility

of bankruptcy. . . . True, we have no campus and buildings here to list as material assets.[5]

He goes on to express appreciation to the Golden Gate Baptist Church for their facilities. He thanked those whose gifts of books raised library holdings to eight hundred items. Among book donors is listed the name of G. W. Keaster, whose later efforts on behalf of the library will be reported in more detail.

The new president pleaded for the churches to continue efforts toward reaching the Christian Education Day offering goal. Though taken in June, it was still more than $3,000 short. He also urged them to enlist others in the Thousand Dollar Club which provided ongoing support for the seminary.

President Herring continued his lengthy report to the convention with some hearty words on "Prospects":

Small are our beginnings. Even so let the mustard seed be small. If and when planted and cultivated latent possibilities soon are manifested out of all proportion to anything that could be seen. . . .

Turn your eyes if you will, to the beginnings of Eastern, Central, Northern, Southern, Southwestern and New Orleans seminaries. Was there ever one whose beginnings were more auspicious than that of our Golden Gate Seminary? Rooted in prayer, grounded in faith, with a planned super-structure silhouetted against and in conformity to the divine will—this all presages a glorious future. Here in this Empire of the West, God seems now to be converging the major streams of the world's life. The confluence of the peoples of all races and creeds seems to be now definitely taking form on the horizons of this Pacific shore. Here the Occident meets the Orient. Here at the edge of the greatest of the seas one sees great seas of humanity. What an area for One to walk who can walk on the sea, and so speak peace to the turbulent waves and raging winds. As people move in by the millions, as deserts are made to blossom as a rose, as the economic capital of the world climbs over the Rockies, as the political capital of the nations looms up by the side of the Golden Gate, . . .

Herring closed his report by offering a rather significant recommendation:

In the light of practically universal desire on the part of our Baptist people, and since it is inherent in any comprehensive and well funded program of education, we recommend that this Convention authorize its chairman to appoint a committee of five to study the matter of opening a Baptist College in and for the state of California. This recommendation would also include the suggestion that if possible under the Lord's blessing and the cooperative efforts of our people the study and recommendation to be so planned as to result in a beginning in the fall of 1947.[6]

Did he want it at Golden Gate? Floyd Looney thought so!

As a part of the seminary report to the convention, a resolution was read by the chairman of the trustees and it was adopted:

Whereas, many brethren at the Miami Convention [1946] proposed that we request Southwide acceptance of the Golden Gate Baptist Theological Seminary, and

Whereas, many since that Convention have voiced individual conviction that it should speedily be so recognized,

Therefore, be it resolved by the Southern Baptist General Convention of California that the Trustees of the said Seminary are hereby requested to memorialize the Southern Baptist Convention in Saint Louis in May, 1947, to appoint a committee of five to make a study of the proposal and to bring back recommendations to that Convention in its meeting of May, 1948.

RESPECTFULLY SUBMITTED,
O. DEAN JOHNSON, CHAIRMAN[7]

R. F. Royal, on the faculty of the seminary while serving as pastor in Vallejo, was elected first vice-president of the California convention. Hollis Burge, a trustee of the seminary, was elected president.

At the meeting of the state board of directors in December, they decided that Floyd Looney be the full-time editor of *The California Southern Baptist*. This required him to relinquish his official responsibility as field man for the seminary.

The budget prepared by the executive secretary and the board of directors again made no provision for support of the seminary from convention funds for the second year. Looney wrote, "The Convention had adopted the child but had refused to support it."[8] The Christian Education Day offering, church budget designations, and special gifts were the only hope. With the departure of Looney as field man, the financial future of the seminary was not bright. In spite of this, however, the state board of directors was asked in April, 1947 to approve the purchase of property for seminary expansion. The property to be purchased was a former lodge building located at Grove and Addison in Berkeley. It was owned by the Calvary Baptist Church. That church had belonged to the Inter-State Baptist Mission but had just voted to seek Southern Baptist affiliation.

The minutes of the seminary trustees' meeting read:

The Board of Trustees of the Golden Gate Baptist Theological Seminary assembled in Oakland, California, on Tuesday, February 4, 1947, unanimously adopted a recommendation of the Building and Grounds Committee as follows:

Be it resolved that we enter into negotiations for the purchase of the property of the Calvary Baptist Church located at the Southeast corner of Grove and Addison for the considerations of seventy-five thousand ($75,000) dollars. The details of payment to be set out in the contract of sale are to be one thousand ($1000) dollars cash, forty thousand ($40,000) dollars as a First Mortgage lien in favor of Mechanics Bank, Richmond, to run 10 years at 5 percent, with equal monthly installments, and the balance of thirty-four thousand ($34,000) dollars to be reduced all or in part by a ninety day campaign among the people in our churches for the raising of funds. If at the end of this period there remains an unpaid balance on this thirty-four thousand ($34,000) dollars, said balance is to be converted into a two year, three

percent second mortgage lien note in favor of the Calvary
Baptist Church Berkeley, interest payable semi-annually and
the principal payable, all or in part, at any semi-annual
interest paying date.[9]

Minutes of the April 2 meeting of the convention's board of
directors indicate that this action by the seminary trustees
was approved. By such action, they committed the convention to a campaign to raise $34,000 for a down payment. We
do not know how the campaign was promoted. The annual
report to the convention in November, 1947 lists $3,623.62 as
having been received by the seminary, designated for property purchase.

As the convention prepared for the Christian Education
Day offering in 1947, the major portion of *The California
Southern Baptist* for June 12 was given to this emphasis. The
front page carried an article written by President Herring.
The offering did not go well. In the August 14 issue of *The
California Southern Baptist* Looney editorialized:

SHALL WE HAVE A SEMINARY?

The President and the Board of Trustees of Golden Gate
Seminary have renewed their appeal for support for our
Seminary. The response to the June 29 offering was in some
instances encouraging but the overall picture is disappointing. . . . They are therefore appealing to us to make a further
effort not later than August 24. Surely our churches which
have not responded will rally to this urgent call. The importance of it cannot be over-emphasized.

The Seminary does not share in the regular cooperative
program percentages. It is dependent entirely upon the
dollar per month club and other special gifts from the
churches. It is certainly hoped that the Southern Baptist
Convention after next year will accept the Seminary and
operate it, but until that time arrives, California Southern
Baptists have no honorable choice other than to support it as
generously as possible.

There are three matters as the editor sees it of paramount
importance: first, the Cooperative Program; second, the

Seminary; third, a generous State Mission offering in October. Other special offerings are good for educational purposes but these three items are the very lifelines of our endeavor in California. We have absolutely no other source from which to secure support except the grants made by the Home Mission Board and the Sunday School Board.

Here it might be noted what resulted from the memorial to the SBC in Saint Louis in May, 1947. A committee was appointed to study the whole field of theological education. Herring reported to the California convention in November that this committee had "just completed its first tour of inspection and fact finding as the work of that committee relates to our Seminary." He went on to plead, "We solicit the prayers of all our constituency that the Lord's will may be surely revealed to the Committee and to the entire Convention."[10] Interest in this matter was heightened by the presence at this California convention of Dr. John Buchanan, representing the SBC. He was chairman of the committee appointed by the SBC to study the matter of theological education, including consideration of the memorial from California.

The seminary's annual financial report is quite remarkable in light of the adopted $10,000 budget for the year June 1, 1946 to May 31, 1947. They had received more than $23,000, nearly half of it from California Baptists. Things looked good indeed until one studied details of the report of the property fund. The amount received for property purchase contained a $5,000 loan. There was also a reference to the Castberg property, a purchase involving a $25,000 obligation. There is no reference in extant records reporting the transaction to obtain these adjoining cottages. Thirty-six hundred dollars had been raised in addition to the loan to complete transactions for the church property and the two cottages. The total debt was almost $100,000. The regular monthly outlay required nearly $600, plus periodic interest payments.[11]

As Herring began his second year, two changes had come in the trustees due to the deaths of C. B. Maxwell and G. E. Armstrong. Leslie E. Sanders, who succeeded Hodges as pastor in Oakland, took Maxwell's place both as trustee and as treasurer. J. M. Cooper replaced Armstrong. This is significant since Cooper was then pastor at Longview, Washington. Messengers from several churches in Oregon and Washington had been seated in the 1946 sessions of the California convention. The constitution had been revised to make this possible. These churches had been in cooperation with the Inter-State Baptist Mission but had become sympathetic toward Southern Baptists.

Several significant additions to the faculty are listed in the 1947-1948 catalog. I. B. Hodges was listed as an instructor in theology. S. G. Posey, who had become pastor of the Calvary Baptist Church in Berkeley, was to teach religious education. J. B. Kincannon was named professor of theology. Kincannon's academic credentials included a Bachelor of Arts degree from the University of Virginia and a Doctor of Theology degree from New Orleans Seminary. A. J. Hyatt, a pastor, was listed as instructor in Greek; and Leslie E. Sanders, as an instructor in homiletics.

The catalog had a strong emphasis on "Practical Activities." These involved community surveys, the beginning of missions, and the establishment of churches. Religious education courses were also stressed. Listings in this area included the Diploma in Religious Education, Bachelor of Religious Education, and Master of Religious Education.

Several students were listed for the 1946-1947 school year (as reported in the 1947-1948 catalog) who went on to complete their work and serve with distinction: Earl Bigelow, California pastor and longtime member of the Golden Gate board of trustees; H. O. Black, director of missions in Monterey Association; J. T. Harmon, Quincy Phipps, and E. E. Hill, longtime pastors in California; Truett Myers of the Radio and Television Commission; and Helen Nixon, first GGBTS graduate to be appointed for service by the Foreign Mission Board.

The status of Isam Hodges obviously changed during Herring's first year. Hodges wrote trustee chairman Johnson on July 11, 1947, expressing shock at learning from Herring that his position was not permanent. He refused a check for teaching summer school until the matter was cleared. Herring reported this to the trustees and asked for their assistance in clarification when they met in August. After that meeting, Secretary L. E. Sanders wrote Hodges on August 22. He reported that "the office of Vice-president is not practical or necessary. Furthermore our adopted constitution does not make any provision for same. In lieu of the two above considerations, the trustees recognize that the office . . . has been discontinued."

Hodges hastened to reply. His letter of August 25, 1947 revealed information he must have received from others. He pointed out the lack of discussion and the absence of a quorum at the trustee meeting and questioned their previous use of the vice-president position. He called for a conference to clarify his position.

Financial support for the seminary had become very critical due to the poor response of the churches. The two efforts to raise money that year, the campaign for the property purchase and the Christian Education Day offering, had fallen short. In November, 1947 the convention adopted a recommendation from Secretary Crittendon and the state board placing the seminary in the budget for the first time. Note Looney's interpretation of this action:

> The convention enthusiastically approved a recommendation of the board that 25 per cent of distributable Cooperative Program funds be channeled through the Executive Committee of the Southern Baptist Convention for world missions and that 75 per cent be retained for mission work in California and that 20 per cent of the state's portion of Cooperative Program funds be allocated to Golden Gate Seminary. This was the first time any recommendation had been made to give money to the seminary except that which came from special offerings. Dr. Crittendon had opposed putting the seminary in the convention's budget on the ground that it had been offered to the Southern Baptist Convention and it would probably delay its acceptance if

California Southern Baptists included it in the Cooperative Program. He contended that theological education was a Southern Baptist Convention responsibility.[12]

Speaking to the state convention in November, 1947, Herring reported that the trustees had adopted a budget of $15,000 for the current year. He stated that the fall enrollment was fifty-eight, forty-one men and seventeen women. Six women had scholarships, one given by the women of New Mexico and the others by California women.[13]

President Herring closed his address with a challenging look ahead:

When we turn our eyes to the unfolding days ahead, we see struggles and hard work to be sure. But work and problems are not to be accepted as a deterrant to effort. Rather do they constitute a challenge to lure and invite. Streaking the gray thus in evidence are many and vivid lines of light and promise. There seems to be a definite and growing consciousness of the Seminary and its needs among our people in all the churches. Too, there is a constantly increasing stream of assurance and help from outside our Golden State, even sufficient, we think, to presage the day of Southwide support and patronage for our school.

During this same convention a report was read by R. F. Royal concerning a children's home. He cautioned, "Already locations and sites for such a home are being suggested, but we have another institution [Golden Gate Seminary] which must be brought beyond the creeping stage and perhaps another which must be given priority. Let us be wise and prayerful that God will give us wisdom."[14] (Could the second "another" be a reference to a college? A committee was making a college study.)

Also addressing the convention was L. A. Brown of the HMB, who, said Looney, "delivered a message on missions which has since been referred to as one of the most inspiring missionary addresses ever heard by a group of California Southern Baptists."[15] Brown later joined the Golden Gate faculty.

During the first meeting of the state board of directors

A view of the seminary complex near downtown Berkeley in 1947, showing the main building and departmental classrooms on the left and the annex on the right.

following the 1947 state convention sessions, possible college sites were discussed. L. A. Watson asked their blessings on an effort in Los Angeles (no money, just blessings). Faulkner reported that they expected a school to open in the San Francisco Bay area by fall. S. G. Posey said that the Bible chair concept followed in Texas was the answer. Scott quoted H. D. Bruce, president of East Texas Baptist College, who said it would cost a million dollars to build and equip an accredited college in California. Someone suggested that George J. Burnett, a former college president, was present and might have words of wisdom. His comments closed the discussion for a time:

> You might as well get it out of your heads that you are in any position to build a university. . . . The state of California is standardized in this matter of education as no other state in the Union and if you started a school that does not measure up to these standards you could not get students for it. . . . I do not think you are ready to start even a college, though you certainly need it.[16]

Faulkner and others in the Golden Gate Association moved ahead with plans for a school which they called Western Baptist University. It was to open in the fall of 1948 with Faulkner as president and E. K. Daugherty as dean. It didn't open. Most of the pastors in the association had no interest in the school and led in withdrawing fellowship from the churches whose pastors were involved. The state board of directors instructed Secretary Crittendon to "write to all state Baptist papers advising them that Western Baptist University had not been recognized and that Golden Gate Seminary is the only school recognized by the Southern Baptist General Convention of California."[17]

Any additional effort in higher education by Southern Baptists in California would have seriously affected the seminary, which, though in a struggle for its life, continued to grow. A total of ninety-one students enrolled in the seminary during the 1947-1948 school year. Texas provided thirty-six of these, California only three. There were fifty-two ministerial students and of these, thirty-eight were serving as pastors of churches or missions.

The new catalog announcing plans for the 1948-1949 year listed new names for faculty and administration: A. L. Aulick, Greek New Testament; and Isham E. Reynolds, guest professor in music (he had served spring of '48). Kincannon was acting librarian and Aulick acting registrar. The Royals were on leave, enrolled in the DRE program at Southwestern Baptist Seminary.

Concerning the library, the catalog stated,

> Our Collection at present includes:
>
> | | |
> |---|---|
> | General and Miscellaneous, about | 1000 volumes |
> | Mary Nelle Lyne collection, about | 300 volumes |
> | B. O. Herring collection, about | 1200 volumes |
> | J. B. Kincannon collection, about | 1200 volumes |
> | S. G. Posey collection, about | 1250 volumes |

(All but 1,000 were on loan.)

To the "awards" section had been added a Diploma in Sacred Music, a Bachelor of Sacred Music, and a Doctor of Theology. Fields of study for the Doctor of Theology award were listed as: Old Testament, New Testament, Systematic Theology, Biblical Theology, Church History, and Missions.

Among students enrolled in the 1947-1948 year were: Sam Brian and Walter Phillips, who went on to serve in the chaplaincy; and R. J. Goodbarn, Dave Chamblin, Foy King, and Sam Jones, longtime pastors in California. E. D. Giddens, George Kendall, and A. J. Hyatt were the first students to enter the Doctor of Theology program.

In an effort to promote the offering for June, 1948, there was a spread in the May 13 issue of *The California Southern Baptist*. An editorial by Looney recounted the history and contribution of the seminary in beginning missions and churches. He reminded his readers that being 2,000 miles from the nearest SBC seminary, Golden Gate was essential in mission strategy. He also stressed the interest being shown by Baptists in nearby states and, indeed, by the SBC leadership. Looney ended his article with, "It is not presumptuous to say that in due course of time Southern Baptists will throw the weight of their influence, the power of their prayers and their material resources behind the Seminary."

Other articles emphasized the seminary's history, needs, scholarships, and contained an announcement of the coming of Aulick to the faculty. A plea by Secretary Crittendon was entitled, "All Out for Golden Gate Seminary."

Looney said, "Golden Gate Seminary, though first opposed by Crittendon, was now in his good graces and was fast becoming the largest theological seminary in the state and was destined to be one of the five seminaries owned and operated by the Southern Baptist Convention."[18]

The financial picture for the 1947-1948 school year ending May 31 was reported by Herring to the state convention in November, 1948. Total receipts of $42,500 represented nearly $17,000 from the Cooperative Program budget and more than $4,000 from church designations. Of this amount $8,000 had been paid in interest and principal on building debts. Less than $600 had been spent on the library.[19] The state convention voted to raise its contribution from 20 percent to 30 percent of receipts in the new year. This was in addition to goals of $5,000 each from church designations and the Christian Education Day offering. Herring was elated with the prospects. If these hopes had been realized, the seminary would, indeed, have been secure. But this was not to be and Herring reacted in disappointment.

Upon recommendation of the college investigating committee, the convention approved the appointment of trustees for a proposed college. No concentrated financial drive was anticipated. No one was encouraged to lessen support of Golden Gate Seminary. Two of the five college trustees chosen were also seminary trustees.[20] The only new name on the board of trustees of the seminary for the year was Robert Hughes to replace Silas Cooper who had left the state. Hughes had succeeded Cooper as pastor at Ventura.

The seminary trustees met in February, 1949 and, with high hopes, expanded the goals set by the convention in

November. They set $12,000 as the goal in church designations and $3 per member for the June offering. This added to the difficulties for California Southern Baptists. The year passed and expectations were not realized. Two central problems faced the state board: the state mission program and Herring's seminary appeals. Looney reported concerning the latter complaint:

> Golden Gate Seminary, through the president, B. O. Herring, and the board of trustees, had adopted and projected a budget which called for a much larger expenditure of money than the state convention had anticipated its receiving. In an effort to meet the budget Dr. Herring was filling the mails with letters concerning the seminary's crying need. Pastors were complaining about his appeals saying they could not comply with his requests without upsetting their local budgets. Dr. Crittendon was charging him with violating the convention's policy by making appeals for funds without the consent of the convention or the board of directors.[21]

One offending letter that had been mailed October 25, 1948, just prior to the annual convention, seems not to have caused much stir until some months later when receipts began to fall short. The letter follows:

GOLDEN GATE BAPTIST THEOLOGICAL SEMINARY
1908 Addison
Berkeley 4, California
October 25, 1948

S.O.S.

FRIENDS OF GOLDEN GATE SEMINARY:
What shall we do about operating expenses? This is not a complaint, but you should know what we face. If things are as our Baptist people want them, then your Seminary servants will abide by that decision.

Our Christian Education Day offering was less than five thousand dollars. The Center note of $4500 had to be paid out of it. So practically nothing was left for operating expenses. Cooperative Program percentages for the Seminary so far this fiscal year are as follows:

June $1153.96
July 1072.72
August 826.17
September 1532.23

Would you want it done? It had to be done. What? We had to use $510 of the September item above to pay the semi-annual interest to Calvary Church. How shall we pay the teachers their small stipends for October! Please pray for us, and if possible send some funds to us today.

SOLICITOUSLY YOURS,
B. O. HERRING

Before discussing reactions to that letter, we turn to activities on the campus. The seminary's first graduation was held May 2, 1949. Three state executive secretaries participated: H. P. Stagg, New Mexico; Willis J. Ray, Arizona; and A. F. Crittendon of California. Clyde J. Garrett, the music leader, was listed as "Head of the Church Music Department." Apparently Garrett had been added to the faculty earlier. His wife was given faculty status at the February trustee meeting. Also participating was F. M. Powell, elected to the faculty in February.

In anticipation of the Christian Education Day offering, the May 12, 1949 issue of *The California Southern Baptist* carried several articles. President Herring again had a message on the front page which seemed to be directed to all Southern Baptists rather than just to those in California. He spoke of the work of the SBC committee on theological education, then answered hypothetical questions about Golden Gate being worthy of support from Southern Baptists everywhere. In listing reasons for support, he stressed location, need, and the wonderful spirit of Golden Gate students and faculty. He closed with:

This young school offers the Southern Baptist Convention an opportunity unequaled in its history. It could be to the Convention what Timothy was to Paul, and if Southern Baptists, through their support would help enlarge this school so that no limitation would have to be placed on its enrolment, there is no way of estimating the thousands that could be won to Christ.

Therefore, the only logical conclusion is that the Southern Baptist Convention should immediately adopt the Golden Gate Seminary and aid in its support.

Crittendon's article in *The California Southern Baptist* was more of an appeal to the churches. He emphasized the need of the seminary along with the shortfall in Cooperative Program receipts. These made a generous Christian Education Day offering a necessity.

At the meeting of the SBC at Oklahoma City in May, 1949, encouraging decisions were made. Floyd Looney of California was chosen to serve on an enlarged committee on theological education. These actions are recorded in the SBC minutes:

1. That it be the purpose and intention of this Convention to project a long range program of theological education seeking to meet the needs as far as possible of all our churches and ministers. . . .

6. That two new seminaries, one in the West and one in the East, be established as soon as suitable sites can be had and adequate plans be made for financing the same without injury or impairment to our existing seminaries. . . .

8. That this Convention appoint a committee of one from each state to promote the long range seminary program in cooperation with this Convention and the several state conventions.

9. That such committee be authorized to recommend sites, enlist financial support, draw up charters, and perform other necessary duties pertaining to the carrying out of the above recommendations.

10. That the memorial relative to the Golden Gate The-

ological Seminary, and all other correspondence relative to the location and establishment of seminaries be referred to this new Committee on Theological Education.

Respectfully submitted,

Douglas Hudgins	John H. Buchanan, Chm.
Wallace Bassett	J. W. Storer
Edgar Godbold	R. Paul Caudill
R. C. Campbell	Wade Bryant
C. Vaughn Rock	Gilbert Guffin[22]

Back in California, Secretary Crittendon called a summer meeting of the executive committee of the board of directors and the committee on missionary nomination and assignment of the California convention. The matter of the Golden Gate Seminary appeals and a problem with R. W. Lackey prompted the call. It was a long meeting, lasting well beyond midnight.

In the course of the evening's discussions the question of Golden Gate Seminary and President Herring's numberless appeals going through the mail came in for considerable discussion. The members of the committee were unanimous in their opinion that Herring had violated the instructions of the convention and agreed to ask him to meet with the board of directors at its next meeting which was scheduled to be held in Santa Cruz, August 23.[23]

Seminary trustees were invited to attend the meeting in Santa Cruz, but for some reason few were present. S. G. Posey, convention president and seminary professor, presided. The dialogue from that meeting sheds light on the crisis.[24] Herring asked to speak first. He thanked those present for all that had been done and then described the plight of the seminary: salaries and bills were due but they had no funds. Both the Cooperative Program receipts and the special offering had fallen short, and he blamed this on a lack of cooperation from the churches. He closed his remarks with a detailed financial report.

Crittendon countered with expressions of sympathy, then

reported that convention needs were going unmet as well. The number of general missionaries needed to be doubled. Help was needed to plant churches in more than fifteen hundred cities and towns in the state. Don Giddens suggested a need to urge SBC action soon on taking over the seminary to relieve the state convention. Mulkey inquired about expenditures for seminary property, then went on to plead that the churches not be asked for more than they could do. Herring was accused of launching a financial drive, but he claimed that his letters simply announced goals set by the trustees. Crittendon said the letters certainly had to be considered as appeals.

Brian stated that the seminary had done more for the work in California than any other agency California Baptists had. Jack Combs then made a motion to send another appeal to the SBC along with details of what the seminary was worth. Looney spoke to Combs's motion:

> As the California member on the committee and not a member of this Board, I know he [Combs] offers that in all good faith, but I hope you don't ask that. We have presented this memorial and we are on the threshold of destiny. I think I can say this committee is almost unanimous in its good will already toward us. In the whole committee meeting in July, almost in the opening moments of the committee, Dr. Storer, chairman of the committee, said to the rest of us that in his opinion the Western seminary is pretty well established. . . . Dr. Buchanan made the motion that the steering committee . . . ask the finance committee of the Executive Committee . . . to recommend to the SBC that 5% of the distributable funds be set aside for each—the Western seminary and the Eastern seminary beginning in 1951. . . . I am honest and sincere in my belief that this committee means business. I believe that if we do one thing in California—demonstrate to all the world that we are big enough to make room in our hearts and lives for free differences of opinion to go ahead and stand together— they are on our side.[25]

Combs withdrew his motion and Posey adjourned the meeting.

Plans for the year 1949-1950 at the seminary were announced through the catalog, reflecting trustee actions at their February 23 meeting. New faculty listings included Dr. and Mrs. Clyde Jay Garrett in music. He is listed as "Director of the School of Music and Professor." Herring reported later, however, that they came to the faculty in the spring to remain only until the fall. They left to join the faculty at Howard Payne. F. M. Powell began on April 16 as professor of church history and homiletics; Royal was designated associate professor and Mrs. Royal assistant professor in religious education. Mrs. Clyde Jackson was named the first full-time librarian.

The catalog reported that dormitories were now operating for young women at 2105 and 2107 Grove Street (the Castberg cottages). An instructional fee of four dollars per semester hour is listed with a note, "On application this fee may be provided by denominational scholarship funds." (An obvious effort to collect the fee from veterans.) There was a new two dollar fee per semester for library use, and the music fees were doubled. Practical activities (field work) were required of all first- and second-year students.

Even though listed in the catalog, Hodges, Averett, and Sanders had left their teaching positions after the 1949 commencement. Herring had tried in 1948 to enlist F. M. Powell, longtime professor of church history at Southern Seminary, but he had declined. Herring had written him again in February, 1949 reporting trustee action, but Powell did not accept immediately. In the action electing him, the trustees also said, "and if he cannot come, to authorize Dr. Herring to continue to search for a professor for the place."[26] Obviously, this reveals the desire to discontinue Hodges though he is not mentioned by name in the minutes.

When Powell agreed to teach church history and homiletics, it eliminated both Hodges and Sanders. Apparently Herring wrote to Hodges reporting this action. Hodges replied on March 5, 1949, closing with:

Permit me to say this further word, that I have always felt, that before the final policies have been determined, and all of the faculty members have been chosen, that I would be offered a permanent place among the instructional staff. I have looked forward to this with joyful anticipation, and this has been so real that I have made many clear cut plans for this. If this should fail to materialize it would be to me an immeasurable disappointment indeed.

With the greatest love for the institution, for you and for what you are trying to accomplish, I remain yours most sincerely and respectfully,

ISAM B. HODGES

There may have been other exchanges, but the next extant letter from Herring to Hodges is dated August 18, 1949. He reminded Hodges of the trustee policy to find permanent replacements for the part-time instructors when finances would warrant it. He reported

with the opening of the fall semester that the professional staff of the Seminary will be sufficient to handle the necessary work without requiring the services of two or three of our former part-time teachers. You are one of these and we trust that the recognition of this condition will be understandingly accepted by you, as an eventuality of a trustee policy.

Hodges was out of town when this letter arrived; but upon his return, he was quick to reply. His disappointment is shown in part of what he wrote on September 1, 1949:

There is no way for me to portray the terrible interruption which has gone on in my heart of hearts since receiving this letter informing me that my connection with the Seminary, for which I have labored and for which I have sacrificed these many years—the best years of my life—has been severed and that not through any will or wish of mine.

Herring answered Hodges on September 12, but the letter has been lost. Hodges's subsequent reply on September 19 gives a clue that he recognized the separation was final. He recounted previous actions and commitments which had given him hope for a permanent place with the seminary, but he did not renew his appeal. He avowed his continued love for the seminary "and what its original design stood for." He wrote further, "that it will always be in my heart a desire to do all I can in any way I can to advance its glory."

Thus ended the official relationship the founder of the seminary had with the institution. Hodges remained in the area, making brief trips back to Arkansas, and finally became pastor of the University Baptist Church in Oakland.

A summary of the financial report of Golden Gate Seminary for the year ending May 31, 1949 shows the material progress that had been made. Nearly $60,000 had been received through the Cooperative Program, special offerings, and fees. In disbursements there was a $17,358.54 item for property expense. Listed in Herring's report to the state convention are the names and salaries of all employed persons. S. G. Posey was considered full time, even though a pastor. He is not listed there as dean but is so designated in other references.[27]

It is interesting to note Herring's appeal to the convention in light of his problem with the state board. After naming the first graduating class of thirteen and making much of the celebration of this event, he made a forceful appeal, then added:

> As we anticipate the favor of all our Baptist people from the Pacific to the Atlantic, let us in each and all our churches take a stand and so positionize ourselves as to let our brethren in other areas know that we are as one in the support of our one institution which is the strong and growing child of our own travail and effort.[28]

As people gathered for that 1949 state convention, they were reviewing the state convention's progress during the five years of Crittendon's leadership (1944-1949). The number of churches in the state had grown from 78 to 225; gifts through the state office were up from $29,900 to $251,200—of this $82,500 came from the churches. There had been a 500 percent increase in total church membership. Sixty-six new churches had been organized during 1949 alone.

Los Angeles Southern Baptists were pressing for a college. They officially established one that year and elected Clyde Jay Garrett as its president, but it had aborted. Crittendon was urging them to hold off until the SBC took over Golden Gate. The seminary was receiving 30 percent of Cooperative Program funds from California Baptists and needed more. For the year ending October 31, 1949, the convention had processed through its office a total of $31,359.03 for Golden Gate.[29]

As California Baptists anticipated the adoption of the seminary by the SBC the next May in Chicago, they voted to continue support during the year. They adopted a convention goal of $110,000 through Cooperative Program gifts from the churches. Golden Gate was to continue receiving 30 percent. In addition, the Christian Education Day offering goal was set at $15,000 and other designations at $10,000.[30]

In the November, 1949 *Golden Gate*, the seminary was called the largest in the San Francisco Bay area. Also, it reported that "Golden Gate Seminary has been accredited by the California State Department of Education for having fulfilled the requirements prerequisite to the conferring of all regular theological degrees. An exhaustive and thorough examination of the organization, faculty, program, and facilities was necessary before the coveted approval was procured. Since the State of California maintains high educational standards, the accreditation of the seminary is a noteworthy event." The Lieutenant Paul W. Bunch Memorial organ, given by his parents, was dedicated in 1949. (Enlarged for use in facilities on the new campus in 1959, that organ was retired in 1978 only after it became impossible to get parts.)

In the meantime, the SBC committee on theological education had been reorganized and enlarged. J. W. Storer replaced John Buchanan as chairman. A special subcommittee was concerned with the western seminary. Floyd Looney served on a seven-member steering committee from the larger committee. When the enlarged committee met, there was considerable criticism from representatives from the eastern part of the country about Golden Gate and the West.

Storer answered those criticisms by saying in the first meeting,

> Now, brethren, I didn't like the name of Golden Gate. Something about it I didn't like. It just had a pentecostal connotation to it somehow. But I went and took a look and I saw that it meant something. I went over with one of our own boys, Wallace Hough, for some meetings. I discovered that as far as Baptists are concerned outside of what those people in that seminary are doing there wasn't anybody doing anything about anything. That's it. I went, I saw, and I am convinced.[31]

President Herring and others in California were in touch with that committee all during those months. After the 1949 meeting of the SBC, Herring wrote the chairman on June 11:

> DEAR DR. STORER:
> Please allow me to file with you and with each member of your honored committee a statement of congratulations on the responsible task which is yours by commitment of the Southern Baptist Convention. . . .
> The Convention has put into your hands consideration of an institution divinely planted and marvelously blessed. Our students come from the states of the nation and from the countries of the world. They hail from the same colleges from which the students come to each and all seminaries. The life plans of about four hundred now in the colleges and desirous of coming this way are in your hands for helping to work out the Lord's will. About two thousand churches that need to be organized in this mighty West are definitely related to the Convention's committal to you. These represent places where there is not now and never has been a Baptist church of any sort. Approximately ten million lost and unchurched people west of the crest of the Rocky Mountains wait for the impact of the living gospel. Our responsibility in that matter is large.
> The Golden Gate Seminary has been correctly founded

and chartered. With one exception, the institution is well-manned. The school is in every way orthodox as measured by the customary New Testament and Baptist measuring rod for that purpose. It now appears that our maximum enrollment of two hundred regular students will be had by next January. Do not hesitate to commandeer our services in any way that your plans and purposes may seem to require. May the Savior point the way for us all.

CORDIALLY IN HIM,
B. O. HERRING

The Western subcommittee for the theological education study consisted of J. W. Storer, Tulsa, Oklahoma; H. A. Zimmerman, Richland, Washington; and C. Vaughn Rock, Phoenix, Arizona. They visited the seminary and the Bay area early in October, 1949.

Following that, things began to move toward a definite recommendation by the subcommittee and then the full committee. Looney said that he sensed victory when Buchanan made the motion that they accept Golden Gate and recommended the establishment of Southeastern Baptist Theological Seminary in Wake Forest, North Carolina. Buchanan further moved that "we request the Executive Committee in making out its budget for the next year to provide $100,000 each for the new schools." Louie Newton seconded the motion, and it carried.[32]

Looney did considerable leg work in making the adoption of the seminary possible. For one thing, the charter had to be redone. In February the state board appointed a committee to do this, but Looney did the work. He and Herring had some differences on this matter. Herring wanted the possibility of college level work to be included, among other things. Looney secured a copy of the New Orleans Seminary charter. He then went to the public library in Fresno, read the requirements for schools and worked out a new document that met California law. He conferred with the seminary lawyer and the secretary of state to get it all cleared. That document is what was presented to the SBC when they acted in Chicago in May, 1950.[33]

On March 1, 1950, Storer wrote President Herring to invite him to attend a meeting of the committee on theological education in Nashville on March 22. He closed the letter with, "I believe you are going to be pleased with the report of the Committee." Herring replied at once that he would be present.

Herring attended the meeting and on returning addressed Storer in a letter of March 27:

> Returning from the Theological Committee meeting in Nashville, I find myself with many and mixed emotions. First of all, I was keenly aware of loss at your own inability to be present. . . . Please allow me to assure you of the sincere regrets of my own heart because of your illness.
>
> At the committee meeting on Wednesday I was thrilled at the privileges that were mine as a guest. . . . It was ground for great joy to see how courageously and assuredly the brethren could vote to recommend the purchase of the Wake Forest properties and at the necessity of expending $1,600,000. Too, my whole being was moved with joy at the plan to pay $300,000 by January 1, 1951. I had been thinking all the while that funds for capital needs were definitely tied up for the other seminaries that plans of that sort could not be made. The explanation was that it might be possible to open as early as the Fall of 1951 and with a maximum enrollment of 150 students. My sincerest congratulations to the 2700 old and well-established churches of North Carolina.
>
> Oh, if our brethren could just see this mighty challenge here! In the Wednesday meeting frequent reference was made to the five eastern states—Maryland, Virginia, North Carolina, South Carolina, Florida. In these states we have over 6200 churches. In California alone we have nearly as many people as in the whole of the five states enumerated, and only 275 churches. Most of them very small, and struggling against problems too serious and numerous to describe. Surely our need here is 10 to 1 greater than anywhere else in our land. . . .

If arrangements can be made for $300,000 for capital needs expenditures at Wake Forest by January 1, then I certainly will rejoice in the accomplishment. The brethren expressed no doubt as to its being done. If the Seminary there can open in the Fall of 1951 with 150 students, again, I say, I will be personally elated.

But here our committee faces an unprecedented need. Here we are a Seminary already in existence. Here we have pending needs for $300,000 for property purchase, expansion and improvement—not next January but *Now*. . . . You will have our unstinted support in making plans for the Seminary child which may be born in September 1951. We have all confidence to believe that we will have yours in equal fashion in the effort to see that the young child which we already have here does not experience serious maiming from malnutrition and inadequate care.

On last Wednesday the brethren took the position that in the older and better established work of the Eastern States the requirements for a campus, buildings, equipment, etc., would be much higher and more expensive and elaborate than in the newer West. Of course, we have no 'requirements' beyond what our people will recognize and provide. However, Berkeley is in many ways the educational center of the world, and especially of the West. The educational and building codes here constitute the center of which the world comes for study. I cannot conceive of a challenge for action in kingdom building that should take precedence over what is offered to our people here. Unhesitatingly do I voice my approval of the Wake Forest recommendation. At the same time I must plead for some definite provision for facilities needed *now* in this mighty western field.

Some of our friends and churches to the east have kindly given to us aid in the past, but have evidently misread press reports about our proposed acceptance by the Executive Committee of the SBC. They have surely interpreted that our current operating expenses are being thereby supplied and have marked us off their list of contributions. Resultantly our plight for the remainder of this calendar year may become serious. If somehow the 1951 allotment could be arranged so that something like $3000 per month for June-December 1950 could be made available, such plan would preclude many hardships in operation.

At the Nashville meeting last week no word was proposed relative to aid for the work here. If the Chicago meeting of your committee announced for Tuesday morning May 9 at breakfast time could possibly initiate a plan for aid, such would not only engender gratitude in our hearts here, but doubtless would please the Saviour and constitute wise denominational strategy. I certainly wish that I might confer with you about it.

GRATEFULLY AND APPRECIATIVELY YOURS,
B. O. HERRING

President Herring saw happening to the seminary what had happened to it in 1945 when it was adopted by the Southern Baptist General Convention of California without provision for its needs. His plea was to no avail, and the struggle for existence which was to mark the institution for at least the next quarter of a century continued. Was it that the SBC saw only a mission project at GGBTS? Was it doubt concerning leadership?

Mention has been made of the criticism of Golden Gate by theological education committee members from the East. The attitude that produced the criticism apparently was unaffected by Storer's response. They found $300,000 at once to purchase a campus for beginning a new seminary in North Carolina. They found nothing to meet immediate capital needs for the school which was already in operation in California.

Herring took issue with the eastern sentiment "that in the older and better established work of the Eastern States the requirements for a campus, buildings, equipment, etc., would be much higher and more expensive and elaborate than the newer West."[34] A survey taken five years later showed that building costs were 40 percent higher in California than in North Carolina. Did these men feel that Baptist church buildings being finer in the East, a seminary campus would have to be finer also?

Few leaders living east of the Mississippi River realized the unique costs and other problems associated with the effort at Golden Gate Seminary. That fact lay at the heart of its struggle for existence. One cannot help wondering what might have been had that committee proposed the kind of immediate support that was needed at Golden Gate.

Duke K. McCall, executive secretary of the Executive Committee of the SBC, visited Golden Gate Seminary in November, 1949. He described it at that time as the "big opportunity." He was very supportive of the seminary as it approached recognition as an SBC institution. After his visit he wrote an article which appeared in the February, 1950 issue of the *Golden Gate*. After speaking of an earlier visit in 1947, he writes of his return, saying in part:

> I returned to find the seminary with an excellent faculty and bulging at the seams with students. The zeal which has always been characteristic of Southern Baptist ministers in not only a carefully planned program, but also a will to work together for the glory of God.
>
> I am rather well acquainted with the pains of birth suffered by the Southern, Southwestern, and New Orleans seminaries. I am convinced that the Golden Gate Seminary is not only to have the shortest and least painful birth experience, but also the briefest infancy. Courageous men have ventured much and sacrificed to serve in the Golden Gate Seminary, but even so, less will be asked of them because Southern Baptists have come to place a proper evaluation upon the training of ministers and missionaries and other religious workers. . . .
>
> The most important and strategic step Southern Baptists have taken with reference to their work on the West Coast is the proposed adoption of the Golden Gate Seminary.

Letters exchanged between Herring and McCall following that 1949 visit reveal Herring's concern as well as McCall's ideas. In response to the normal request for budget data preceding the meeting of the Executive Committee, Herring had written McCall for clarification on what was needed from Golden Gate. After providing the data, he pleaded for some consideration of support during the last half of 1950. McCall replied on January 30 with words of concern but without any promise of possible assistance.

The trustees of Golden Gate were to hold their annual meeting in February, 1950. Anticipating that time, Herring wrote McCall for suggestions on their approach. McCall replied with some suggestions:

> The trustees elected at the SBC in Chicago, May 9-12, 1950, are elected effective at that date. It will be necessary, however, for the present trustees of the GGBTS to continue to function until the actual transfer of property can be effected. Since the support from the SBC does not begin until January 1, 1951, I should not think that the SBC trustees would be concerned with the operation of the seminary prior to that date. . . . Frankly it would be my suggestion that your trustees proceed as though they were to continue in office with the understanding that their actions must be reviewed by the new board January 1, 1951 and may at that time be amended or recinded.

On March 24, 1950, President Herring wrote McCall, following his March 22 meeting with the theological education committee in Nashville. Noting the plans for the prospective new school in North Carolina, he asked for similar treatment. He begged that consideration be given to "a baby already born," equal to that given to "one whose coming is anticipated several months away." He again reported that the churches had begun to slacken their support, thinking that they were soon to receive SBC funds. He pleaded for help with operating funds.

McCall's answer on April 4 was short and sympathetic without giving much assurance that help was on the way:

> I appreciate your letter and would assure you that I am going to do everything in my power to provide some capital

needs funds for the Golden Gate Seminary at the earliest possible date.

Like you, I do not see at this time how the proposal of the brethren can be carried out with reference to the 1951 capital needs. That is one of those things which will have to be worked out in the pre-Convention sessions in Chicago.

Herring seemed to find some encouragement from Mc-Call's letter for on April 7 he wrote: "Your letter of April 4 is ground for thanksgiving. I am happy to be re-assured that you are going to do everything in your power to provide some capital needs funds for GGBTS. As you work there . . . a host of workers here will pray."

Everything during the spring of 1950 focused on preparations for the Chicago meeting of the SBC in May. An enlarged edition of the *Golden Gate* was prepared for distribution at the Convention. With pictures and descriptions of many Western scenes, it bore a welcome signed by J. B. Lawrence and Fred McCaulley, HMB, President Herring, and state secretaries Stagg, New Mexico; Crittendon, California; Ray, Arizona; and Milam, Oregon-Washington. That issue of the *Golden Gate* also announced the coming of D. W. Deere as head of the Old Testament Department and Joe McClain as associate professor of New Testament.

Summarizing the accomplishments of the seminary during his fourth year, Herring issued a statistical sheet. Enrollment had reached 188 from 28 states and 3 foreign countries. Texas provided 54 and California was up to 35. Ninety-eight were pastors of churches or missions. They had established 26 missions and organized 10 churches during the year. Students had reported 149 baptisms and nearly 200 other additions to their churches.

All were anticipating the action of the Southern Baptist Convention in Chicago, and they were not disappointed. The SBC minutes record the action:

27. J. W. Storer, Oklahoma, brought the report of the Committee on Theological Education, with the following

recommendations which were adopted after discussion . . .:

Recommendations

Bible Schools

1. . . .

2. . . .

3. . . .

Western Seminary

4. We recommend that the location of the Western Seminary be the present site of the Golden Gate Seminary at Grove and Addison Streets, Berkeley, California.

5. That the articles of incorporation be as follows:

6. That the Convention proceed to elect trustees as prescribed in the articles of incorporation, and take such legal steps as are necessary to establish same, and to acquire the assets of the Golden Gate Seminary, with the understanding that no liabilities will be assumed except those existing as of May 8, 1950, unless approved by a majority of the trustees elected by the Southern Baptist Convention at the time the liability is incurred.

7. That the transfer of ownership and control of properties of the Golden Gate Baptist Theological Seminary of the Southern Baptist [General] Convention of California shall be made on or before January 1, 1951.

8. That we instruct the Executive Committee of the SBC to advance funds to provide the expenses incident to the said transfer. . . .

Respectfully submitted:

J. W. Storer, Okla., Chairman	Claud B. Bowen, N.C.
C. Vaughn Rock, Arizona	A. E. Tibbs, S.C.
John H. Buchanan, Alabama	W. Fred Kendall, Tenn.
R. C. Campbell, Arkansas	Wade H. Bryant, Va.
Lucius M. Polhill, Kentucky	Lewis A. Myers, N.M.
A. Lincoln Smith, D.C.	Otto Sutton, La.
Thomas Hansen, Florida	Wallace Bassett, Texas
W. A. Burkey, Kansas	Floyd Looney, Calif.
Louie D. Newton, Georgia	James Heaton, Mo.
Vernon Richardson, Maryland	J. Paul Carleton, Ill.
Douglas Hudgins, Mississippi	H. A. Zimmerman, Ore.[35]

Golden Gate Seminary was officially a part of the SBC family but a more leisurely program of absorption was anticipated than what actually transpired. The Committee on Boards of the SBC was instructed to bring nominations for the Golden Gate board of trustees. The number and distribution were spelled out in the adopted articles of incorporation contained in the basic recommendation. These articles stated that they "shall be elected . . . in such manner and for such terms as may be from time to time prescribed by the said Convention . . .; except, however, that ten of said trustees shall be selected from the State of California, and one-fifth of the entire members shall retire each year upon the election of their successors."[36] At that time, the SBC constitution and by-laws called for one member from each cooperating state with 25,000 members in their churches. For some reason, however, two were chosen from Texas and have been ever since.

Trustees elected were: California: Harold Dye, Louis Hendricks, H. F. Burns, Fred Leach,* O. Dean Johnson,* and Hollis A. Burge (Burge, Johnson, and Scott were carry-overs from the California convention's elected board); Tennessee: J. L. McMillen*; Texas: E. H. Westmoreland and P. D. O'Brien; New Mexico: Floyd Golden*; Missouri: B. A. Pugh; Arkansas: B. K. Selph; Georgia: Guy Rutland, Jr.*; South Carolina: G. H. Mahon*; Illinois: T. W. Nelson; Mississippi: Glen E. Wiley; Virginia: Joseph H. Cosby, Jr.; Arizona: Roland E. Beck*; Alabama: Oscar A. Davis; North Carolina, Clyde E. Baucom; Kentucky: E. T. Moseley; Florida: Elwin Skiles; Louisiana: Otto Sutton; Maryland: Paul M. Tharp; Oklahoma: John W. Raley; District of Columbia: M. P. German (* laymen).[37]

An organizational meeting was called for the trustees who were in attendance at the Chicago Convention. E. H. Westmoreland was chosen as temporary president of the board. He appointed committees to begin functioning and to be prepared to report at their first regular meeting.

Letters of encouragement and congratulations poured in to President Herring from many quarters. J. M. Price (of Southwestern) wrote July 21, 1950, "It will give you new support and backing and will take quite a load off of your shoulders besides guaranteeing a future otherwise exceedingly difficult." This was a belief expressed by far too many without knowledge of the struggles that were to mark the school's existence for years to come.

Mrs. R. N. Underwood of Needles, California, wrote on July 22, 1950:

> Ever since I met you as you were on your way to the Convention I have realized I should write you. I want to tell you I could lend you around $1000.00 at least until your money starts from the first of the year through the SBC. I feel I should let you use it anyway, and my wish is that I could make it a gift, but I can't do that now. . . . my income is very small but my needs are the minimum.

President Herring was concerned about what California Baptists would do between the SBC action and the actual takeover of the institution January 1, 1951. His fears were justified as was demonstrated in the response to the Christian Education Day offering. Receipts were less than one-fourth of the year before. While support through a percentage of the Cooperative Program increased, total support from the state dropped $3,000 for the year. At the same time, a house next door to the seminary's main building came on the market May 1, and Herring felt compelled to buy it.

After the SBC meeting in Chicago, Guy Rutland and his pastor, Dick Hall, visited the seminary. A thorough study of all the facilities and the financial records enabled Rutland to assist President Herring in his planning. He presented the case for Golden Gate at the SBC Executive Committee meeting in June. Westmoreland, Rutland, and Hall accompanied Herring to that meeting.

As a result of Rutland's visit, numerous letters were exchanged between him, Herring, and Westmoreland. It was apparent that something would have to be done to provide for operation of the seminary for the remainder of 1950. Herring wrote a letter to each trustee on June 19, which combined a welcome to the board with an official notice of a called meeting. It was set for August 9-10 in Berkeley.

In anticipation of this meeting, Rutland sent his committee members a detailed report of the finance and property situation. He also described their assignment from Westmoreland "regarding all matters that pertain to the future plans and policies of the seminary." Arrangements for funds to operate the rest of 1950 had to be made and a budget for 1951 prepared. Consideration had to be given to property needs as well. His report also revealed the net worth of the seminary to be just short of $175,000.

It is an amazing evidence of the Lord's leadership that twenty-six of the thirty elected trustees were gathered on August 9. The minutes indicate that only McMillen of Tennessee, O'Brien of Texas (who never did attend a meeting), Davis of Alabama, and Moseley of Kentucky were absent.[38]

I. B. Hodges was present and was asked to speak about the early history of the school. The afternoon session was given to a consideration of the proposed constitution and by-laws as prepared by B. A. Pugh and his committee. They voted to make the fiscal year January 1—December 31. President Herring was asked to report for June 1—December 31, 1950 and then for the calendar year thereafter.

The nominating committee presented the name of Westmoreland as president of the board and Skiles as vice-president, and they were elected. Rutland's committee proposed borrowing $120,000 from a Nashville bank to combine all obligations (set at $117,929). They proposed a budget of $41,358 for the remainder of 1950, stating that the anticipated income would be approximately $17,000 short. The Relief and Annuity Board of the SBC would advance $20,000 without interest to be repaid out of 1951 receipts. The proposed budget for 1951 anticipated an income of $181,225 and expenditures of $176,389 and was adopted.

The board voted to petition the board of directors of the California convention to continue the 30 percent of its receipts to Golden Gate. Raley and Burge were asked to draw up the petition which was sent to Crittendon. He replied that

California Baptists could not do the other things needed if they continued that level of support. The California convention did allocate 10 percent of their 1951 receipts to Golden Gate. They also continued the Christian Education Day offering in their program (50 percent to Golden Gate; 50 percent to California Baptist College). These efforts provided nearly $18,000 in 1951 for the seminary.

The trustees also voted to take a like appeal to the Baptist conventions of Oregon-Washington, Arizona, and New Mexico. (Leaders of these state conventions replied that their mission needs prevented such action. Their support of Golden Gate would continue through the Cooperative Program allocation through the SBC.) The Executive Committee of the SBC was asked to secure a $120,000 loan to refinance the seminary liabilities.

Herring was elected president of the seminary. He then presented names of faculty members for election. These included those already serving plus some new ones. C. A. Insko was proposed as associate professor of church history (according to minutes, but we know it to be preaching, with Powell continuing in history). Wilbur Martin was named head professor of music. L. A. Brown was suggested for comparative religions and missions and Jack W. Manning was proposed for registrar.

Trustees spent Thursday morning inspecting the property in Berkeley and a property in San Francisco then voted to remain at the Berkeley location. They also voted to negotiate with Calvary Baptist Church for adjacent property. The Church Architecture Department of the Baptist Sunday School Board was asked to draw plans for the future development. The trustees set 500 students as the number toward which plans should be made.

The president's recommendations for the faculty were approved with the understanding that the faculty-personnel committee pass on the qualifications of each one. The next trustee meeting was set for June, 1951, preceding the SBC sessions in San Francisco. O. Dean Johnson, chairman of the former board of trustees, spoke of the "glorious mountaintop we have reached in the Golden Gate Seminary." He expressed appreciation to the board in taking up where they had left off.[39]

The executive committee of the board met two weeks later at Beulah Park, Santa Cruz, California, with Rutland, Raley, and Skiles absent. The committee approved a requirement for students to secure health insurance if they did not already have it. They requested the SBC Executive Committee to grant $5,000 at once for repairing the roof, purchasing chairs, pianos, and so forth, while awaiting the clearing of the bank loan. President Herring presented the papers which were to be signed by the former trustees, transferring the property to SBC ownership without going through escrow.

The former trustees (Southern Baptist General Convention of California elected ones) met October 31, 1950 in Bakersfield. They approved the transfer of the property to the new board, signed the prepared document, and adjourned, ending their responsibility.[40]

The first semester of school, during which the SBC assumed control, opened September 5, 1950. The enrollment was 177, coming from 25 states and 4 foreign countries. Fifty-three colleges were represented. According to a report in the annual of the state convention that fall, there were additional members of the instructional staff. These included: NeVoy A. Gerbracht, assistant professor in music; and O. Dean Johnson, business manager.[41] Johnson apparently began in October, 1950 and remained until September 1, 1951.

With the prospect of growth in the student body, Herring was very conscious of building needs. On September 14, 1950 he wrote Rutland:

> Too, I wonder if I might inquire as to whether or not we may expect someone from the department of architecture to visit us at a reasonably early date in order that we may begin to make some plans involving our proposed expansion. I could wish that we might have some plans sufficiently developed to be available for observation by our many friends who will be coming to us next June. I do not know

that it would be possible for anything to be done beyond the mere matter of making such plans available for that observation [the SBC meeting in San Francisco].

In the meantime, Rutland expressed concern to Herring about expenditures for repairs and equipment for which there were no funds in hand. He wrote on September 23, 1950, "I would advise both yourself and the Executive Committee to go slow on commitments or promises based on securing this capital loan. We feel that it is certain to go through but there is the chance that it might not." In listing the up-to-the-minute obligations for Rutland, on October 24 Herring wrote:

> The pianos and office equipment certainly seem to be absolutely necessary for us to do our work. We are getting by with 49 chairs instead of the 100 which we needed. At a very early date now we will be getting into the building next door planned for the Music Department and some rather extensive alterations and re-decorating will be absolutely necessary.

He continued his plea that some of the bank loan money be saved for this.

With the enlarged faculty, the added facilities, and the growing student body came greater financial burdens. These were all the more apparent with the delay in securing the loan for operation until the SBC allocations began January 1, 1951. The anxiety of the president was reflected in a letter to Westmoreland in October, 1950:

> On this October 11, duty requires that I report our financial plight to you. The date for the semi-annual interest payment to Calvary Church was yesterday . . . $750, and we have nothing with which to pay. Also, we have many current bills due yesterday, and we are faced with the impossibility of payment. You will recall that the operational expenses for September-December 1950 were figured on the basis of a replacement of those funds temporarily used for capital needs. We have been under the necessity of continuing these capital needs payments until now. We have exhausted

our operations funds and still don't have anything for the above matters.

He then listed items which had been purchased out of operating funds. Three additional items of capital improvement which he felt impelled to secure would cost enough more to make the total over $9,000. He ended his letter with "I see no human way for us to preclude almost unbearable embarrassment."

The executive committee of the trustees had voted in August to delay payment of the Castberg and Wendering notes. This would leave some $29,000 for a down payment on additional property. The conditions of the loan as approved in Nashville made this impossible, however, since it was specified that the debts be paid.

Herring wrote Rutland with copy to Westmoreland on November 7, informing them of an impending meeting in Nashville. It was a meeting of the capital needs subcommittee of the SBC Executive Committee. He reminded them that a request had to be prepared and suggested that perhaps the three of them should get together. A figure of $1,500,000 had been mentioned for Golden Gate. His list of priorities included an administration and classroom building and several units of student housing.

Before hearing from Rutland, Herring wrote again on November 10, pleading his case for necessary expenditures: "I do not see how we could operate a rapidly growing institution such as is this for 6 to 8 months without the purchase of other items where we find ourselves in such imperative need. Here are some things involving obligations which we could not escape (costing $3,153)." He went on to list needs for typewriters, desks, filing cabinets, and so forth for the business office and for the music department. He also asked that loan monies be allowed to pass through the seminary's bank account toward an "improved standing with officials in the bank." The financial plight is further revealed when he closes his letter with: "Especially, may I say that our expenditures of operating funds as previously set out above leaves us for these several days in great embarrassment with some of our staff, and I pray and trust that all possible speed may be had in caring for this item."

On November 15 Rutland sent checks representing the loans from the Nashville bank and from the Relief and Annuity Board. In the accompanying letter he said, "I will be glad to meet with you and Dr. Westmoreland in Houston on some convenient date." He continued his letter in answer to some of Herring's requests:

> I appreciate the fact that you would like to run these amounts through your local checking account, but the bank in Nashville asks that these be paid direct so that they would be reassured.
>
> In our various correspondence you set out that you have spent about $8,000 on such items as pianos, roof, office equipment, alterations and improvements, furniture and equipment for dormitories, tools, arm chairs for classrooms, hardware, etc. As you know, we have no provisions made to take care of these items in our budget before October of 1951, and I would suggest that before you make any expenditures you work closely with the Executive Committee to see your way through before proceeding with them. I realize the necessity, yet we are not in a strong enough financial position to make commitments beyond our estimated income.

We do not have in hand the agreements reached in the meeting of Westmoreland, Rutland, and Herring in Houston. However, Herring apparently thought he was to bring a proposal for their consideration, but he reported to Westmoreland in December:

> Each one present was handed a paper, a copy of which is enclosed. . . . Of course, I noted that action had already been taken. When it came my turn to make remarks I mentioned my awareness of what had been done and that perhaps my statements would not be to any point as far as committee action was concerned, since the vote had already been taken. However, I begged their indulgence since I felt

that my duty to you and our Trustees would require that I report the results of the Houston conversations.

The meeting with the SBC Executive Committee was disappointing for President Herring. The proposed allocation for Golden Gate for their second year under SBC operation was the same as before ($100,035) along with $150,000 for capital needs. (And that is what was voted when the SBC met in San Francisco in June.)

Herring wrote Rutland on January 8, 1951:

> Just prior to our recent meeting in Houston I talked with Dr. Westmoreland about the matter of putting our music building in shape. He suggested that since it could be handled personally and locally that I should go ahead provided that the total cost would be no more than $5000. We have done so and I wish you could see the building now. . . .
>
> You would be interested in knowing that upon the going of Dr. Posey to the State office in Fresno and the resultant vacancy in our faculty here, we have arranged for Mr. Manning to take part of his teaching duties. . . . In that way we will effect a saving of $250 per month. . . . We are doing our best to inventory every phase of our seminary life with a view of reducing the expenses for 1951. The trustees have the whole-hearted co-operation of the entire administration and staff of the seminary in attacking that problem.

Both Westmoreland and Rutland continued their emphasis on economy in the immediate future. Westmoreland wrote on January 22: "If it is in the realm of possibility, I wish that we might resolve to live within our anticipated income until such time as we can secure a greater support from the Convention. I give you this as my sincere conviction." Rutland had written on January 19:

> With apologies for being persistent, I urge that regardless of our budget approved at our meeting, you make every possible effort to adjust your expenses to the amount of your foreseeable, assured income for 1951. Nothing would

place us in a more favorable light with the Convention than to do the very best job possible with what we have and keep within our income.

To supply the many needs which he saw, Herring continued to write friends across the Convention to let them know of material deficiencies. Writing to one friend on February 14, 1951, he said,

A local firm has 5 good reconditioned pianos on their sales floor. They were valued at $1080. They offered them to us for $500. We had to have them. We must have faith to believe that God will impress a friend somewhere to enable us to pay the bill. The same is true relative to some lighting fixtures for the studios and practice rooms, and materials for cabinets and shelving.

Posey became executive secretary-treasurer of the Southern Baptist General Convention of California on January 1, 1951. Other changes in personnel were proposed by President Herring as he began to plan for the new catalog. In a letter to Rutland in March, he reported his planned reduction in teaching force. Hyatt, Townsend, Mrs. L. A. Brown, and Mrs. Royal were not to be continued beyond the current session ending May 1.

In the meantime the school year was drawing to a close. The enrollment had reached 222 for the year. Texas sent 52, Oklahoma 27, and now California had 27. There were 22 in the graduating class April 30.

In the *Golden Gate* prepared for use at the Convention, the practical activities report for 1950-1951 was given. There were 466 additions by baptism and 754 other additions to churches through the efforts of students. Forty-one students were working with foreign language groups. During the year, 14 new churches and 27 missions were organized.

A cordial invitation was extended to all who attended the Convention in San Francisco in June to visit the seminary. Free transportation was provided for those desiring it. Fred McCaulley was general chairman of the local arrangements committee. Wilbur Martin of the faculty was the Convention organist.

In anticipation of the trustee meeting, the president, board chairman, and finance chairman were all busy with plans. On April 20, 1951 Herring wrote Rutland:

> I am sending to you a copy of some blue print sketches which were sent to me a few days ago by the Architectural Department at Nashville. I am wondering if many of the Trustees perhaps still have at least an inner urge that we should get the acreage accommodations for our future building operations. If you think it wise, I will undertake to find some data on possibilities and have some suggestions along that line by the time of our meeting on June 15.

He seemed to be having some second thoughts about any further development in the present location.

Rutland answered on May 4:

> It is my opinion that the trustees believe that it will be necessary to move our institution to some nearby location where there is adequate grounds before we can sell the Convention on financing an adequate building program for us. I understand that is the very reason that we were required to liquidate our entire loan at Nashville out of this year's reserves in order that we would not have additional funds to expand on our present location without again clearing through the Executive Committee.
>
> I do think it would be wise if you would look for a location of approximately 25 acres or more, that would be suitable for the location of our seminary and when Dr. Westmoreland and I arrive, we could examine the possibilities with you and make a recommendation to our Board of Trustees as to some definite action.

Herring replied on May 8, assuring Rutland that information about possible locations for a new campus would be secured. Herring also repeated his pledge to practice economy in operations no matter how much they needed materials.

The trustees met June 15, 1951 at the seminary, following chapel where Westmoreland had spoken. Nine were absent. Westmoreland announced that the capital needs survey committee of the SBC would visit the seminary on the Monday following. All trustees were invited.

The finance committee recommended that all reports regarding finances being sent to the SBC be cleared through the trustee executive committee. Rutland asked that a financial report be sent to all trustees since they, as well as the finance committee, were responsible. All expenses not in the budget were to be cleared by the executive committee. They also requested the California convention to continue support. The securing of a business manager was to be cleared through the faculty personnel and curriculum committee and the finance committee. The administration was instructed to operate within the budget. The minutes record next:

> Mr. Rutland presented some plans for our further expansion of the Seminary. Some plans for building whether on present location or on new location. Also possible plans for the next four or five years to take care of the needs within that period of time.
>
> Motion was made that the Board present the Survey Committee with a listing of minimum needs as to buildings, girls dormitory, boys dormitory, apartment building, administration, etc., with estimate of cost and request that be set up in the budget and allocated to us as rapidly as possible. Motion was seconded and carried.[42]

Resolutions of appreciation were adopted for the Executive Committee of the SBC and Relief and Annuity Board for their help during the year. Floyd Golden, chairman of the faculty and curriculum committee, reported that they had gone over the curriculum and courses of study and recommended adoption. Resignations from the previously mentioned teaching force were accepted along with that of O. Dean Johnson. The administration was instructed to require all resignations to be presented in writing. A tenure policy was to be considered next year. They asked John Raley to work with President Herring and Albert McClellan in presenting the seminary to the SBC sessions in San Francisco. After setting a salary of $4,500 for heads of the departments and the registrar, they adopted the budget for 1952 as revised.

On Monday of the Convention week the SBC committee that had been asked to restudy the capital needs program visited the campus. The committee consisted of H. W. Tiffany, Virginia, chairman; Louie Newton, Georgia; Boyd Hunt, Texas; George B. Fraser, D.C.; and J. W. Storer, Oklahoma.

Golden Gate Seminary received considerable attention during the Convention. Using a California brick as the symbol, trustee chairman Westmoreland gave the seminary to the Convention in a presentation to SBC president, R. G. Lee. In making the seminary report to the Convention, Herring emphasized its phenomenal growth of over 400 percent in four years.

During the Convention, the second national meeting of the seminary alumni association was held, with 150 in attendance. Berkeley mayor, Laurance L. Cross, gave greetings, and Westmoreland was the speaker. Don Giddens was succeeded by Robert E. Townsend as national president. SBC seminaries, boards, and agencies were well represented.

An article appearing in the August *Golden Gate* reported that more than two thousand from the Convention visited the seminary in Berkeley. "It was a WESTERN convention, and yet, the Baptists who came from all sections of the nation were never more in perfect unity and spiritual harmony." The Golden Gate article quoted a Tennessee *Baptist and Reflector* editorial:

The San Francisco Convention will stand out in the minds of many who attended it as one of the greatest among our sessions in recent years. Dr. E. H. Westmoreland, chairman of the Board of Trustees, Golden Gate Seminary, said he believed it was the providence of God that the Convention voted to go to San Francisco, and was held here the year

Golden Gate Seminary actually came under the control of the Southern Baptist Convention.

A highlight of the summer news at the seminary was the announcement that the Baptist Sunday School Board had authorized a gift of $25,000 toward the library. There seemed to be no question in anyone's mind that the seminary would relocate, hopefully in or near Berkeley.

There was much excitement as plans for the opening of the fall semester neared. Summer school attendance had been at a record high, including twenty-five new students, mostly from other schools who earned credits to transfer. An enrollment of 200 was expected in the fall, including a record 100 new students, according to the *Golden Gate.* Two men were added to the faculty as associate professors: J. B. Nichols in religious education and James H. Walker in church music. When enrollment was completed, 192 students were on hand.

Meeting in connection with the California convention October 31, in Fresno, the alumni association voted to raise $2,500 to buy pews for the seminary chapel. A goal of $30 was proposed for each former student.

A most electrifying announcement appeared in the November, 1951 *Golden Gate.* The SBC Executive Committee had adopted a recommendation that Golden Gate receive a total of $1,000,000 over the next five years for capital needs. Herring announced this in November—though it still had to be voted by the SBC the next May.

In the same issue of *Golden Gate,* Chairman Westmoreland expressed gratitude to God for leading Southern Baptists to San Francisco. He said in part:

> Meeting in the heart of a great mission field, messengers to the Convention returned to their homes with gratitude in their hearts that Southern Baptists already had in operation a full-fledged seminary to serve the crying need for trained workers in this challenging mission area. . . . The President, faculty, staff and trustees believe that the future of the seminary is secure. It has won its way into the hearts of the

people, and such support as is necessary for its future growth and expansion will be provided in time. We believe that the hand of God planted it at the "World's Crossroads," and we believe that the will of God will guarantee its perpetuity. . . . Plans are already underway for the development of a stronger faculty, the standardization of the curriculum and the establishment of policies and procedures that will guide the institution through this period of "growing pains."

Some of those "growing pains" were beginning to appear as that article was being read. The faculty had begun to express different opinions on the seminary's direction. Probably the central issue was the matter of an academic *versus* a practical emphasis. There was also some disagreement over the graduate *versus* the basic degree efforts.

Perhaps it is appropriate to comment on the transition through which theological education in America was passing at the time. During the last century and well into the twentieth century, theological education consisted basically of biblical, theological, and historical studies. Such a pattern lingered much longer in England and on the Continent, even being the dominant one for the first half of this century. The practical or applied courses, such as religious education and church music, were often considered inferior in content and value.

At our various seminaries, some professors insisted on an academic approach to the neglect of practical courses that were also needed. In fact, religious education courses had to be forced into the curriculum in some schools. The degree of acceptance of practical courses varied from professor to professor and school to school. However, as late as the 1930s there were professors who described courses Dobbins and Price taught as busywork and not solid theological fare.

One seminary described itself as "The School of the Prophets"—in short, a "preacher school." In that school, there was a lack of emphasis on practical or how-to courses. As late as 1934, the seminaries' curricula left no room for electives and no layman had yet enrolled. Many thought that the religious education and music courses were disciplines which should be provided by Baptist colleges. This idea was still present in some quarters in 1957 when the SBC voted to establish Midwestern Seminary.

Golden Gate Seminary was begun because of a felt need for practical help for church staff members, primarily pastors. Preparation was needed in all areas, including religious education and music.

Early leaders at Golden Gate Seminary came with the conviction that the academic and the practical should be blended into the curriculum to provide total preparation for ministry. However, as the faculty grew, there were those whose training and focus often relegated practical disciplines to a lesser place. This divided the faculty and affected many decisions that were basic to the life of the school.

Notes from the 1951-1952 diary of a faculty member shed some light on the conflict:

> Jan. 5_____ came in later than usual. . . . (Theologs are trying to root out Rel. Ed.) Jan. 16. Disturbing times: faculty dissension. Jan. 22. Advisory Council (heads of departments) met this afternoon. Rel. Ed. took a beating: but the Lord is working it out to His glory. Jan. 29: Faculty meeting this afternoon—rather harmonious except for Dr._____'s grumblings. We hope everything is settled concerning Rel. Ed. Truly, the Lord has won the victory—not we ourselves. Feb. 22: . . . group is having meetings again. Feb. 26: Faculty meeting was "rough." Feb. 28: We know that our Heavenly Father will win the victory in our seminary. Oh for a richer fellowship!
>
> March 7: Voted against D.R.E. at Golden Gate. Not ready for it! . . . November 12: . . . Faculty meeting stormy. Wanted to give power to appoint committees to faculty instead of president. The amendment carried, asking the president to appoint committees, subject to faculty approval.[43]

The diary reveals that the conflict was over what kind of school Golden Gate was going to be and how the administration and faculty would relate. There were both practical

curriculum problems and personal conflicts—especially between President Herring and Professor Powell (with Dr.
Deere as Powell's able assistant).

When Herring came to see that he could not get the faculty
together, he asked Powell to resign at age sixty-five. Herring
wrote Powell on November 21 suggesting that he exercise the
option of retiring as of December 31, 1951. A bomb dropped
on the school could hardly have caused more disruption.

The faculty was at odds, and President Herring asked
trustee chairman Westmoreland to involve the executive
committee of the trustees in resolving the conflict.

The executive committee meeting was held in Berkeley
December 11, 1951. Herring did not attend because he was in
the hospital. After interviews with some faculty members
and considerable discussion, it was determined that several
would have to leave the seminary. There was also general
agreement that the president had gone about as far as he
could in leading the school. Everyone seemed to feel, however, that he should continue as a teacher. It was agreed that
he should not have his status changed in the same action that
dismissed faculty members.

The outcome of the December trustee meeting is revealed
in a letter from Chairman Westmoreland to each of the
trustees dated December 30:

> The Executive Committee was called into emergency ses-
> sion at the request of President Herring, a crisis having
> arisen among the members of the faculty. Dr. Herring had
> written a letter on November 21 to Dr. F. M. Powell, Head of
> the Department of Church History, suggesting that he volun-
> tarily retire from the faculty as of December 31, 1951. Dr.
> Powell could do so by exercising the option to voluntarily
> retire at age 65. Dr. Herring sent the letter after a conference
> with Rev. H. F. Burns, Chairman of the Executive Committee,
> and Dr. Floyd D. Golden, Chairman of the Committee on
> Faculty Personnel and Curriculum. This action created a state
> of emergency and it seemed imperative for the Executive
> Committee to be called into session. Every member of the
> committee was present, including the president of the Board

of Trustees. In executive session, the president of the
Seminary and the members of the faculty were interviewed
one at a time. Following these interviews, we drew up and
adopted the enclosed Findings and Directives. These were
read to a called meeting of the president and the faculty. No
discussion was allowed to this report but all seemed agreea-
ble to this action.

The Executive Committee will have further recommendations to make to the meeting of the Board of Trustees, when
it convenes in Berkeley, February 13-14, 1952. It is imperative
that we have a full meeting of the Board at that time.
Decisions will be made that will affect the destiny of our
institution.

Since my return to Houston, I have received Dr. Herring's
resignation, dated December 15, 1951. . . . This action further
emphasizes the importance of our Feb. meeting.

In the February trustee meeting, after Herring's letter was
read, the trustees went into executive session. The minutes
report that,

Dr. Golden was then called upon to give a report of incidents
leading to the calling of the emergency session. Dr. Westmoreland and Dr. Golden both stated that the fellowship in
the instructional staff of the seminary had been broken and a
serious rift had developed between the faculty and the
president. Because of this condition, President Herring had
asked for a meeting of the executive committee.[44]

The report of the executive committee was then read to the
trustees, "prefaced by reading the resignation of Dr. F. M.
Powell."

The minutes of the February meeting of the board record
the report of the executive committee:

The Golden Gate Baptist Theological Seminary is a phenomenon in the life of Southern Baptists. It is here because
of the vision, work and often sacrifice of our brethren in
California, and represents the brightest hope the denomination has for successful Christianization of this great territory.

Your Executive Committee is keenly conscious of the necessity of conserving all that has gone into the seminary life, and at the same time matching its problems with courage and faith that its rightful destiny be achieved.

The major problem before us at this moment is that of leadership. President Herring has tendered his resignation. In studying this matter in light of all related problems, highlighted with the good of the seminary as a primary consideration, your committee has a recommendation whereby it feels that we can serve the best interest of the institution.

We happily recognize that there is a place for all the laborers in the vineyard of the Lord. Did not one say that there are many laborers . . . some apostles, some preachers, some administrators, some teachers, etc.? A reference that individual men possess specific gifts for various tasks in the Master's vineyard, and that there is a reward for every laborer.

Anxious to have the continuing services of Dr. Herring added to his labors of the past, and recognizing that his lifetime preparation and experience lie in the field of Christian service other than administration, that administrative duties have been arduous, unpleasant and restrictive of his best energies in the major fields of teaching and preaching, your committee, after full deliberation, prayer and consultation with each other submit the following three-fold recommendation:

1. That the resignation of Dr. F. M. Powell be accepted and his services be terminated immediately and that his salary continue through the summer term of 1952.

2. That Dr. Herring's resignation as President of the Seminary be accepted, but that he be requested to continue in full authority as president until a successor has been chosen and installed.

3. That the President of the Board of Trustees and the Chairman of the Faculty Committee confer with Dr. Herring regarding a new relationship with the seminary, and a new assignment of duties in which his abilities as

a teacher and preacher be utilized to capacity service
for the seminary both on the campus and throughout
the territory.

4. That a committee be appointed to draw up suitable
resolutions of appreciation of the work of Dr. Herring as
president of the Golden Gate Baptist Theological Seminary and that the resolutions be the official statement
of this board.

The trustees acted upon the recommendations one at a
time. They voted to accept Powell's resignation, effective
immediately. (Powell later requested that they consider a
delay of one week in order that he might make arrangements
for his graduate students and this was granted.) The vote on
Herring's resignation was taken and accepted. The other
recommendations concerning Herring were adopted. They
then granted him a month's leave of absence due to his
illness.

A committee of five was chosen to find a new president.
The officers of the board, E. H. Westmoreland, Floyd
Golden, and Earl Bigelow, were to serve and they were to
choose two others. They chose Elwin Skiles and P. Boyd
Smith.[45]

The acceptance of resignations from Herring and Powell
did not end the matter. Others were to be dealt with by
interview, and the minutes reflect the actions taken. In due
time those interviews were held and Golden was asked to
report. The committee made its recommendations. After
much discussion and a series of motions, amendments, and
votes, all faculty members except one were retained.

Other actions of the trustees in their annual meeting in
February are worth notice. They elected Paul Mason, business manager of First Baptist Church of Lubbock, Texas, as
seminary business manager, to begin service March 15, 1952.
They voted twenty-five-dollars-per-month increase in faculty
salaries retroactive to January 1, 1952. A student loan fund
was established with funds received from Mr. Wasson of Big
Spring, Texas. The total was $7,500 including $1,550 on hand
"for such purposes from five Memorial trusts." They also

visited a possible site for the new campus near the Caldecot Tunnel in Oakland. When they returned, they approved the 1953 budget of $192,300. Rutland then recommended:

> That we get an option on the property and to bring someone out from the architectural department of the Sunday School Board for counsel. It was recommended that the two pieces of property be considered, the one being the property adjacent to the proposed site. The two properties constitute approximately 97 acres . . . motion made that the finance committee and the president of the Board of Trustees act as a committee to proceed to get an option on both pieces of property if possible. . . . Confidence was placed in this committee to use their own discretion as to the money it would take for the option and the worth and value of the property.[46]

Westmoreland appointed a committee of Wiley, Brantley, and Selph to draw up resolutions expressing appreciation for the work of B. O. Herring. Future meetings of the trustees were set for Miami, Florida, Tuesday, May 13, 1952 and the annual meeting in Berkeley in February, 1953.

Immediately following the trustee gathering, J. W. Storer was at Golden Gate to deliver lectures in the annual Bible conference. He had visited the seminary on many occasions during the preceding three years and knew it as well as anyone outside the state. His heart was heavy when he returned home.

In conversation with fellow Oklahoma pastor Harold Graves, Storer said, "That school is going to die unless they can get a new president soon."

I asked, "And who are they going to get?"

Storer's reply was, "I don't know, but I think they are going to get you."

"What!" I exclaimed. "You can't be serious." But Storer was serious and produced a copy of a letter he had written to E. H. Westmoreland.

I shared this experience with a dear friend, Gus Carleton, a few days later. He replied, "Good. You go out there as president and I'll come to teach church history for you." I did and he did, but many things would transpire before the July 1 date when I would assume the presidential responsibility.

President Herring's resignation had been accepted, but he was to serve until his successor was chosen. In the meantime, he was elected president of Grand Canyon College in Phoenix, Arizona. He left the seminary on April 1 to assume his new duties. Westmoreland appointed A. L. Aulick as acting president. He served until the new president arrived. There were forty-one graduates in the commencement exercises.

Among the 41 graduates of the class of 1952 were several who became foreign missionaries and many others who have served well in California and elsewhere. They were a part of a total of 248 students who had enrolled at Golden Gate during the 1951-1952 year.

Aulick wrote to Westmoreland on April 28, telling of his plans to attend the SBC in Miami and reporting that enrollment for the summer looked good. He expressed concern for someone to replace Carl Halvarson in public relations.

Acting President Aulick reported to the trustees in Miami that McClain had resigned to accept a church in Texas.

When the trustees met on May 13, they accepted resignations of both Halvarson and McClain. They then asked Rutland to report on the progress of negotiations for the proposed site for seminary development. He presented Hardie Bass, architect with the BSSB, who stated that he felt the site was usable. Rutland quoted a price of $140,000 for the 47-acre parcel but said that no price had been set for the 50-acre piece. Selph moved and Burns seconded, "that the Finance Committee purchase both pieces of property at a maximum of $220,000. Motion carried."[47] The only other action taken in that meeting on May 13, 1952 was in response to a recommendation of the president search committee. The trustees present were Westmoreland, Rutland, Harwell, Raley, Cosby, German, Skiles, Pugh, Mahon, Burns, Bigelow, Selph, Tharp, and Day. The minutes read:

Dr. Westmoreland gave the report of the Committee appointed to find a new President. Dr. Westmoreland reported that the Committee earnestly sought the Lord's will and were unanimous in recommending Dr. Harold Graves of Bartlesville, Oklahoma, for the new president. A complete explanation of the work of the committee and how it had arrived at the decision was given by President Westmoreland. A motion was made by B. A. Pugh and seconded by Bernes Selph that Dr. Harold Graves be elected as our new President. Dr. German then spoke in favor of the motion and very favorable comments were heard from many Board members. President Westmoreland then asked the Board to kneel in prayer and seek God's guidance in the final decision. Brother Selph led in the prayer. The motion to elect Dr. Graves carried unanimously.

G. H. Mahon made the motion and Joseph Cosby seconded it that the Finance Committee, in consultation with Dr. Graves, set the salary for the new President. Motion carried.

Dr. Harold Graves, who had been asked to wait in the hotel lobby, was then brought and presented to the Board. Dr. Graves, after being told he was unanimously elected the new President, said he was surprised and humbled by the action of the Board and that his decision must be wrought through prayer. He asked the Board to join with him, praying that the Lord's will might prevail.

Mr. G. H. Mahon made a motion that Dr. Aulick continue until Graves assumes the role.[48]

Graves had not known that the full board of trustees (fourteen of them) was meeting in Miami. He had not talked with a single member of the president search committee. Though he knew four of them, he did not know at that time nor for years afterward who was on that committee. John Raley had asked Graves to meet with the committee during the SBC meeting in Miami. Expecting nothing to come of it, Graves made no mention of it to the chairman of deacons in Bartlesville nor to his children. Preceding the SBC gathering, the Graveses spent a week on a HMB tour of Cuba, arriving back in Miami on Monday. On Tuesday afternoon a call from Westmoreland confirmed the eight o'clock appointment.

While Graves waited, he visited with a friend of seminary days. They talked past eight o'clock. John Raley came for him, his usually ruddy complexion blanched white, obviously greatly agitated. Graves asked, "What's wrong with you, John? Are you sick?"

Raley replied, "No, I'm not sick. Come on with me and you'll see what it's all about." As they entered the room, everyone stood and cheered, much to the confusion and amazement of Graves.

Westmoreland introduced Graves to the trustees and each of them to him, along with Aulick, the only non-trustee present. Only three members of the president search committee were present: Westmoreland, whom Graves had known from service with him on an SBC committee; Skiles, with whom Graves attended seminary; and Bigelow, whom Graves had known as a student at OBU and pastor in Oklahoma.

Following the introductions, Westmoreland turned to Graves and announced, "I have the honor of informing you that you have been unanimously elected president of Golden Gate Baptist Theological Seminary."

Graves exclaimed, "What? I don't know what to say. We'll have to talk about this. I'm surprised and humbled by your action. I'll have to do a lot of thinking and praying about a decision."

Trustee members began, one after the other, to share their thoughts and convictions. Many of them, like German and Rutland had not known Graves until he was mentioned for the post. Several were emotional in saying, "If God isn't in this, then I don't know how to know his will." There was general agreement on several aspects of the type of man that was needed as president. Graves seemed to possess several of the qualifications that made him look right.

They wanted a pastor; he had been one for seventeen years. They wanted someone familiar with educational institutions; he had been on the OBU board of trustees for four years, serving once as chairman. He had served on the board of The Southern Baptist Theological Seminary for six years. He had also served on the board of directors of the Oklahoma Baptist Convention and as president of that state's convention for two sessions. They wanted one who could work with other Baptists, especially Northern Baptists; he had been a pastor in the North for five years and had grown up in Illinois where Northern and Southern Baptists existed side by side.

They wanted one who could work with all kinds of Southern Baptists, especially pastors, graduates of either Southern or Southwestern; he was a graduate of Southern and had worked among graduates of Southwestern for eleven years in Oklahoma. He had earned the Doctor of Theology degree and had served the denomination on association, state, and SBC levels in many capacities. He seemed to be just the man they sought.

He, on the other hand, loved the pastorate, was happily situated in a church where he had been for seven years. A new educational building was nearing completion, and the future looked bright for pastor and people. His family was happy. At age forty, with a good church staff that gave him time to prepare, he might even become a good preacher. How could he leave?

Returning to the Convention that night, Graves discovered that everyone seemed to know what had transpired. When he saw Gus Carleton, Gus covered his face, remembering what he had said a few weeks earlier. The next day Westmoreland introduced him to the SBC at the time of the Golden Gate report. Graves asked for their prayers during the time of his difficult decision.

Soon after the Convention meeting, Graves went to Berkeley to meet with Westmoreland and Rutland. He looked the situation over, met with the faculty, and sought further information on which to base a decision. He had not visited the campus a year earlier when the SBC met in San Francisco. He had visited it in 1948, however, while on

Harold K. Graves when elected president of Golden Gate Seminary in 1952

vacation with his family in the West, at which time he met S. G. Posey. During his visit now he got a much clearer picture of the needs and possibilities, but still could not see leaving his church.

In the meantime OBU awarded him the Doctor of Laws degree. President McCall of Southern Seminary spoke at the ceremonies. Graves's parents were also present. Both McCall and Raley sought the aid of the elder Graves in leading to a positive decision, but he declined to interfere. It took weeks of thought, conversation, and prayer before a clear decision came. The combination of experiences that came together to fit the man for the post was impressive. The evident conviction of the trustees in the Lord's leadership helped as well. He became convinced.

On Monday, June 9, Graves left for Nashville, Tennessee, to attend the SBC Executive Committee meeting. It was the first of a long series of such meetings he would attend over the next twenty-five years as president of Golden Gate. A week later he and his wife went to Berkeley to find a house. On their way, they met Fred Fisher in the Dallas airport.

In December, 1952 Harold K. Graves was inaugurated as the third president of Golden Gate Seminary. Among those present for the service were, from left, Porter Routh, J. W. Storer, Graves, J. D. Grey, and E. H. Westmoreland.

The first faculty to serve under the Graves administration in 1952-1953 included, from left, Wilbur Martin, R. Fletcher Royal, J. B. Nichols, J. B. Kincannon, Jack Manning, Chester A. Insko, A. L. Aulick, Harold K. Graves, Derward W. Deere, Fred L. Fisher, and L. A. Brown.

Graves talked with Fisher about joining the Golden Gate faculty.

The Graveses stayed in the Clairmont Hotel while visiting the seminary. It is situated in a beautiful garden estate in the foothills of Oakland. The setting, the fresh flowers all about, and the fresh strawberries for breakfast had impressed the president earlier. It had helped offset some of the drab appearance of things about the seminary facilities, and Graves was anxious that it do the same for his wife.

They were inside twenty-eight houses in two days but 874 Contra Costa felt more like home. The kitchen would have to be redone and a half bath added on the main floor, but that was the house. The executive committee of the trustees met in a few days and purchased the home as the official residence of the president. The most impressive thing about the house was the view of the city, the bay, San Francisco, and the Golden Gate Bridge. Remodeled, it became a very livable house and adequate for most things for the seven years it was occupied by the president and his family.

Returning to Bartlesville, the Graveses spent the following weeks preparing for the dedication of a new educational building at the church and packing to move. On July 8, after the dedication service on the seventh, the Graves family started their drive to California.

Notes

1. Golden Gate Baptist Theological Seminary, *Catalog*, 1946-47, p. 6.
2. Ibid., p. 10.
3. Board of Directors, SBGCC, Minutes, November 5, 1946.
4. Ibid.
5. Southern Baptist General Convention of California, *Annual*, (1946), p. 18.
6. Ibid., p. 24.
7. Ibid., pp. 24,25.
8. Floyd Looney, *History of Southern Baptists*, p. 117.
9. Trustees Minutes, GGBTS, February 4, 1947.
10. SBGCC, *Annual*, (1947), p. 64.
11. Ibid., pp. 60 *ff.*

12. Looney, pp. 119-120.
13. B. O. Herring, SBGCC, *Annual*, (1947), p. 63.
14. R. F. Royal, ibid., p. 98.
15. Looney, p. 125.
16. Board of Directors, SBGCC, January 13, 1948.
17. Ibid.
18. Looney, p. 146.
19. B. O. Herring, SBGCC, *Annual* (1948), pp. 61-63.
20. Looney, p. 153.
21. Ibid., p. 163.
22. Southern Baptist Convention, *Annual* (1949), p. 44.
23. Looney, p. 164.
24. Transcript of meeting, state board of directors and seminary trustees, August 23, 1949.
25. Ibid.
26. GGBTS, Trustees Minutes, February 23, 1949.
27. SBGCC, *Annual*, (1949), pp. 65-70.
28. Ibid., p. 71.
29. Ibid., p. 47.
30. Ibid., p. 17.
31. Looney, Tape of Conversations, November 8, 1978.
32. Ibid.
33. Ibid.
34. Ibid.
35. Southern Baptist Convention, *Annual* (1950), p. 38,39.
36. Ibid., p. 411.
37. Ibid., pp. 10,11.
38. GGBTS, Trustees Minutes, August 9-10, 1950.
39. Ibid.
40. Trustee Minutes (state convention elected board) October 31, 1950.
41. SBGCC, *Annual* (1950), pp. 63-65.
42. GGBTS, Trustee Minutes, June 15, 1951.
43. Diary, Claudia Royal, 1951-1952.
44. Trustee Minutes, February 13-14, 1952.
45. Ibid.
46. Ibid.
47. GGBTS, Trustee Minutes, May 13, 1952.
48. Ibid.

(EDITOR'S NOTE: *Chapters 4, 5, and 6 summarize the period the author served as president of Golden Gate. Writing about oneself is sometimes awkward. Most of the time Graves refers to himself in the third person. For variety in style there are a few places in which he refers to himself in the first person, as on p. 121 in this chapter.*)

4
Developing a New Image
and Home

By the time the Graveses were settled in Berkeley, it was just six weeks before the fall semester was to open. The new president was determined to make changes in the seminary buildings that would give a fresh new image. He had already begun to develop some ideas on improvements and sought others as the days passed. Better use had to be made of the space, and a little paint could work wonders. A plan began to evolve and walls were changed as students in need of work were employed. An attractive suite of offices providing space for the president, business manager, and registrar was developed on the main floor. Library space was enlarged with the moving of several offices.

An old house across Addison Street with a new twelve-unit motel complex was leased to provide housing and dining facilities for single students. The two houses formerly used as dorms were converted to classroom and office space. All these facilities and the chapel were painted. Nothing could be done at once about seating in the chapel where every kind of folding chair ever made must have been represented. Everyone was pleased with the changes, even city officials, since everything done was an improvement. All was in order by the opening of school except parking—and that problem was never solved.

Fred Fisher was elected to the faculty by the trustee executive committee. He and his family were on hand for the fall semester. A graduate of Oklahoma Baptist University and Southwestern Seminary, he had been at Hardin-Simmons University for six years as head of the department of religion.

The trustees had made a serious effort in the February meeting to set things in order concerning the faculty. Several had departed but others had questions raised about them that left the air a bit unsettled. Powell had not been replaced in church history. L. A. Brown was asked to teach the required course.

While the new president was getting acquainted with the faculty, he discovered that the problems of the year before had left scars and tensions. Some of the faculty had little to do with each other. The Graveses invited the men and their wives to their home as couples, in small groups and as a whole. Most meetings of the faculty wives that first year were held in the Graves's home.

The president faced the first faculty meeting with anxiety and with much prayer. He preached at the San Mateo church on the Sunday before school opened and spent the afternoon contemplating what he would say to the faculty the next day. He rested on the assurance that God had called him to this position. Therefore, God would provide the proper words and the right approach. Graves received a good response. He spoke his mind with as much grace as possible, resting in the confidence that there was a way to develop a good spirit and harmony. He was willing to visit with individual faculty members to promote the desired harmony.

President Graves sensed the need for building harmony among the students as well. He felt that he had been able to develop that in the pastorate through preaching and Bible exposition. He sought through the daily chapel services to achieve the same goal at the seminary. Unless there was a special guest, he spoke in chapel every day he was on campus. He was always in reserve when the special guests did not show, as was sometimes true.

During the meeting of the SBC in May following Graves's election, many people with influence on the decision-making level had urged him to go to Golden Gate. They assured him that they would seek to supply the resources. In letters and in conversations at the June SBC Executive Committee meeting in Nashville, these assurances continued. In effect, they said, "Go to work, discover what is needed, and we will do our best to provide it." They were sincere in those words, and they had the power to provide. What they were not prepared for was the extent of those needs or the cost of supplying them. They neither knew the California situation nor what was involved in developing a viable program that far from the center of Southern Baptist life.

The president found himself engaged in a battle from the beginning in an effort to inform and convince the SBC leadership. Operating a seminary in the San Francisco area was unlike anything Southern Baptists had ever attempted. Most leaders could not grasp this nor get away from assuming the needs at Golden Gate were the same as those at the other seminaries. This concept was shared to some degree by the other SBC seminary presidents.

There was a general consensus that Golden Gate should relocate its campus, but remain in the San Francisco area. The East Bay was preferred, near the University of California at Berkeley and other good educational institutions. Actions by the trustees in February and again in May had authorized obtaining an option on a parcel of land in Oakland. This decision was interpreted to the new president as being subject to his approval.

Thus as Graves began his service he was faced with developing a new spirit on campus among faculty and students; with improving the faculty; with renewing and enlarging the current facilities; and with locating and developing an entirely new campus. Given the credit rating, the physical appearance of the facilities, and its reputation (or lack of it) among the educational institutions surrounding it, his was a formidable task. The business community had no reason to take the operation seriously. The academic community took little notice of them. The religious community considered the SBC to be the problem child of the Christian world. It seemed imperative that all these fronts be attacked at once.

The president joined the Chamber of Commerce and the Kiwanis Club of Berkeley. He joined the Commonwealth Club of California in San Francisco. He went to every academic function—inauguration, convocation, dedication, and so forth—to which he received an invitation.

The Oakland land had to be considered at once. A real estate agent called regularly. The potential campus site had much to commend it—location, view from its summit, even price, at a possible $220,000. On the other hand, it was rugged, with sharp differences in elevation, and the usable acreage was relatively small. The president needed help in a proper evaluation. A good architect was essential.

Hardie Bass of the BSSB Architecture Department had been seeking an architect in California for assistance with church buildings. A pamphlet came across his desk advertising redwood, picturing a beautiful school plant and the likeness of a young architect, John Carl Warnecke, who was responsible for the design. Bass wrote Warnecke for some materials which he found impressive but which indicated that the firm was perhaps too large for his purpose. He sent the material to his longtime friend Guy Rutland, who sent it back to the West Coast to the new president of Golden Gate.

Warnecke and his father, Carl, a recognized leader among architects of the world, came to the seminary in response to Graves's call. The three visited the proposed site. In a week or ten days, a detailed evaluation of the site was on the president's desk. The report said that the site could be developed but at great expense. The architects recommended finding a more usable location. The advice had cost nothing, and an association was begun with John Carl Warnecke which continued more than a quarter of a century.

The seminary administration and the architects were often together. Graves and Warnecke spent a week visiting Southwestern, New Orleans, and Southern seminaries. The new campus at New Orleans was under construction. They

visited the BSSB and the SBC offices in Nashville. This gave
Warnecke a better knowledge of who Southern Baptists are
and what their older schools had done. Graves kept in touch
with trustees Westmoreland and Rutland and with other
members of the executive committee of the trustees. By the
time the full board met, the seminary owed Warnecke
$12,000. The trustees were being asked for an additional
commitment of $21,000 for work to determine basic needs
and to evaluate proposed sites.

This was the largest task Warnecke had undertaken up to
that time. He and his associates became part of the team
looking for a site for the new campus. Among the first sites
considered was the Mira Vista Golf Club in El Cerrito. The
grounds were privately owned but available to those who
wanted to play golf. The architect's preliminary studies
indicated that 100 acres would suffice. The president knew
that he needed the services of a good attorney for assistance
in such a transaction. He went to the seminary's bank, The
American Trust Company, for advice. A name was given to
him and, though assured that he probably would not be
available, an appointment was arranged.

The president went to see Edward D. Landels of Landels
and Weigel in San Francisco. He found a most personable
man, very easy to talk with, and one who knew who Baptists
were. His grandfather, William H. Landels, had been a
Baptist pastor in London, a contemporary of Charles Had-
den Spurgeon, and, with him, a cofounder of the British
Baptist Union. While not a churchman himself, Landels was
interested in the seminary and would be glad to help. And
help he did over a period of nearly twenty-five years. His
integrity, wisdom, and reputation paid off for the seminary,
especially in many critical situations over the first decade of
the association. He has been a true friend.

The Mira Vista golf course consisted of 150 acres and a
price of $650,000 was agreed upon. A firm offer of $250,000
was secured for the fifty acres in excess of that needed by the
seminary. So the cost of the 100 acres was to be $400,000. The
owners produced an option agreement that was not accepta-

ble to Landels so he set about to rewrite it. In the meantime, seminary trustee leadership advanced the date for the annual meeting from February, 1953 to December, 1952. They could act on this purchase as well as hold inaugural ceremonies for the new president. Things were looking good for a new campus that, with some remodeling of existing buildings, might be used in the fall of 1953.

The excitement and anticipation was not to last long, however. It turned to anxiety as there appeared signs in the Richmond-El Cerrito community that all was not well in the sale of the golf course. Propaganda described a Baptist seminary in that location as being something similar in impact to that of a prison, a mental hospital, or an industrial school. It would affect property values. Where would the people play golf for such a price? An editorial against the seminary appeared in the Richmond *Independent-Journal*. The city manager of Richmond sought to lead the seminary to consider some other site in the area.

As a result of these efforts, the property was withdrawn from the market. The young president was left to face his first trustee meeting without the major agenda item. It was a dark hour that affected all activities, including the inauguration. Chairman Westmoreland was relieved to learn that the president's inaugural message had been prepared in a much brighter atmosphere. The ceremonies went off very well, and the tone was positive. The seminary was on its way.

The Mira Vista Golf Club matter served some very good purposes even though nothing seemed good about it at the time. It brought the seminary and Landels together. It introduced Golden Gate Seminary and Southern Baptists to the San Francisco Bay area business and financial community. Any group that could talk in terms of $650,000 in cash in 1952 had to attract attention. Bank and real estate people of the highest caliber became acquainted with the seminary administration. Even in its failure, the transaction caused the seminary to gain a stature it was never to relinquish.

Enrollment in the seminary in September, 1952 attained an all-time record of 199. Students came from 25 states and 5 foreign countries. Opening festivities brought an exciting time for the new president and his family. L. A. Brown brought the convocation address on the evening of September 2. It was followed by the first reception for the seminary family in the new president's home. It seemed as though hundreds came to be greeted by President and Mrs. Graves and Professor and Mrs. Aulick.

That reception was the responsibility of the president's wife. She was nervous about such a task as she and her husband considered accepting the place of service at Golden Gate. In their close association with the Oklahoma Baptist University and the Raleys, they knew about the place Mrs. Raley filled. For her it was appropriate and beautiful, but not the kind of role Frieda Graves felt comfortable with at all. Her husband assured her that she should function in the manner that was comfortable. She proved equal to the occasion that first evening as she was on the scores of other occasions over the next twenty-five years.

There were many joyous times of fellowship in the Berkeley house, as well as in the more spacious new home on the campus in Marin County later. Receptions came in all sizes from a dozen guests to hundreds. Besides these, there were numerous luncheons and dinners for visitors, sometimes for only one guest but often many more. Many came on short notice. In addition, Mrs. Graves was hostess and tour guide for many trustee wives and others accompanying official visitors to the seminary.

The other major project that Mrs. Graves pursued was the association for the wives of students. The faculty wives were able assistants in these efforts. With some measure of success the group tried to help the wives of students get a wholesome view of their role as the wife of a minister or other church staff member. Fellowship among the faculty wives was developed and maintained through monthly meetings in various homes. As I review the twenty-five years of service at Golden Gate, it is hard for me to imagine those years without the marvelous support of Frieda. During many of

Photo by Faulkner, San Francisco, CA

Frieda Kommer Graves

those years I was away more nights than I was at home. Our task was performed as a team, and I am grateful.

The trustee executive committee met in November and elected Carlyle and Elma Bennett of Los Angeles to the faculty in church music. They were both natives of Indiana and graduates of Southwestern Baptist Seminary. They were currently on the staff of Temple Baptist Church and teaching at California Baptist Seminary.

A special chapel service was held Wednesday morning, December 10, to recognize the graduation of six students. E. W. Hunke, Jr., received the first diploma signed by President Graves. That evening the Golden Gate Choir presented Handel's *Messiah*, continuing a tradition begun in 1950. Bennett was the tenor soloist. That was his first appearance before a Golden Gate audience since joining the faculty.

In the meantime, the Southern Baptist General Convention of California meeting in San Jose elected Professor A. L. Aulick as its president. At the preconvention meeting of the state convention's board of directors, Graves asked that the seminary receive no more money from the Christian Education Day offering. He was concerned that the new California Baptist College (CBC) get all the support from the state that was possible. CBC President P. Boyd Smith was not so sure, and neither were the seminary trustees. It was eventually done, and history has proven the wisdom of that suggestion. It was far better to volunteer than be voted out of that offering as the life struggle for CBC developed.

At the December trustee meeting, actions were taken concerning the golf course. Other actions included agreements for continuing the services of both Landels, the attorney, and Warnecke, the architect. Even though the golf club property had been withdrawn, approval was given to purchase the land should it be made available. Specific action was also taken to discontinue consideration of the Oakland property discussed in previous meetings.

Trustees also elected Kyle M. Yates, Jr., as instructor in Hebrew and archaeology to begin in the fall of 1953. Upon recommendation of President Graves, they voted to discontinue offering the Doctor of Theology degree. Aulick was elected to emeritus status but was asked to remain on a part-time basis for the 1953-1954 year.

Thus, the first full board meeting after the election of the new president came to an end. J. W. Storer, chairman of the SBC Executive Committee, stayed over and had dinner with me and my family. During the evening, I excused myself and retired to the study. From there I had a view of the bay and San Francisco. I thought of how Jesus must have felt as he wept over Jerusalem. I expressed aloud my resentment of the secular and material-minded community which had won a battle against the seminary. With tears in my eyes, I vowed that this setback would not be permanent. God would have his way. This site or a better one would be secured, and the seminary would move ahead.

When an opening for a professor in church history needed to be filled, Graves remembered what W. A. Carleton had said at one time. He knew of none better qualified than Carleton. He tried to enlist him that summer but to no avail.

William Augustus Carleton joined the seminary faculty in 1953 as professor of church history. He was elected academic dean in 1956 and vice-president in 1959. In 1970 he was named Distinguished Professor of Church History upon his retirement from Golden Gate and Dean Emeritus in 1972. Carleton died in 1980.

Mrs. Carleton (Opal) recalls the visit of the Graves to their home in Ponca City, Oklahoma, soon after the decision to assume the presidency at Golden Gate. Graves urged Carleton to consider becoming professor of church history. Opal remembers the statement, "Of course we can't pay you what you're earning as a pastor. Opal, you'll have to get a position as a schoolteacher." She was surprised. She did not want to return to the classroom after an absence of more than fifteen years. They declined the invitation.

Unknown to Opal, Carleton later wrote Graves, saying that he could not get away from the pull to teach church history. He wanted to know if the position were still open. Graves responded in the affirmative and set a date to visit Carleton in Oklahoma in January. Carleton then visited the seminary and agreed to accept the position if elected. Graves also wanted Carleton to assist in administration. He had no one with whom he could discuss overall problems who had enough denominational experience to help aid in basic decisions.

When Carleton became convinced that God was calling him to serve in California, things became critical in their household. Opal could not be reconciled to the idea. A dear friend saw her sitting alone weeping after others had left a meeting in the church. He asked, "Have you talked with the Lord about this, Opal?"

She replied, "Of course not. It's too ridiculous to mention to him." That caused her to pray however. Her simple prayer was, "Lord, if Gus is supposed to go, help me to change my attitude." In a week she became so excited about the opportunity that had Carleton changed his mind she would have been disappointed. Opal obtained a teaching position, entered San Francisco State University to earn a master's degree, and served for twenty years as a teacher and counselor. They were fruitful and enjoyable years.

At the Missionary Day service on January 30, Baker J. Cauthen, secretary for the Orient for the FMB, was the speaker. Thirty-five students responded for mission service. President Graves and his family missed this great service due to the death of his father, whose funeral they were attending in Illinois.

The annual Seminary Bible Conference was held March 2-5, 1952. President Graves was the leader, speaking on the Sermon on the Mount under the title of "The Kingdom Man."

Loren Williams of the Baptist Sunday School Board was the leader of the first annual Church Music Conference held in March, 1953. No activity of the seminary across the years has affected the churches in California more than these conferences. The contrast between what was and what has come to be is perhaps best illustrated by the growth of the choir festival. Only four choirs participated the first year (1954) the festival was included in the conferences. Most of the program for the evening was provided by the seminary chapel choir. The festival grew until in 1963 there were fifty-three choirs in attendance, too many to continue the practice.

Enrollment in the seminary for the 1952-1953 year reached 246, 6 above the previous year. Texas provided 41 students, California 29, Oklahoma 28, Arkansas 21, Tennessee and New Mexico 14 each, and Mississippi 12.

Commencement for 41 graduates was held April 25, 1953,

with trustee chairman Westmoreland as the speaker. Immediately following these exercises the chapel choir left for an extensive tour of churches and colleges en route to the SBC in Houston. They sang just before President Graves addressed the Convention.

GGBTS trustees met at South Main Baptist Church during the Convention. Thirteen trustees were present to consider the report of the president and recommendations from the faculty personnel and finance committees. They voted to accept the resignation of J. B. Kincannon, professor of theology. A permanent faculty salary scale was adopted along with a schedule placing each faculty member. It was also agreed to study the matter of Social Security for seminary personnel.

W. A. Carleton was elected associate professor of church history and assistant to the president. He was named *assistant* but he was an invaluable *associate* in administration for the seventeen years he served. Clyde Francisco of Southern Seminary was invited to be guest professor for the 1953-1954 year. The budget year was changed to begin August 1, 1953, and the revised budget for the new year as presented by the finance committee chairman, Rutland, was approved. The budget had been prepared by Mason and Graves before the Houston meeting. Prior to the meeting, Rutland went over the budget with Graves, asking for meticulous explanations. President Graves soon heard his own words being used to explain the budget to the board.

In connection with the financial reports, Rutland asked the trustees to authorize the sale of the bonds and stocks from the William Conover estate. In the spring of 1952, the seminary needed additional funds to continue operation. The trustees had appealed to Porter Routh and the Executive Committee. At first there seemed to be no way they could help. On the very day Routh received the seminary's request, a notice of the settlement of the estate of a Baptist layman was received. The residue of the estate was to go to The Southern Baptist Theological Seminary or "to any other seminary which Southern Baptists may then own." Golden Gate needed $50,000. The legacy was almost exactly that. The Executive Committee allocated it to Golden Gate.

It seems strange that no reference is made in the minutes of this meeting to the problem that had developed with the Veteran's Administration. Apparently, other pressing needs and the excitement of prospects for the future caused them to take another financial blow in stride.

The problem with the VA began one day in mid-April. A large package arrived at the seminary, consisting of an inch thick stack of legal-sized sheets of paper. It was the record of the purchases from the seminary book store of each military veteran. The cover letter from the VA addressed to President Graves said, "The Seminary has been improperly reimbursed for books and supplies provided to students who were veterans in the amount of $27,930.31." On the individual sheets were listed many books and supplies that were not on the list of required texts.

Graves remembered that late in the fall of 1952 an auditor from the VA appeared at the seminary, asking to see the financial records of all the veterans. He was given access to the files. When his task was completed in late January, 1953, he left without comment. The receipt of the package in April was the next thing that was heard from him.

After recovering from the shock of the statement, "Please remit by return mail," the president made a hurried call to the VA in San Francisco. He, Business Manager Mason, and the veterans' coordinator at the seminary, Jack Manning, went to plead their case. They made two points. One was that, in the earliest days of the school, the library was so inadequate that some sets of books were needed by individual students. The other point was that some courses were added each semester after the lists were provided to the VA, and texts for these had not been listed. The arguments prevailed to a degree, and the bill was reduced to $20,624.65. Payment of that amount wiped out the reserves that were beginning to accumulate.

President Herring had had the idea that each veteran was entitled to an allowance of $500 for books during his seminary career. The audit sheet for each man contained that figure at the top with charges made against it. Ultimately, there appeared on each record a final entry of *merchandise,* with the figure opposite absorbing the exact balance of the beginning $500. VA officials said that no such allowance was ever a part of their program. So the seminary, in effect, purchased more than $20,000 worth of books and supplies for preachers' libraries.

About this time, it became apparent that the golf course was not going to be available for purchase. The search continued for a suitable campus location. Properties in the East Bay from Milpitas on the south to San Pablo on the north and Lafayette on the east were studied. Down the San Francisco peninsula, property at Millbrae and San Jose were considered.

In the spring of 1953, the state of California sold bonds for the construction of a bridge connecting the East Bay and Marin County, replacing the ferries. Up to then Marin County had not been considered seriously as a seminary location. The people looking for a site had felt that it could not provide the necessary housing and employment for students. The new bridge enabled students to find housing and employment in the East Bay. The Freitas Ranch and Strawberry Point were two pieces of property given primary attention.

The Strawberry Point land was exciting. It had been in the news a few years earlier as a proposed site for the United Nations. It was reported as not being for sale since plans for development of the remaining 250 acres had already been approved by the county.

Delay in locating just the right campus site had not slowed the process begun by the architect and seminary administration. They were busy developing the basic guidelines— indicating needs, style, and relationships necessary for a seminary campus, wherever it might be located. The scope of these efforts was reflected in materials provided for the December, 1952 trustee meeting. A bound volume was produced which began with a message from the president. After giving a bit of history of Baptist education, he said:

> We feel extremely fortunate in obtaining John Carl War-
> necke, AIA, and his staff of fine architects, engineers,
> planners and researchers to make these preliminary stud-
> ies. . . .
>
> Mr. Warnecke shows us that we need 100 acres of land. We
> want to remain in the Bay Area—for reasons too many to
> enumerate. But where is there 100 acres of land available in
> this area which is in a good neighborhood, close to transpor-
> tation, accessible to main highways, and not too distant from
> suitable housing and possible secular employment for stu-
> dents?
>
> A site worthy of this program must have the possibilities of
> beauty in development. A place of prominence on a rising
> hill would be preferred. The surrounding homes and free
> areas need to be of the highest type. Besides, we want the
> community to desire such an institution. There is not the
> slightest desire on the part of any of us to force our way into
> any community. We want, . . . to become a part of the city
> where we live and study and work, and we hope that the
> satisfaction and pride may eventually become mutual.

In introducing the work they had done, architect John Carl
Warnecke said:

> California climate and California weather and California
> architecture can no longer be separated. The planning of the
> site and design of the architecture itself will be, must be, the
> natural effect of natural causes—the natural expression of
> the functions involved, and we therefore will frequently use
> the term "functional architecture." At the same time, those
> traditions and associations of the Southern Baptist churches
> so dear to every one of you, will always be borne in mind.

During the fall months of 1952 and the first months of 1953,
meetings were held between the seminary faculty and the
architectural staff. They stated topics for consideration each
week, such as: an analysis of the academic, spiritual, and
practical considerations; extracurricular functions; student

facilities, housing; offices; classrooms; the library, and so forth. At each meeting a reporter would read to the seminary people what had been said earlier for any necessary clarification or correction. The entire faculty and staff of the seminary were involved.

After his return from the SBC in Houston in May, 1953, President Graves again addressed the problem of a site. The architects had gone about as far as they could until a specific site was selected. One day, while Graves was sitting with Warnecke and his staff, Warnecke asked, "What about Strawberry Point?"

Graves replied, "It is not for sale."

"Who owns it?" Warnecke asked. Graves did not know, but Warnecke called a man he knew for an answer. The property was owned by Sam Neider, a man described as hard to deal with and not available to many people. When asked who might get to him, the reply was Bruce Madden of Oakland. What a coincidence! Madden was the man with whom President Graves had worked in connection with the golf course.

Graves called Madden at once and told him they were interested in seeing Strawberry Point. A few minutes after Graves and Madden had finished their conversation, Madden called back, setting a time for the next day. Madden picked up Graves, then Warnecke and Neider in San Francisco; and they drove across the Golden Gate Bridge to Marin County. They left Highway 101 at Ricardo Drive, went through housing over the ridge, and south along East Strawberry Drive. Only six or eight houses were on East Strawberry Drive at the time. The road soon ran out, becoming only tracks for the car along an old railroad right-of-way.

A half mile later they left the road and set out across pastureland, turning west, and then north up the slope of the hill. At the elevation of 205 feet, the view was magnificent. There were a few live oak trees, a few cedar trees, and many beautiful wild flowers. Neider began by saying that none of the shoreline was for sale. They drove to Neider's temporary office to look at aerial relief maps. He gave one of these to Warnecke for his study and a possible proposal. They did not see Neider again for many months.

Warnecke and his staff analyzed the maps and produced sketches that indicated what and how much land might be needed. They specified some 129 plus or minus acres, including three quarters of a mile of shoreline on the west side of the peninsula. With this in hand, the bargaining began. Madden said that Neider would not set a price, but he knew that he would not take less than $5,000 per acre. If the shoreline were to be considered, that would take at least an additional fifty dollars per front foot. Such prices were out of the question, but it was apparent that Neider would indeed sell some land for cash. He was anxious to have a shopping center developed.

Consideration of the Mira Vista golf course property had given President Graves some sense of property values. He had determined that $400,000 for about 129 acres in its undeveloped state might be reasonable. Meeting in Warnecke's office with Madden, the president rejected the figures being proposed and indicated what the seminary might be willing to do. A secretary was called in as the president began to dictate an offer with some conditions advised by Landels, the seminary's lawyer.

A two-page document was presented by Madden to the owner. Later it was refined by the attorney and put in the form of an option. Only negative responses were received from Neider at first. After a month of negotiations, there was a verbal agreement to accept. It took another month to get Neider to sign the option.

Even before the papers were signed, President Graves asked Chairman Westmoreland to alert the trustees of a possible special meeting. When the option was signed, the meeting was called. Porter Routh was alerted about a possible meeting of the SBC Executive Committee to approve a necessary $150,000 loan.

The trustees gathered at the seminary on Thursday, September 17 for chapel then moved to the president's office. After introducing his associate, W. A. Carleton, Graves proposed an agenda and schedule which was adopted. They had lunch in the new dining facility with the faculty and then drove to Marin County to inspect the proposed site.

The day was not ideal. It was overcast, and the wind blew so hard on the high hill that the men needed to hold their hats in place. Many things impressed the trustees, but it was evident that not all were agreed on the site. Several raised questions. Some California men had campaigned in the state against a move to Marin County. One trustee told Graves that, if this was what he wanted, a selling job would have to be done. Graves replied:

> It is obvious how I feel in having called for spending the money for the special trustee meeting. The architects will present the case, answer questions, and the trustees will vote their convictions. If they are not sold by the facts, then selling the idea to the SBC leadership would be impossible. No argument or pressure will be applied.

After dinner in the seminary dining room with the faculty, the trustees retired to the Shattuck Hotel. President Graves gave a brief survey of events leading up to the consideration of Strawberry Point. He explained that he had offered the owner $400,000 for the approximately 129 acres and now had an option to purchase. He presented Warnecke and his staff. By use of maps, drawings, diagrams, and words, they laid before the trustees the possibilities of the proposed site. The trustees remained until after eleven o'clock listening and asking questions. They decided to make no decision until the next morning.

The next morning the meeting was reconvened, and the trustees resumed discussion. Guy Rutland gave a brief explanation of how the purchase could be financed. Chairman Westmoreland then asked each member of the board to give his personal reaction to the site and its possibilities. The period that followed was quite exciting, as one man after another had his say. Some confessed their earlier opposition and strong efforts to defeat any such consideration. Each closed by saying, "I am convinced. This is the place. I am

ready to vote." President Graves again gave details of the
option agreement. Of the $400,000 offered, $150,000 was to
be retained in escrow to pay for certain improvements agreed
to by Neider.

Action by the trustees was recorded in their minutes:

> Motion was made by Floyd Golden that the Board of
> trustees of Golden Gate Seminary exercise the option to
> purchase site of 129 acres more or less on Strawberry Point,
> Marin County, California, for the location of the new campus
> of the Seminary. The motion was seconded by Paul Tharp.
> The motion carried unanimously.[1]

Several actions followed to implement that decision. They
authorized paying the expenses of members of the SBC
Executive Committee to a meeting in Nashville on September 24 to approve the loan. The money was to be secured
from the First American National Bank of Nashville and
repaid from capital funds due Golden Gate in 1954. President
Graves was authorized to sign contracts, to pay half of the
cost of joint improvements, and to instruct the architect to
begin plans for developing Strawberry Point.

While all these transactions were going on, many significant things transpired at the seminary. A. L. Aulick had died
August 5 and a memorial service was held for him in Berkeley. After the funeral Mrs. Aulick left the city, never to visit
the seminary again. The Carletons lived in the Aulick home
for a few weeks. The Clyde Franciscos lived there during
their year at the seminary. In late August Golden Gate was
host to the second annual meeting of the Western Baptist
Religious Education Association with 110 present. Among the
participants was Elmer Gray, pastor at Santa Ana, later to
become a trustee, then faculty member, and ultimately dean
of the seminary.

Miss Isma Johnson, who had worked with Carleton in
Oklahoma, came to serve with the registrar, Jack Manning.
Two men were asked to serve for the 1953-1954 year in place
of the late A. L. Aulick. A. J. Hyatt, pastor in Richmond,
California, and former faculty member at Golden Gate,

Photo by R. L. Copeland

The rolling hills and serene countryside of Strawberry Point in Marin County, across San Francisco Bay from Berkeley, made an ideal location for the seminary's third home. The peninsula, extending into the bay, had been selected as a recommended site for the United Nations building had it been constructed in San Francisco. After the New York site was chosen, the property became available to the Southern Baptist Convention in 1953.

taught beginning Greek. Robert Stapp, a 1952 Bachelor of Divinity graduate and a Doctor of Theology candidate in Greek and pastor at Yuba City, taught second-year Greek. With this assistance in the New Testament area, Fred Fisher was free to offer the required course in systematic theology.

A building across Grove Street was leased by the seminary to house a dining facility, the child-care program, and several faculty offices. A large house four blocks away was purchased as a residence for women students. Nine Baldwin pianos were added in the music building, two of them grand pianos.

The fall enrollment was 15 percent above any previous term. Derward Deere brought the convocation address, followed by a reception at the president's home. The first of four missionary days for the year was held October 1. Alton Reed of the Annuity Board spoke of the use of radio and TV in evangelism and missions. Willis Ray, executive secretary of Arizona, spoke of the challenge of the West.

"Practical Activities" were reorganized into six groups under the general leadership of Jack Manning and the student chairman, Warren Smith. Each group had a student chairman and one or more faculty sponsors. The six groups were: Pastors, Teaching and Church Activities, Racial Minorities, Evangelistic, Church Extension, and Baptist Student Union.

Relocation was several years away, yet the purchase of a site for the new campus lifted the spirits of the entire seminary family. It was hoped that the move might be made in four years. It soon became apparent, however, that resources would not be available to complete enough construction for a move to be made before six years. Yet everyone wrote friends about this grand move to occupy such a dramatic site as though it would be soon.

As the seminary family observed the Christmas season in December, 1953, it had much for which to be grateful. They had come a long way in a year since the disappointment over failure to obtain the golf club site. God did, indeed, have something better.

The trustees met for their annual meeting in February, 1954. Graves reported that enrollment had reached 273 for the year, another record. There was still a need for additional classroom, office, and library space in the present location. Calvary Baptist Church, which shared the seminary facilities, was planning an additional classroom building. The logical location for it was on the lots owned by the seminary. The trustees approved the arrangement.

Personnel proposed by the president included James W. McClendon of Louisiana to be assistant professor of theology and J. Lyn Elder, also of Louisiana, to be associate professor of Christian psychology. Graves and Elder had met when the latter was a beginning student at Southern Seminary. Elder had served in the military during World War II. He then completed graduate work, planning to teach Christian psychology. As Graves planned his convention visit to Louisiana in the fall of 1953, he decided to discuss with Elder the possibility of teaching at Golden Gate. Before he could arrange this, a letter came from Elder inquiring about a conference. Out of that meeting came a visit, election, and more than twenty-five years' service to Golden Gate Seminary.

At the February meeting of the trustees, architect Warnecke and his staff presented preliminary drawings and gave explanations concerning the progress they had made since the campus site was purchased. There was considerable discussion with general approval of the ideas presented. The site utilization plan was adopted, looking toward consideration of the completed master plan at a meeting during the SBC in Saint Louis.

J. W. Storer, president of the SBC, was the Missionary Day speaker in February, and Francisco led the annual Bible conference. Hines Sims was featured at the second annual music workshop. Roland Leavell, president of New Orleans Seminary, brought the baccalaureate sermon on April 22. President Graves gave the address the next day for the sixth annual commencement. Thirty-three students graduated.

Summer school opened May 25 with fifty enrolled. During

that week President Graves released to the press word concerning the completed master plan. The *Berkeley Daily Gazette* of May 25, 1954 said:

> The Strawberry Point development is shaping up as one of the most ambitious religious undertakings of modern times, with adequate financial support, progressive architectural planning, and above all, a spiritual impetus in both faculty and students which places the whole operation on the level of a modern religious epic.
>
> Dr. Graves pictured the Southern Baptists . . . as coming to California little more than a decade ago, and in accomplishing the organization of some 400 churches in that time . . . the explanation being that the preachers and then the churches followed the people who came here during the war years.
>
> He then pictured the young Golden Gate Seminary here, . . . as literally bursting its walls in its need for enlarged quarters and a student body of nearly 300 which would grow to 500 within another few years, and thence to 1000 or more in keeping with the proportions of other such institutions.[2]

Recalling the purchase of property on Strawberry Point in Marin County, the *Gazette* continued with a quote from President Graves:

> We have been told by the architect that we can by 1959 have a basic plant to accommodate 500 students, and that this will cost $4,000,000. A complete plan for 1000 students, with living accommodations for both single students and families, will require a full 10 years to build, and a total expenditure, according to present estimates, of $9,000,000. We have every confidence that this dream will be realized.

On his way to the meeting of the SBC in Saint Louis, President Graves went by El Monte, California, to address the first commencement exercises at California Baptist College.

The trustees met in Saint Louis on June 3. I reported that 20 new missions and 10 churches had been organized by students during the year. There were 648 conversions reported, 466 baptized, and 375 other additions to the churches. I told the trustees that I had discovered a Berkeley part-pay clinic which would accept seminary students at a minimal cost.

I reported that McClendon was teaching a summer term and that Elder would arrive soon. McClendon, a native of Louisiana, was a graduate of the University of Texas. He earned theological degrees from Southwestern Baptist Seminary and Princeton. A brilliant student and a member of Phi Beta Kappa, he had served as a pastor for several years. Deere had been given a year's leave to teach at Southern Seminary. (The trustees did not act on this decision but consultations had been held with Chairman Westmoreland and instruction committee chairman Golden before the decision was made for Deere to be away.)

The master plan for the new campus as prepared by the architect was presented and after much study and discussion was adopted. The architect's request to proceed with several items was broken down and voted on separately. They authorized complete preliminary drawings for mass grading, first-stage landscaping and erosion control, and site utilities. They asked Graves and the building committee to study additional recommendations of the architect. They were to work with him in preparing preliminary sketches on four or five buildings in the academic group.

Before proceeding with an account of their efforts, let's return to the matter of the leave for Derward Deere. When President Graves arrived in 1952, the division between faculty members was quite apparent. After Professor Powell left Golden Gate, the leader and strongest voice for Powell's curriculum concept was Deere. Deere and Graves had visited in Louisville on several occasions in previous years. Deere had been pastor of the Buffalo Lick Baptist Church, succeeding Graves. Graves felt very strongly that there was an important role for religious education and church music. He had a very high regard for Deere, however, and hoped to influence him to accept the concept of a broad and balanced curriculum.

Deere had made considerable progress and Graves was able to answer Deere's critics by reporting an improvement in attitude during the previous two years. Nevertheless, by the end of his second year, Graves was convinced that some changes needed to occur if fellowship were to be maintained. When it was learned that help was needed at Southern Seminary in Old Testament for the next year, Graves was willing for Deere to fill a temporary position there. McCall extended an invitation.

The president was to be in Kentucky in the fall, so he planned a visit with Deere. Upon arrival in Louisville, Graves found a message from Deere requesting an opportunity for lunch together. At the luncheon Deere vowed his loyalty to Golden Gate and commitment to becoming a good member of the team. He returned and became a fine teacher and loyal faculty member. He was in poor health much of the time, missing an entire year at one stretch, and ultimately came to a premature death with a heart attack. Many servants of the Lord all over the world owe their love for the Old Testament to this good teacher, Derward W. Deere.

A building committee was authorized by the trustees in February, 1954 and chosen by Chairman Westmoreland and President Graves. Committee members were E. H. Westmoreland, Guy Rutland, John Raley, Floyd Golden, and Clarence Kennedy. The trustees gave the committee and the president authority to decide on many issues, including what and when to build within the prescribed guidelines. They held their first meeting in October, 1954. After a session in the architect's office, they visited the new campus site and some buildings in the area to get acquainted with styles and materials being considered. Discussions along the way gave the architect and his staff general reactions of the committee members to their proposals.

The committee instructed the architect to prepare:

a. Complete preliminary drawings of all building scheduled for initial stage of construction.

b. Semi-complete preliminary drawings of all such other buildings as may influence the determination of finish grades.

c. Working drawings and specifications for all mass grading, storm sewers, and landscaping of the site and preparation of bidding documents for such portions of the work as can be encompassed within the current budget.[3]

The building committee members were well qualified by training and/or experience for their task. Rutland was a graduate of Georgia Tech and an associate in the family construction business. Raley had been building at OBU for twenty years. Golden had spent a like number of years in campus construction as president of Eastern New Mexico University. Westmoreland had led in church building. Kennedy was a local businessman, acquainted with matters unique to the California scene. They were a good team. On numerous occasions Rutland flew in from Atlanta to spend the day with Graves. After assisting in decisions, he flew overnight and was back in the Georgia legislature the next morning. Always traveling at his own expense, he was like a local consultant.

There were other significant happenings involving Golden Gate during the summer of 1954. I attended my first meeting of the American Association of Theological Schools at the University of Chicago. Golden Gate made application for associate membership in the AATS that year. There I met, by chance, my neighbor, President Sandford Fleming of Berkeley Baptist Divinity School.

Association with President Fleming led to many fine activities involving the two seminaries during the next several years. They promoted a rally in connection with the visit to the San Francisco Bay Area of Townley Lord, president of the Baptist World Alliance (BWA) and its executive secretary, Arnold Ohrn. They sponsored a fellowship dinner, held at Golden Gate, honoring Dr. and Mrs. Lord and Dr. and Mrs. Ohrn, attended by the two faculties and their spouses. These dinners continued for many years, alternating between the two schools.

The finance committee of the SBC Executive Committee has had an almost impossible task in stretching the available resources among the agencies. For their December, 1954 meeting, they were looking for ways to reduce their load. One idea was to allocate a lump sum to theological education and let the presidents divide it. "No more money to the seminaries until the presidents have a formula for distribution," they said. That plan looked good on the surface, but it did not prove so in application. It was somewhat like asking the several children in a family to divide the weekly allowance.

The 1956 allocation for theological education voted by the SBC in May, 1955 was $1,800,000. Seventy-five thousand dollars of that ($15,000 from each school) was designated for the Seminary Extension Department (SED). The remainder was to be divided, according to a formula prepared by the presidents. Sixty-five percent was divided among the schools for the first 300 students. With only 238 enrolled, that was all Golden Gate received. With the $15,000 for SED, GGBTS's total was $249,000. Other percentages of the total were added for each 100 additional students. The formula took no notice of the peculiar needs of any school due to location or other circumstances.

During discussions leading to the preparation of this formula, and in subsequent years of applying it, there were many tense moments. Attitudes toward Golden Gate were revealed. One president brushed Golden Gate aside by stating flatly that all they needed was $150,000. When asked by President Graves when he was authorized to speak for Golden Gate, he realized he was out of order and apologized. Neither he nor the others had any real knowledge of the peculiar needs of that seminary. In mission territory, away from the center of SBC activities, Golden Gate was in the most expensive area in which Southern Baptists were doing business.

The first state chapter of Golden Gate alumni was organized during the California State convention in November, 1954 with Byron Todd as president. The California convention president and both vice-presidents elected that year were Golden Gate graduates.

On campus, November was a busy month. Golden Gate was host to the state Baptist Student Union Convention where 421 participants registered. Also visiting the campus was Elmer West, secretary for missionary personnel for the Foreign Mission Board. He addressed the Mission Fellowship, spoke in chapel, and conferred with prospective missionaries. Wilfred L. Jarvis, pastor of Central Baptist Church, Sydney, Australia, and vice-president of the BWA was the speaker for the second missionary day of the session.

Ralph Herring spoke at the annual Seminary Conference held in January, 1955. On February 2 one of the finest missionary addresses ever delivered at Golden Gate was given by missionary John N. Thomas of Colombia, South America. As the trustees gathered for their meeting in February, 1955, the seminary family was on a high plane of spiritual excitement with a growing spirit of oneness.

The president's message to the trustees included news of a total enrollment of 277 for the year. He reported that there were more than 600 additions to the churches where students labored. Six new missions had been started and 16 churches organized. There was a superb faculty spirit and evidence of a growing appreciation for the seminary throughout the convention. Recognition as an associate member of AATS had come after recommendation of sister seminaries in Berkeley and San Anselmo. Attitudes toward Golden Gate were changing.

The capital needs allocation for Golden Gate through 1958, though $2,283,000, was still $2,000,000 short if the new campus were to be occupied in 1959. Hope was expressed that this amount might be allocated for 1959 and 1960. The committee on capital needs for the SBC Executive Committee was made aware of the need. They had been advised of a recent study, reported in the *School Board Journal*. That study indicated that building costs for school structures in the San Francisco Bay area were 43 percent higher than in the location of any other SBC seminary.

The trustees adopted a faculty recommendation that the seminary curriculum be organized in three areas instead of the traditional four. This was a further effort to provide an integrated emphasis across all disciplines rather than the institution being divided into schools. The three areas are Christian Sources and Origins (Old Testament; New Testament; Hebrew; Greek; and Archaeology); Christian Life and Thought (Theology; Church History; Christian Ethics; Philosophy of Religion; and Missions); Christian Work and Worship (Preaching; Evangelism; Religious Education; and Church Music).

The faculty wanted to meet the need of all its potential students. In an effort to make instruction fit previous preparation, they requested permission to provide separate classes for those without college degrees. In the years that followed, this group became so small that the plan was later dropped. There was begun at this meeting of the trustees an action that became almost automatic in the years of growing inflation. The faculty salary scale was revised. It continues to be revised in an effort to provide an increasing percentage of available resources for faculty and staff personnel.

There were further efforts to strengthen and stabilize the faculty. Faculty status was limited to full-time teachers and full professorships were to be offered only to those with earned doctorates. (This rule was sometimes set aside in special cases.) President Graves reported that an IRS ruling made possible a housing allowance for ordained faculty members. The trustees voted that the books of the seminary be set up to allow for this. Unordained faculty had a portion of their Social Security paid by the seminary which partially offset the difference between them and the ordained faculty.

The building committee asked the architectural staff to present details of their work. After much discussion, the following action was taken:

> Motion was made by Dr. Caudill, seconded by Mr. Mahon, that we (1) adopt the preliminary building plans as presented by the building committee; (2) approve the building time schedule as presented, on the basis of anticipated annual

income from the Cooperative Program and other sources; (3) authorize the building committee to proceed accordingly, including the letting of contracts; and that we (4) hereby reaffirm our purpose to conform to the financial plan of the Southern Baptist Convention in this raising of all funds for our building program, and pledge anew our unfailing support of the Cooperative Program. The motion carried unanimously.[4]

The minutes record that "Oscar Davis led in a prayer of thanksgiving following which the entire group joined in singing the Doxology." This is all the more significant since the trustees were meeting in the conference room of the architectural firm of John Carl Warnecke and Associates in San Francisco. Those walls may have never heard such before.

With the move to Marin County now possibly only four years away, the trustees were concerned with disposition of the Berkeley property. Both they and Calvary Baptist Church wanted the church to remain a functioning entity in that strategic location. An agreement was reached whereby the church could purchase the main seminary building for what the school had invested there. The seminary was to have full use until it moved and the right to make alterations and additions as might be necessary.

As I began preparation of my report for the SBC in Miami in May, 1955, I was able to note several significant signs of progress. Of the 277 students enrolled, 57 were from Texas, but California was gaining with 38. For years 25 percent or more of the students had come from east of the Mississippi River. Even though 31 states and the District of Columbia were represented, the student body was becoming more Western and international.

In the March, 1955 issue of the *Golden Gate,* I continued my appeal for commitment to the task of learning how to witness to and serve in the secular culture about the seminary.

The call now to those present and to those who look from afar is to strengthen the stakes and make the gospel message effective in Pacific Coast culture. There is a heart hunger among the people. Yet they are so busy, so preoccupied, so absorbed with things that they are almost numb to the gospel.

Get angry, criticize, characterize, philosophize as we will, men by the millions are lost about us, and we have the only hope. It will take the keenest minds, the finest skills, and the most absolute dedication we have ever known. There is no place for the soft or undisciplined. This task, as perhaps no other in Baptist history, calls for the best men our churches have to offer. There is no promise of glory here; no place for overnight fame to be gained. All that can be promised to the student, minister, or other called-of-God person is a task that will challenge his best, tax his mind and heart, and bring forth proof that we serve a great God.

Members of the faculty and student body were heavily involved in the Simultaneous Crusade of Southern Baptists in the spring of 1955. Baccalaureate speaker for the last of April was Dr. Allen W. Graves, pastor in Tulsa, Oklahoma, and my brother. I gave the commencement address and conferred degrees and awards on forty-six graduates.

At the meeting of the trustees in Miami, the president reported that seventeen new churches had been organized by Golden Gate students during the past session. He recommended, and the trustees elected, Clayton K. Harrop as an instructor in New Testament. A native of Kansas, graduate of William Jewell College and Southern Seminary, Harrop had only his thesis to complete before being awarded the Doctor of Theology degree.

Word came during the convention of the approval of the plan for development of the new campus by the Marin County Planning Commission. Working drawings to begin the grading were nearing completion and Graves reported negotiations with a contracting firm, the Guy F. Atkinson Company, to do the work. They had offered a price of 39.3¢ per cubic yard. Rutland had assisted the president in the negotiations and was convinced that the price was reasonable.

The trustees discussed the matter and decided that, in the

best interest of all concerned, the project would be put out for bids. This was done and the Atkinson Company was the lowest bidder, using the same figure as in previous negotiations. A contract was signed in June, 1955, and the first work began in October. Their superintendent, Mr. Hendricks, saved the seminary thousands of dollars by his suggestions. When all was done, Robert Atkinson, nephew of Guy, founder of the firm, figured their cost for the operation and returned their profit. In all, 638,000 yards of soil were moved, culverts placed, and so forth. Later movement of soil in actual construction brought this total to nearly 1,000,000 yards of material moved without leaving a scar.

During the summer of 1955, a beautiful color rendering of the new campus layout was hung in the lobby of the seminary building in Berkeley. This helped to heighten excitement.

The fall semester opened on August 29 with an increase of 15 percent in enrollment, with 96 new students. The 50 students from California almost matched the number from Texas. OBU still led the colleges, but with 8, Grand Canyon alumni were coming in larger numbers.

A two-day orientation program for new students was instituted that fall. L. A. Brown introduced Northern California and the Bay Area with its needs. President Graves spoke on the "Spirit and Purpose of the Seminary." W. A. Carleton led a panel discussion about the student's workload. The students were taken for a driving tour of San Francisco and over the Golden Gate Bridge to the new campus site in Marin County. Madge Lewis introduced them to the library. Royal spoke on study habits. Later in the week J. Lyn Elder addressed the new students on their personal adjustment. Following this initial experience with orientation, the faculty decided to add presentations by state convention personnel and some tests that could assist in the educational task.

On October 14, 1955, groundbreaking ceremonies were held on the new campus site. The service was attended by the seminary family, several trustees, the architect, John Carl Warnecke, Posey and several from the state convention office, and C. E. Boyle, editor of the *Pacific Coast Baptist*, represented the Washington-Oregon Baptist Convention. Visitors also included many from nearby churches and friends from Marin County.

The ceremony was described in the *Tiburon Peninsula Pelican*:

> The day was overcast last Friday . . . on the high headlands of Strawberry Point overlooking the Golden Gate and the great city across the bay. However, the several hundred Southern Baptists assembled there with a Bible and a bulldozer, didn't mind the weather. This was a great day in California for their faith and will become a mark in the history of Marin.[5]

Chairman Westmoreland said:

> This is the day the Lord hath made, especially for the Golden Gate Baptist Theological Seminary. . . . We believe the Lord has led us here. . . . this marks a new departure for Southern Baptists and especially for Southern Baptists of California as they launch out into a new program. . . . No student can study in the buildings to be erected here and have little thoughts.[6]

To climax the groundbreaking ceremonies, Graves and the building committee boarded a huge D9 Caterpillar bulldozer. With Guy Rutland driving, they began to move dirt. Not much work was done before the rains started that fall, but the grading moved into high gear the next summer. At its peak the process moved 15,000 yards of earth each day.

R. Paul Caudill was the speaker for the second Missionary Day, December 2. He was pastor of the First Baptist Church, Memphis, Tennessee, a seminary trustee, and longtime chairman of the BWA relief committee. The Oratorio Choir gave the first of their five presentations of Handel's *Messiah* that evening at the First Southern Baptist Church in Palo Alto. Other appearances that year included one at First Presbyterian Church in Berkeley and on the aircraft carrier *Oriskany,* based in Alameda.

With the enrollment of students in January, 1956, the accumulative figure went over the 300 mark for the first time to 331. During the process of registration the 1,000th student to enter Golden Gate Seminary was enrolled.

Golden Gate was making news in many ways. Claudia Royal's book, *Storytelling*, came off the press that spring. Deere's translation of Amos and Hosea for *The New Berkeley Version* of the Bible was offered for sale in printed form. Clinical pastoral training became available for Golden Gate students under the direction of Lyn Elder. The Baptist Missionary Pilot-Training program was begun by students.

As the trustees gathered for their annual meeting in February, 1956, Graves had some exciting things to report. Sixty percent of the students enrolled were now employed on church staffs, and all others were busy in some way. There was evidence that perhaps as many as 400 students might be enrolled in Golden Gate before the move to the new campus.

The trustees elected David Appleby of Wayland Baptist College as assistant professor of music. G. S. Dobbins was elected distinguished professor of church administration for the coming session. He had taught at Southern Seminary for thirty-six years. The president suggested that at seventy years of age Dobbins might be expected to serve two or three years, maybe even five. As a matter of fact, he was elected each year for ten years, moving to Marin County with the seminary and continuing to teach until he was eighty.

Clayton Harrop was advanced to faculty status as assistant professor of New Testament, having received his Doctor of Theology degree in January. Southern Baptist educational history was made in 1956 when Golden Gate became the first seminary to elect a dean. The trustees changed William A. Carleton's title from administrative assistant to dean. Since faculty members conferred with him on academic matters when the president was away, it seemed logical for him to have that responsibility all the time. Other SBC seminaries soon changed their directors to deans.

Other personnel changes included the transfer of Jack Manning to director of field work with Isma Johnson succeeding him as registrar. Manning continued to teach evangelism. A. J. Hyatt was elected librarian and instructor in New Testament effective April 1, 1956, and Madge Lewis was named supervisor of technical and readers' services. An additional house was purchased at 1905 Grove as a residence for women students. Because of two beautiful royal palm trees on the front lawn, it was immediately named "The Palms."

A committee of trustees had been appointed earlier to recommend constitutional revisions. The committee proposed naming two trustees from the Washington-Oregon convention territory, reducing the number from California to eight. The doctrinal statement was changed from "that contained in Pendleton's Manual" to that adopted by the SBC in Memphis in 1925. The trustees also voted to purchase pews for the chapel with the understanding that they would not be included in the sale of the building when the seminary relocated. Each piece of equipment and furniture was being purchased with a view to its use on the new campus.

The April, 1956 *Golden Gate* carried an interesting article that reflects the life of students during these years. Eugene V. England wrote:

> "I Led Three Lives" is the way the "typical" Golden Gate student may describe his life in Seminary in years to come, for he fills the position of husband and father, employee, and student. A few are not satisfied with this triple role and add a fourth—that of Pastor, Minister of Education or Minister of Music in one of the nearby churches.
>
> Married students constitute approximately 77% of the current student body with some 80% of these having children. To provide for these families and finance a seminary education, he works a "swing" or "graveyard" shift in one of the local plants, odd hours at a part-time job, or he may receive some assistance such as that from the Veterans Administration. In great numbers, however, working wives fill in the financial gap.
>
> With all this, the "typical" student finds time to accomplish his original mission and prepare for an expanded

future service. It is not an easy life, but it is an immensely rewarding one.

England, a member of the 1956 graduating class, joined the administrative staff a dozen years later. The baccalaureate preacher on April 26 was Arnold Ohrn, secretary of the BWA. Graves addressed the graduates the next day and conferred forty-eight degrees and awards.

The trustees met in connection with the SBC in Kansas City in May. The most significant action they took was to authorize the architect to prepare working drawings for all construction planned for the initial stage of development. Trustees were advised that the Washington-Oregon convention was not yet large enough to qualify for representation on the board. The constitution change voted in February was set aside until the Washington-Oregon convention had grown.

In June, 1956 the seminary cohosted, with Berkeley Baptist Divinity School, five Baptist leaders from the USSR. These included Alexander Karev, secretary of the All-Union Council of Evangelical Christian Baptists and Jakov Zidkov, president and pastor of the Moscow Baptist Church. Karev addressed a Baptist rally sponsored by the two seminaries and the Bay Cities Baptist Union. On a two-day visit to Yosemite National Park, Zidkov was hesitant to ride in the car Mrs. Graves was driving. He did, however, and when asked by Graves in Rio four years later if he remembered eating cucumbers in Graves's home, he replied, "I remember you as the husband of that good woman driver."

The June, 1956 edition of the *Golden Gate* carried Graves's comments concerning the denomination and Golden Gate:

> I never attend an annual meeting of the SBC that I do not come away with a new sense of gratitude for our denomination. . . . Specifically, what is being done for Golden Gate Seminary is thrilling to behold. . . . Baptist eyes are focused on the Far West and what the seminary will do in realizing the potential here.
>
> The results encourage us to believe that our investment is sound. Of the 533 Southern Baptist churches organized in

California, 142 were organized by students while attending Golden Gate Seminary. Sixty additional churches were organized by ex-students and an additional 91 had some assistance from former Golden Gate students.

The SBC investment in Golden Gate was indeed large, yet many did not understand why the demands were so heavy. The capital needs allocations stretched the imaginations of the most farsighted friends of the seminary. One such person was chairman of the finance committee of the SBC Executive Committee, Douglas Hudgins. He and Graves had been neighbors during seminary days and the friendship had continued across the years. In the summer of 1956 he wrote Graves, saying in substance that he and others felt like the architect for the new campus thought the SBC had an endless supply of money. Graves answered Hudgins, encouraging him and anyone else to visit the seminary and meet the architect.

An exchange of letters followed between Hudgins, Porter Routh, and Graves. A meeting at the seminary was set for September. Hudgins, Curtis English, a committee member and a contractor from Virginia, and Porter Routh, executive secretary of the SBC Executive Committee came. The building committee of the trustees was present and after chapel they and the visitors left for the new campus site, crossing the new Richmond-San Rafael Bridge which had opened September 1. Only one deck of the bridge was in use because the approaches to the other deck were still being completed.

As the group entered Marin County, the visitors observed scores of new houses under construction in Greenbrae and Corte Madera. The piling was being driven for a new overpass on Highway 101 at Corte Madera. Arriving on campus, just three miles further on 101, they saw heavy earthmoving equipment rolling everywhere. The cars easily followed the construction roads, stopping at various points for explanations. From there the group went to the Alta Mira Hotel in the hills of Sausalito for lunch.

It was a beautiful day and the bay was dotted with sailboats. By that time the three visitors were numb with the sights and experiences of the previous hours. English commented that he had seen more construction work that morning than in months back home. After lunch the group drove across the Golden Gate Bridge to San Francisco and the offices of the architect.

Warnecke outlined the steps through which the architects and the seminary administration had gone in developing an understanding of the needs and in producing the plans for providing the facilities to meet those needs. It was a lengthy presentation, punctuated with many questions and answers. When it was over, Curtis English was the first to speak.

> I have been in the contracting business all of my life for my father was a contractor. I have seen many plans and built structures of many types but I have never seen a program more thoroughly researched and planned in my life. The only criticism I would have is the idea of building housing out of wood. I do understand, however, about earthquakes and of course those redwood exteriors add permanency. I see no place to cut. The seminary must have the money they are asking for.

Routh and Hudgins followed with their approval of that judgment. The request for Golden Gate in the new capital needs program had been $2,500,000. The men who had come to tell the seminary to lower its sights went away champions of Golden Gate's cause. The allocation determined by the SBC Executive Committee in December and approved in the Chicago Convention in 1957 was set at $2,400,000. Of this amount $2,000,000 was promised for 1959 and the remainder at a rate of $100,000 per year.

The fall semester of 1956 opened August 28 with enrollment up 15 percent. There were 102 new students. For the first time California, with 58, led the states in providing students. Faculty offices had been removed from the balcony of the chapel during the summer. But even with balcony seating available, the chapel was strained to capacity with the crowd which came to hear Fred Fisher's convocation address.

Among matters reported by the president to the trustee

executive committee in September was the record in the practical activities program for the past year. Some 4,590 sermons had been delivered, 1,044 conversions reported, and 1,545 additions by letter to churches pastored by students. Thirteen new missions had been started. It had been a banner year for this active mission force at work in California. One student had driven more than 600 miles, round trip, each weekend to continue a mission begun the summer before and to get it organized into a church.

Actions of the trustee executive committee included assistance to the Calvary Baptist Church in securing a loan to complete payment for their new addition. The trustees heard a report from the building committee, then authorized the president to move ahead with plantings when the grading was completed. Architect Warnecke had asked Lawrence Halprin, a landscape architect, to plan this phase of the development of the new campus. His plans called for the planting of more than 4,000 trees and shrubs in addition to grass and other ground cover for erosion control. Contracts were let in October and work was begun before the winter rains. Planting was completed after the rains ended in early spring of 1957.

The first Missionary Day for 1956-1957 was held September 26. The featured speaker was Floyd Looney, editor of *The California Southern Baptist* whose subject was "Southern Baptists' Second Chance in California." He recounted the story of Baptist beginnings in 1849 and then again for Southern Baptists in 1936. This second effort, twenty years old, had been greatly helped by Golden Gate Seminary. Two Golden Gaters, Peter Chen and Amelio Giannetta, spoke of the progress of work in the Bay Area among Chinese and Italian people respectively.

The second Missionary Day, December 6, was addressed by Theodore F. Adams, president of the BWA and pastor of the First Baptist Church of Richmond, Virginia. In connection with his and Mrs. Adams's visit to the area, two Baptist rallies were held: one in San Francisco and one in Oakland.

Among the changes to be noted in seminary life during the

fall term that year was the name of the organization for student wives. The name was changed from Lambda Delta Sigma to Seminary Wives Fellowship. It later became Seminary Women's Fellowship.

An all-out effort was made to receive a sacrificial offering for the Lottie Moon Christmas emphasis in December, 1956. The goal was exceeded when $3,222 was given. The seminary family not only practiced missions in their personal efforts but, in spite of their own needs, also shared financially in the world task.

The annual meeting of the seminary trustees came in February, 1957. The president's report read in part:

> This is the fifth annual report I have brought to you. These have been five years of study, trial, error, planning and some production. First, the faculty needed attention for strengthening, stabilizing, and enlarging. Ten members have been added, plus Dr. Hyatt in the library.
>
> Second, space and equipment had to have attention. Classroom, library, office, and auxiliary space has been added. The chapel has been completely renovated. . . . Adequate dormitory space has been provided, and with the addition of a staff member, the problem of other housing and secular jobs has been solved.
>
> Third, the problem of an adequate permanent campus has been tackled and in measure is being brought to quite a satisfactory solution. . . . The master plan has been accepted and progress is being made in development. . . .
>
> The fourth task has been one of public relations, locally and denominationally. Nothing has been more gratifying than seeing the institution become accepted by our neighbors: theological schools, business and professional groups, and the community. . . .
>
> The year 1956-57 has been a record year in almost every way. 348 students have been enrolled. They came from 32 states, the District of Columbia, Hawaii, and six foreign countries.
>
> . . . The library now boasts of more than 17,000 titles.

Trustee actions included an expression concerning health insurance for the faculty and staff. A committee was asked to study the matter and bring recommendations. They were also asked to propose a sabbatical leave program. Royal was granted a sabbatical leave for the next school year, the first provided by Golden Gate. Mrs. Royal was given an expression of appreciation for her long service as a member of the faculty. She was asked to consider continued instructional duties in elementary education when they returned. The Bachelor of Sacred Music degree was discontinued and a certificate in church music was added for those not qualified to study toward the Master of Church Music degree.

The trustees named Paul Mason "Clerk of the Works" for the construction and asked that a house be built for him at once. A study of possible faculty housing was also instituted. An account with the SBC Foundation was approved, with $10,000 from the current budget to be placed there.

The new librarian, A. J. Hyatt, wrote in the March, 1957 *Golden Gate* of the ministry of a seminary library. Though a freshman librarian, he was no freshman in theological education or in service to the churches. He contrasted library use in the thirties to today. Then it was a reading room for students with their textbooks. Now the approach called for a library to provide a wide range of sources to be used by the students. He also mentioned the expanded use of visual aids and the growth of microfilm production. Music materials and periodicals were given their place. He ended his article by making sure that no one had the antiquated idea that libraries were places to "keep" material. "The staff of our library desires to make it a valuable helper to every student, every faculty member, and to nearby pastors."

Ted Lindwall, the first native Californian to graduate from Golden Gate, was chosen president of the senior class. Later he and his wife, Sue, entered service in Guatemala through the Foreign Mission Board. Commencement was held April 25-26, with Carl E. Bates, pastor of the First Baptist Church of Amarillo, Texas, as the baccalaureate preacher. Graves addressed the students the next morning and conferred thirty-three degrees and awards. Among those receiving the Master of Religious Education degree was Geil Davis. She was asked to join the teaching force of the seminary in the field of elementary education and director of the child-care program. She continued in service to the seminary, soon being added to the faculty, and remaining until poor health forced early retirement in 1978.

The Chapel Choir went on tour each spring for many years. The tours served to enhance public relations and effectively recruit students. A letter from a church music director in Longview, Texas, received after the 1957 tour reflects the impact of the tours:

> Thank you for sending your choral group our way. . . . It was not a program, and it was not music used merely as a concert. We felt we had attended a profound worship service. We have not seen anything so accurately worked out . . . nor have we heard anything that sounded better musically.

Bennett prepared good programs that mixed songs by the choir with those by soloists, smaller groups, the organ or piano, or any other instrument that might be used by a choir member.

That letter emphasized what Graves learned early in his service with the seminary. When representatives of Golden Gate presented Christ and led the people to worship, there was a good response. Brief comments about the school were sufficient when the people had their hearts warmed by the devotional part of the presentation.

There was exciting news for the trustees as they gathered in Chicago May 29, 1957, during meetings of the SBC. The capital needs recommendations were adopted, allocating $2,000,000 to Golden Gate in 1959. This assured completion of construction in time to occupy the campus that year. Grading and planting contracts had been completed. Bids for the installation of utilities were to be opened in July and for the construction of major buildings in the fall of 1957.

Actions taken by the trustees included the approval of a

program of hospital, disability, and life insurance for the faculty and staff. It was not much, but it was a start. The insurance program grew until a truly fine program developed, completely financed by the seminary.

An alumni breakfast was held during the Convention. Byron Todd was elected president, succeeding Earl Bigelow. The featured speaker was G. S. Dobbins. Commenting on the unique opportunities of Golden Gate Seminary, he said,

> The seminary must help Southern Baptists to devise and put into operation a suburban strategy; to see in Golden Gate Seminary a unique opportunity for clinical training or practice; to see a field of missionary training such as exists nowhere else on earth; to accept the opportunity to live one's vision.[7]

The action of the SBC in approving the recommended capital needs budget for the next five years was not received with enthusiasm by everyone. When a pie is divided, increasing the size of one piece inevitably reduces the size of others. Such is the case in dividing a fixed dollar allocation for capital needs expenditures. As the committee began reporting its conclusions in December, 1956, there were rumblings from several seminary presidents.

The older schools were facing curtailment in their development because of the cost of the new campus at Golden Gate and the new seminary in Kansas City. The SBC voted in Chicago to open Midwestern Seminary in 1958 and to allocate construction funds for it. Southern Seminary was especially sensitive to this action since the new Boyce Library was being built. It was hoped that it might be completed for dedication in connection with the meeting of the SBC in Louisville in 1959. With $2,000,000 going to Golden Gate in 1959, Southern could not get the help from the Convention that was expected. Therefore, President McCall turned to Southern's alumni for needed resources.

Each seminary goes through critical times in needing capital funds. Golden Gate was in one of those times since it was establishing a new campus. The older and more estab-

The building committee charged with the responsibility of developing the master plan for the Marin County campus is shown conferring with the renowned architect John Carl Warnecke, left. The committee was composed of, from left, Harold K. Graves, E. Hermond Westmoreland, Guy W. Rutland, Jr., Clarence E. Kennedy, John Wesley Raley, and Floyd D. Golden.

lished seminaries had to operate with reduced capital funds temporarily. That fact was painful for Graves as he had to personally deal with the implication that Golden Gate Seminary had gotten funds that would normally have been allocated to other seminaries.

In the July, 1957 issue of the *Golden Gate*, trustee Chairman Westmoreland wrote of "Five Years in Retrospect," which spoke of the progress since Graves had been elected president:

> Golden Gate Seminary today stands on the threshold of realizing a dream that five years ago seemed far distant and well-nigh impossible. With the adoption of the new five-year Capital Needs program at the recent Chicago Convention, the construction of the first phase of development on Strawberry Point was guaranteed. The fall session in 1959 should see our seminary housed and functioning in new facilities on this attractive site. Harold K. Graves will view with satisfaction the fulfillment of a dream which he largely fashioned and to which he has devoted himself with boundless energy and unfaltering vision.

> Faced with the cramped buildings and limited space available in Berkeley, he set himself to the task of finding a site suitable to the needs of a growing institution. Refusing to be discouraged by temporary frustrations of his plans, he continued the quest until he found a site that exceeded the fondest hopes of the trustees and the fairest vision of all our Baptist constituency . . . on a beautiful peninsula, hard by the Golden Gate Bridge. . . . Only the seminary at Ruschlikon in Switzerland will even rival the site in natural setting and in panoramic beauty.

> One of the leading architectural firms on the West Coast was engaged to draw the master plan and to recommend the proposed development of the campus. This firm has caught the enthusiasm and vision of our president and, after years of research and study, has produced a set of plans that will make our seminary one of the most distinctive theological institutions in America. They have captured the functional design of our Baptist institutions and have added the con-

temporary character of California architecture. With consummate skill they have planned a building program that will attract and inspire, while still remaining economical in cost of construction. When completed, the campus will represent the faith and dream of one man, above all others—our president.

While giving himself, without reserve, to this stupendous task, Dr. Graves has not neglected the welfare of the seminary at its present location. These five years have witnessed building expansion, the strengthening of the faculty, the improvement of curriculum, the enlargement of the library, growth in the student body, and the general elevation of spirit and morale on the part of faculty, students, and our Baptist forces on the Pacific coast. The seminary has gained stature with every passing year and today occupies a position of respect and confidence in the minds and hearts of all our neighbors, as well as among our own Baptist people in the entire territory of our convention.

The trustees of Golden Gate Seminary are grateful to Southern Baptists for their prayerful interest and their generous support in all our plans for the continued growth and spiritual ministry of our institution. We believe that the seminary will prove worthy of such confidence and will in the future serve in a way that will justify such investment. We are grateful to God for His blessings and favor which have attended us during these days of growth and development.

In commenting on the SBC actions concerning Golden Gate at the Chicago Convention, Graves said in the July, 1957 *Golden Gate*,

We observed our anniversary in Chicago. Seven years ago the SBC took over the reins of this institution. And what a wonderful anniversary it proved to be! . . . [the actions taken] shows the confidence the convention has in our fine trustees and the seminary family as a whole. Faculty and students alike have had their share in building this confidence. . . . The challenge for all of us now is to build an institution that will justify the confidence expressed. With such equipment of faculty, staff, and physical facilities, surely there is a new day for Baptists in the West.

With the opening of the fall semester in 1957, excitement was in the air as everyone caught the spirit of progress and promise. Bachelor of Divinity students entering that fall would complete their studies on the new campus. There was a record number of new students which pushed the enrollment to an all-time high.

The faculty and administration became interested in offering classes to prepare students to minister to the deaf. In 1957 dactylology (sign language) was offered for the first time. Men and women trained at Golden Gate have made significant contributions in Southern Baptist life because of this preparation. Glen C. Prock, a druggist turned missionary for the HMB, was the teacher.

Edmond Walker, Golden Gate alumnus, spoke on the first Missionary Day of the new school year. As a pastor and then assistant executive secretary for Southern Baptists, he discussed the challenge of the California cities. He cited the need for 503 additional churches in Los Angeles County. Nearly 700 others were needed in 28 cities of more than 50,000 population if Southern Baptists were to be up to the norm for cities in the United States. Sharing the program with Walker, was Dobbins, just home from a world tour. He spoke on "Re-thinking Our Mission Strategy." "One hundred years hence how will historians characterize our age?" he asked. "The age of change! . . . The change has been so rapid that it has affected us in the field of missions. . . . Just as strategy is essential in military aspects, now it has become one of the great essentials in missionary advance."[8]

Graves reported to the seminary family that four contractors were busy on the new campus and that others would soon be added. Costs were continually rising, and he asked them to pray that right decisions would be made related to the problems of increased cost. When L. R. Elliot, longtime librarian at Southwestern, visited Golden Gate library, he was impressed with its 20,000 titles and the fact that it was surpassed by few other theological libraries in the Bay Area in breadth and depth.

Fifty-one mission volunteers were interviewed by Edna Francis Dawkins, assistant personnel secretary of the Foreign Mission Board during a week in November. H. Cornell Goerner, secretary-elect for Africa, Europe, and the Near East, was the speaker for Missionary Day in December.

Work began in earnest during the summer of 1957 for the Billy Graham Crusade to be held in San Francisco, April 28-May 25, 1958. Graves was a member of the executive committee planning the crusade; Earle Smith of the Bay Cities Baptist Union served as chairman. Walter Smyth, of the Billy Graham Association was the resident director. The committee met almost weekly. Besides Smith, Graves became well acquainted with Robert Munger, pastor of First Presbyterian, Berkeley. Lowell Berry, president of BEST Fertilizer Company, also joined his circle of friends. Berry became a regular contributor for aid to Golden Gate students and has continued the practice. He has especially helped in bringing students to the seminary and attending evangelism seminars.

The development of a formula for the distribution of Cooperative Program funds to the seminaries in 1956 had several flaws and did not solve many problems. When the SBC Executive Committee met in December, 1957, the presidents reported their inability to agree. The finance committee asked them to return to their negotiations until they could agree. Several trustee board chairmen including Robert Naylor of Southwestern and Westmoreland of Golden Gate were accompanied by their presidents.

This session was held in a small room where most had to stand. The discussion was heated, and the air tense with emotion. But after an hour or so, a compromise was reached. The larger schools agreed to share the available funds so that the smaller seminaries could live. All thought the agreement was understood, but when the chairman of the finance committee reported, Southwestern seemed to have done all the sharing. Nevertheless, the report was adopted. That was not the last tension-filled meeting the seminary presidents had.

With the assistance of the SBC Executive Committee, the presidents asked a team of educational consultants to develop a more acceptable formula for distribution. The team consisted of Oren Cornett, executive secretary of the Education Commission of SBC; Doak Campbell, president of Florida State University; and Harold A. Haswell, of the Texas Baptist Education Commission. The new formula was to include such factors as size, cost of theological education in general, and efficiency of operation. After much discussion and many revisions, a formula was finally approved by the presidents in October, 1958. It was proposed to the Executive Committee for use in the 1960 allocation.

As large contracts began to be signed for construction on the new Golden Gate campus, it became apparent that cash flow was going to be a problem. It was impossible to correlate the outflow with incoming funds from the SBC. Most of the capital needs allocations were paid in August and September, after the basic operational funds had been distributed. Contract payments came monthly.

A construction loan that might reach $1,000,000 was needed. Graves went to his friend, James K. Dobey, assistant manager of the Berkeley office of the American Trust Company. Dobey was a bit taken aback with the amount, but said that he would talk with top management. All he had to go on were letters of commitment from the SBC Executive Committee and, as Dobey said later, "President Graves had an honest face." In any event, the commitment was secured and a line of credit was extended up to $1,000,000 at the rate of 5 percent. A maximum of $700,000 was borrowed. Most if it was repaid before the end of 1959.

On Friday, November 22, 1957, bids were opened for the first major construction—administration and classroom buildings, cafeteria, and recital hall. In spite of continuous reminders from the architect that prices were rising, the bids were a shocking $500,000 over estimates. After much discussion, a contract was signed eliminating the recital hall and the connecting music practice rooms. A change order adjusted what was to be built to provide for a temporary chapel and practice rooms. (The recital hall was to have been the chapel in the first stage.) Construction began at once.

With the beginning of the spring semester in January, 1958, the enrollment reached a record of 384 students. Now the seminary family could say, "Next year, we move to Strawberry Point." It was going to be an interesting eighteen months before the move. On January 24 bids were opened for the construction of housing on the new campus. Like the earlier bids, they, too, were far above estimates. Some very badly needed family housing units had to be deleted. (If seventy-five more units could have been built at that time, another 100 students might have entered Golden Gate and its enrollment been maintained at that level.) The contract provided for the two dormitories and family housing, including studio, one-bedroom, and two-bedroom type units.

The trustees held their annual meeting in February. Also attending some of their sessions was Brooks Hays, president of the SBC. Hays spoke in chapel and at the joint dinner for the trustees and the faculty. The president's report to the trustees dealt largely with the progress of the building program. Most of the first phase development was either complete or under contract. Conversations with the fire district personnel were revealing. It was so small at the time, and the campus development so large, that the seminary would have to pay for fire protection. It was determined that the seminary should lease land and build a firehouse for the district. Lease and amortization payments by the district would be credited toward the cost of fire protection to the seminary. No other SBC educational institution known to this writer pays for fire protection. It has cost Golden Gate several hundred thousand dollars.

The president also reported that the seminary was required by the water district to pay a share of a new water storage and pressure tank. The use of the sewer connection also called for an annual fee. In addition to these costs,

California churches and schools also pay sales tax (6 percent in Marin County). The total of these items is more than $25,000 a year which Golden Gate has paid that is not required of any other SBC seminary. One school even pays no tax on income-producing property. This is one of the variables not included in the early formulas for distribution of funds.

Several changes in the academic programs were approved by the trustees. The Master of Sacred Music degree was changed to the Master of Church Music degree and was also to be offered in combination with the Master of Religious Education degree. The Bachelor of Religious Education degree and the Bachelor of Theology degree were dropped, having been offered with a two-year college prerequisite. The desire was to eliminate the college prerequisite that put the seminary in competition with Baptist colleges. Mrs. Bennett, who had been half-time as a faculty member, was given the title of instructor without faculty responsibilities. In all the years that she taught, her load was never light, sometimes nearing the full-time level. Her contribution cannot be overemphasized.

The finance committee recommended that the seminary assume the entire premium cost for hospital and disability insurance for the faculty and staff. This was approved along with a proposal to enter the new "Ministers' Security Plan" of the Annuity Board. The seminary paid the entire 10 percent on the salary of each faculty and administrative staff member. The board also agreed to move each faculty member to Marin County who wished to move.

Chairman Westmoreland read a letter from Wallace Hough, pastor of the First Baptist Church of San Rafael. Speaking for the Redwood Empire Baptist Association, he expressed appreciation for the assistance rendered by several trustees who had helped to purchase land for a church to be located near the new campus.

A number of people had been thinking of establishing a church in the fast-developing neighborhood near the new campus. Graves learned of the realignment of the Tiburon

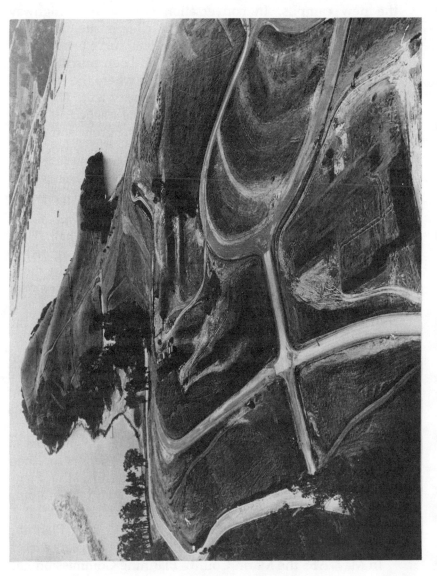

The initial phase of construction on the Strawberry Point campus focused on developing the terrain and laying out a basic network of roads.

Boulevard just beyond East Strawberry Drive, an entrance to the new campus. In conversation with a state highway engineer, he discovered a possible church site. It was a banana-shaped parcel of land located on a curve between the old road and the right-of-way that had been purchased for the new highway. It was a mountainside where the cut at the center line of the new road would be sixty feet. The three acre parcel would just about be the space needed. It was a dramatic location for a church building. Surely somebody would need the dirt that would have to be removed to prepare the site for a church building complex.

The owners were descendants of the family that once owned Strawberry Point. In due time a price of $30,000 was agreed upon. The HMB paid half of it. The president appealed to the trustees for help with the other half. They and their churches provided $7,500. The owners agreed to carry the remainder. So, in 1957, two years before the move to Marin County, land was secured for a Baptist church near the campus. The Redwood Empire Baptist Association was the legal owner, though it did not contribute toward the purchase.

The trustees were glad to learn that a site had been purchased for a church. All felt that the church should have its orientation toward the community. The church has sought to do this in spite of the fact that across the years half of its members have been seminary related.

In a letter to the trustees accompanying the minutes of their February meeting, I expressed appreciation for their support. I asked for their prayers concerning the many decisions I had to make daily in connection with the building program. I especially asked to be remembered on April 3. That night I had to go before the Marin County Planning Commission to appeal a ruling made nearly two years earlier.

In May, 1955 the Marin County Planning Commission had given tentative approval to the plan for the development of the new campus. Graves was in Miami, Florida, at the SBC meeting. Since the planning commission gives no formal notice to property owners of their actions, Graves did not

Evangelist Billy Graham preached the baccalaureate service at Golden Gate Seminary in May, 1958. Here he helps President Harold K. Graves with his academic robe.

learn that their approval was contingent upon the construction of a road along the west side of the seminary property until near the end of 1957. It would connect the end of the peninsula (not owned by the seminary) with the major road. Lacking rules that cover institutions like the seminary, the commission treated it like any other developer. Such companies would of course pass on these costs to the buyers of lots in their development.

In the *Independent Journal* of April 4, 1958, there was a report of the action of the planning commission the night before. They had voted four to one to require the seminary to build the road. It was described as a "lengthy and heated argument between seminary officials and attorney Bryan McCarthy, representing Sam Neider, Strawberry Point developer."[9]

Commissioner Niels Shultz, Jr., cast the lone dissenting vote, declaring that "Since everybody benefits, everybody should participate." The majority opinion was expressed in the words of Commissioner Mrs. Alfred Azevedo, "We get down to the irreducible problem: If the seminary doesn't build the road, who does?" She went on to say that, "a precedent has been set for any developer of land to provide circulation through the land. I just can't see my way clear to throwing out that precedent."

While being convinced that no court in the land would require this of the seminary, it was too late for any such action. Construction had to continue if the campus were to be occupied in 1959 as planned. Each new contract called for permits that caused the seminary to face the demand for that road. The day of reckoning finally came on July 1, 1959. That morning, with the campus complete, the utilities hooked up and working, the moving trucks were loaded and ready to roll to Marin County. The president had to produce a bond guaranteeing construction of the required road in two years before the trucks were allowed to move. That road cost in total outlay in excess of $135,000.

Commencement exercises were highlighted by the appearance of Billy Graham as the baccalaureate preacher on May 1, 1958. He was in the area for the crusade which opened Sunday, April 27, at the Cow Palace in San Francisco. There was a record number of seventy in the graduating class.

It had been a great year in many respects. The students reported preaching nearly 7,000 sermons with 1,342 conversions. Their preaching was in English and six other languages. Students also worked among the deaf, blind, migrants, and in rescue missions.

Every visit to the new campus by the seminary family during the summer of 1958 revealed amazing progress in the construction. Graves found it almost impossible to keep from going there daily. Even on the day of his daughter's wedding, August 1, he and Nancy made a trip. Nancy remembers it as a time the determination was made concerning the color of the porcelain panels beneath the windows in the academic buildings. With construction of outside walls and rooms completed that summer, the winter rains would not slow the pace.

Barring some catastrophe, it did seem that the move a year hence was assured. Catastrophies could happen. An earthquake shook the Bay Area in the spring of 1957. This caused the seminary to seek insurance from Lloyds of London against any damage from such a shake during construction. From time to time, changes had to be made in location of a structure due to unstable ground for foundations. One day, during the grading process in 1956, the earth movers had dumped 100 yards of fill where a road was to be built. When they returned from lunch, the fill had all disappeared. Drillings revealed that this was the old seabed and the mud was thirty-five feet deep. Fortunately the alignment could be changed and there was enough fill material available to create acceptable compaction.

There was much excitement in the air as plans were made for the beginning of the final year in Berkeley. The enrollment was down but CBC and Grand Canyon continued to increase the number of students they provided.

Dean W. A. Carleton brought the opening academic address, speaking on "Baptist Territorialism Among Baptists in America." Basing his remarks on actions of the SBC and its mission boards, he proclaimed that no limits had ever been placed on where they should work. What had been done because of Baptist concern for people continued to be the order of the day. He predicted that Southern Baptist work would soon be in each of the states in the United States. He lived to see that realized.

The first Missionary Day of the year on October 1 was shared by A. L. Gillespie of Japan and Roland Hood from the Washington-Oregon convention. Hood told of what several couples had done in beginning work in their convention. In almost every instance, he said, "another fine couple from Southwestern Seminary." Afterwards Graves said he hoped that in ten years Hood would be able to report on more work being done by Golden Gate graduates. Hood was a friend of Golden Gate and said that he would watch for the contributions of Golden Gates graduates.

When the second semester opened, the accumulative enrollment for the year was thirty-four short of the previous year. The opening of the new seminary in Kansas City and the tight economic situation were ample explanations for the decline. As a matter of fact, all of the SBC seminaries except Southeastern dropped in enrollment that year.

Golden Gate was host for the annual joint faculty dinner with the Berkeley Baptist Divinity School on January 22, 1959. The group heard from C. O. Johnson and G. S. Dobbins. Johnson was living in Oakland near his son Ralph who was president of Berkeley Baptist Divinity School. Ralph Johnson and Graves were in Southern Seminary together and had continued their friendship. C. O. Johnson was teaching preaching and evangelism at BBDS in his retirement from the pastorate of Third Baptist Church in St. Louis, Missouri.

The Seminary Conference in February, 1959 also featured this Baptist veteran and Dobbins. Johnson spoke three times on "Preaching to the City." Dobbins reported on his efforts as cochairman of the Bible Study and Training Commission of BWA. The two leaders spoke to appreciative audiences, including the Baptist military chaplains, who now met regularly during this annual conference.

In commenting on the recent Seminary Conference, Graves wrote in the March, 1959 issue of *Golden Gate*:

> We had the privilege of hearing two honored leaders of Southern Baptist Convention life for the past quarter of a century. These two . . . spoke on widely different themes. . . . Yet to the amazement of us all, they came out at the same place with us as we looked at our modern task. We saw that the day of the chapel emphasis on the mission field is fast passing into that of the church organized for study and training. We heard the veteran city pastor say that the day of the popular appeal of a 'name' preacher and a dominating public worship service is passing in favor of the well-organized city church using its people to reach the city for the Saviour.
>
> . . . This is no new emphasis. It is rather that of the New Testament. Jesus charged his followers to take the Gospel to every person. The effectiveness of the first church was little short of a miracle. . . . They who might have been despised became the dominating factor in their society.

With all the facilities of the twentieth century at our disposal, dare we to think in smaller terms than they? To be sure, times have changed and the pattern of life for men is revolutionized with transportation as it is and with television and other mass media for communication. Yet these can be used for God and his glory. America is fast becoming urban. This brings new problems to us who think like country people—but the problems have answers, and God has wisdom and to spare.

The trustees met in Berkeley for the last time in February, 1959. In his report to them, Graves called attention to the fact that he was in his seventh year as president. In Jewish terms, it was the end of an era and the beginning of another. He recounted the changes that had come about and drew contrasts in many areas. All was ready now for the big change to the new campus.

He commented on the recently adopted formula for distribution of SBC Cooperative Program funds to the six seminaries:

It will give us additional funds only after we get well beyond the 400 mark in enrollment. We must have at least 150 new students this fall to justify [obtain] this kind of support. Nearer 200 would be much better. . . . The economic picture is very much improved both from the increase of jobs and in the development of San Francisco as an area of work. It looks good at this stage to encourage students to come.

He had expressed strong doubts to Oren Cornett concerning the ability of Golden Gate to live within the limits of the new formula. Cornett quickly agreed that this would be hard without a marked increase in enrollment at Golden Gate. "But," he added, "everybody knows that Golden Gate will have 75 to 100 more students this fall." As a matter of fact, there were fewer students when the seminary moved to the new campus, and financial woes were compounded.

He closed his report to the trustees by emphasizing concern for faculty housing in Marin County. The trustees were urged to assist if possible. Then he said,

This new era brings with it many problems of support and personnel, but they are less ominous as we face them in the light of what has been given us with which to work. Jacob worked seven years and got Leah for his labors. The next seven years seemed less burdensome because of Rachel. So may it be with us as we think of the new facilities compared with the old.

The trustees authorized the president and faculty, in consultation with the building committee, to name roads and buildings. Those chosen reflect the wide range of interests. The four academic buildings were given names honoring late professors at Southern (John A. Broadus and A. T. Robertson) and Southwestern (B. H. Carroll and W. T. Connor). The dormitories memorialized George W. Truett, the preacher, and Kathleen Mallory, worker with women. Housing villages took the names of missionaries: Gill, Maddox, Bagby, and Oliver and Foreman of South America were chosen for one. Rankin, Carey, Wallace, and Rice and Judson from the Orient were used for the other.

Major roads honored California Baptist leaders of a century earlier: Gilbert, Shuck, and Willis. The first two Golden Gate presidents, Isam Hodges and B. O. Herring, were honored with the entrance roads. J. W. Storer, the chairman of the committee recommending Golden Gate to the SBC in 1950, rounded out the selection for road names. The trustees also instructed this committee to "follow the policy of naming the buildings after deceased persons only unless a substantial contribution would warrant their naming the building after a living person."

A policy was approved to lend up to $2,400 to each faculty member who needed assistance in purchase of a new house in Marin County. Interest was set at 3 percent with the total to be amortized in ten years. Loans were considered as advance salary and therefore as belonging to the faculty member as he arranged for additional financing.

April 1, 1959 was a significant day on the new campus.

With some flourish, the power was turned on by PG&E. It was another sign that all would be in readiness for the move.

Commencement time was advanced to April 16. A majority of the seminary family were involved in simultaneous revivals being conducted in California April 19-May 3. W. Morris Ford, pastor, First Baptist Church, Longview, Texas, was the baccalaureate preacher. Graves addressed the group and awarded diplomas to fifty-eight men and women. The final Doctor of Theology degree awarded by Golden Gate was given to Robert Stapp. He had been delayed in completing his degree because a flood covered his home in Yuba City, California, destroying all his dissertation notes.

The SBC met in Louisville, Kentucky, in May, 1959 to help Southern Seminary celebrate 100 years of history and dedicate the new Boyce Library. It was announced at the Convention that Midwestern Seminary in Kansas City would occupy its new campus that fall.

Golden Gate trustees met during the Convention, and I gave a report concerning the final preparations for the move to Strawberry Point. I emphasized that every economy possible would be practiced. All realized that the sheer size of the operation would call for greater operational expense. My major concern for the new school year was enrollment. The seminary administration was telling prospective students about good prospects for housing and jobs in the East Bay and in Marin County. Many students, however, who were currently enrolled were writing very discouraging letters to their friends back East. This had a very devastating effect on the enrollment of new students that fall.

The trustees still hoped to sell the basic campus buildings in Berkeley to the Calvary Baptist Church. They worked out and approved the best possible financial structure, but all their efforts came to nothing in the end. The property was a burden to the seminary for several years. The church finally decided that they could not carry the load. Certain parts of the property were rented for some time, but this income did not cover the cost of insurance and taxes. It was finally sold.

It would have been much better to have deeded the property to the church, the state convention, or the HMB the day the seminary moved. It would have provided a good center for Baptist work in the heart of the city.

Returning from the SBC, the president came through Oklahoma where he and his family attended graduation exercises at OBU. Their daughter, Nancy, and her husband, Homer McLaughlin, received degrees. In the brief time after returning home before leaving for Hawaii, the president arranged for the medical staff of the infirmary on the new campus. Dr. John Lee became the staff physician, and Dr. Binkley provided obstetric services. Dr. B, as he was fondly called, brought many a preacher's kid into the world. He served the seminary family for ten or twelve years. Dr. Lee remained for seventeen years, rendering invaluable service to several generations of student families.

E. W. Hunke was elected president of the Alumni Association of Golden Gate at their meeting held at the SBC in Louisville. Hunke led the alumni to raise funds to construct a stone entry marker for the new campus. A beautiful wall of native stone with bronze lettering spelling out *Golden Gate Baptist Theological Seminary* stands today at the main entrance. Hunke wrote in the June, 1959 *Golden Gate*:

> A beautiful gateway is associated with almost every event in religious history. . . . There are . . . 300 biblical references to gateways.
>
> The gate in Biblical history was a place to meet friends. A 'broad place' was provided by the gate and became the center of public life. The gate was the place of legal tribunal and having a seat among the elders in the gate was a high honor. Kings held special audiences in the gate and God's prophets and teachers came here to herald his message.
>
> The Golden Gate is a symbol of American life and hope. Our seminary founders could not have chosen a more significant name for our institution. We rejoice as Golden Gate Baptist Theological Seminary moves to Strawberry Point, BUT, we have no gateway to our beautiful campus.
>
> . . . Seminary friends are invited to join hands with us in

providing this entry. "To possess the gate is to possess the city" was a military fact in the days of old. Is not a gateway just as important to our cause?

As the seminary prepared to occupy this beautiful new campus, Graves grew philosophical and wrote in the May, 1959 *Golden Gate*:

Most of us at one time or another have spent some time considering "what might have been if." As I think of . . . Southern Seminary in the celebration of her centennial, I think of that institution's history and am thrilled. Only God himself can measure the influence and outreach of that great school. Not only have her professors and presidents been men of wide influence, but her alumni have permeated the life of Baptist churches and institutions the world over.

The "what might have been" comes in when I remember that there was begun in the same year that Southern Seminary began, a similar institution on the West Coast, in San Rafael, Marin County, California. The noble founders of this institution were motivated by those same ideals and purposes which stirred in the hearts of Boyce, Broadus, Manly and Williams. Harvey Gilbert was not so well known and his Baptist constituency was not nearly so numerous or strong. We now know that the difficulties incident to the distance from strong Baptist support and in connection with the Civil War made the life of the young western institution very short. (We recall that a similar fate was almost the end for Southern Seminary.)

Now, what might have been the western institution's history had it lived for a century? What sort of Baptist witness would California now have? How different would the culture of our state be? We can only guess at answers to these and other questions, and such guesses would serve no purpose. The realities are that Southern Seminary begins a second century of noble service, and Golden Gate Seminary takes up the torch laid down so many years ago. With our 15 years of history already written in this general area, the move is only a change in scenery, but with renewed challenge because of enlarged facilities and inspiring surroundings. Just as the move to "The Beeches" in Louisville gave Southern Seminary a new lease on life and enlarged service, so our new campus on Strawberry Point enlarges our horizons and stirs us to renewed dedication.

June 30 came and everything was ready—well almost everything. Classrooms, offices, and halls were filled with boxes labeled "Strawberry Point." Trucks were being loaded but could not move until the Marin County supervisors gave permission to occupy the new campus. At four o'clock that afternoon Graves appeared before the supervisors, but the document he had was not acceptable. They agreed to see him again the next morning. He left and quickly had the attorney make the required adjustments. The seminary had to guarantee that by September 1, 1961 a road would be built around the west border of the campus.

Graves was present for the appointment at ten the next morning, July 1, and the document was approved. He ran to a phone and called Paul Mason to say, "Get the trucks rolling!" The switchboard was activated and the business office opened. Henceforth, the address for Golden Gate Baptist Theological Seminary was Strawberry Point, Mill Valley, California 94941.

Notes

1. Trustees' Minutes, September 17-18, 1953.
2. The *Berkeley Daily Gazette*, May 25, 1954.
3. Trustees' Minutes, October 12-13, 1954.
4. Ibid., February 15-16, 1955.
5. *Tiburon Peninsula Pelican*, October 19, 1955.
6. The *Golden Gate*, November, 1955.
7. Ibid., June, 1957.
8. Ibid., October, 1957.
9. The *Independent-Journal*, San Rafael, April 4, 1958.

5
Coping with the Searching
Sixties

Golden Gate Seminary occupied its new campus at the end of the fifties. The first year in the new location reached over into the next decade—the searching sixties. People everywhere were searching for meaning, for purpose, for values worthy of one's effort. Were these to be found in science, as illustrated by new developments in atomic research or space exploration? Were they to be found in the social restructuring of life? Or were there other answers?

Golden Gate prepared to enter that decade with new facilities, new surroundings, and with the determination to be a part of the army of those who would seek answers in God's Word and its application to life. Everyone associated with the seminary sensed the challenge of the situation. There was much to be done but there was more with which to do it. In the new locale away from busy city streets, there was beauty and peace. Yet with San Francisco, the Bay, and one of the bridges in full view there was no sense of being isolated or detached from the multitudes.

Several members of the faculty and staff began searching for houses in Marin County early. Some moved before the seminary did. Even though prices seemed very high at the time, their purchases proved to be fabulous investments for those who have retired and sold their homes.

Difficulties prevented the move of the president until the weekend before school opened. During the actual move, a dozen or more people called, asking if the opening reception were to be held in the new home. That house held a fascination for people that one could hardly imagine. Everyone who visited the campus wanted to see it, and many who did not get in peeked through the windows. On several occasions, members of the family would look up to see a face pressed against the glass.

Perhaps the unique nature of the house explains part of the fascination. Unlike the traditional president's home on most Eastern and Southern college campuses, this house is one story, with the Oriental influence so common in California. Instead of brick and columns, there is glass and stained wood. The furnishings reflect the same Oriental simplicity.

Southern Baptists in the area were proud of the new campus and wanted to show it to their friends. Those tours usually included the president's home. The people wanted to see the inside as well as the outside. They would call or ring the door bell at all hours of the day or evening. One pastor in the area had been to the house with his guests so often he became somewhat of an authority on it. When a member of the family would be leading that man and some of his friends toward the living room, the self-appointed tour director frequently went another way and showed the bedrooms, baths, or some other room. People opened closet doors, drawers, and even the refrigerator.

The Graveses had worked closely with the architectural staff for six months designing the house. They didn't want a three-story house like the one in Berkeley, so this is all on one floor. Circulation of visitors during large receptions was important, as was the possibility of opening doors to let them flow outside. Dozens of receptions were attended by groups in excess of 150, often 200, and one brought 350 to the house in a one-hour period.

Mrs. Graves and I wondered if a house designed to meet entertaining requirements would ever feel like a family home. Well, we lived there for eighteen years and could never be satisfied in a house again that was not open with plenty of light and room to move about. The view from the home included San Francisco, the Bay, the hills, the fog, the highway, and the ever-present wildlife—which included deer, rabbits, quail, fox, and an occasional raccoon or skunk.

The seminary officially opened its Marin County campus on July 1, 1959. The buildings at that time included three housing villages, a men's dormitory, a women's dormitory, a cafeteria and student center, a classroom building, and an administrative office building.

It was an ever-changing panorama. Mrs. Graves spent nearly half the nights alone, but she still thinks of it as being the most inspiring place to live. Ten Chapel Drive hosted thousands while we lived there.

On August 25 the Mill Valley Rotary Club held its regular Tuesday luncheon in the seminary cafeteria and toured the facilities. I had made my first address to that group in March, 1957. I joined the club in March, 1959, served as its president in 1964-1965, and served Rotary International as governor of District #513 in 1969-1970. The Mill Valley club gave $1,000 to the Rotary Foundation in 1973 in my honor, naming me a Paul Harris Fellow. Upon my retirement, scores of Rotarians and several clubs contributed toward a scholarship fund at the seminary in my name. I have continued to maintain contact with hundreds of friends of the seminary through this medium.

The July, 1959 *Golden Gate* carried an article about the opening of the fall semester which read in part:

> After an absence of 100 years, the Southern Baptist Convention will open the doors of a theological institution in Marin County. . . . Dr. Carleton, dean and newly elected vice-president, was not only enthusiastic about the prospects of the approaching school year, but was devoutly grateful as he considered the future of Golden Gate Seminary in the West.

With the move of the seminary to Marin County, Southern Baptist mission forces had planned an invasion of the county as well. In addition to the mission which began in the seminary chapel, three other missions were reported on in the July *Golden Gate*, "located in San Anselmo, Mill Valley, and San Geronimo Valley." The San Anselmo mission began well with largely imported (seminary) members and flourished as a church for a few years, but in due time closed its doors. It was later revived as a mission of the Tiburon Baptist Church and relocated in Fairfax. It continues as a church, experimenting with some innovative programs in an effort to reach the people of Ross Valley. The Mill Valley church had a

The faculty at the time the campus moved from Berkeley to Mill Valley in 1959 included, top row from left, J. Lyn Elder, James W. McClendon, R. Fletcher Royal, Phil Tilden, and David P. Appleby. Middle row from left, J. B. Nichols, Clayton K. Harrop, Fred L. Fisher, Jack Manning, and Kyle Yates. Front row from left, Chester A. Insko, L. A. Brown, W. A. Carleton, Harold K. Graves, Gaines S. Dobbins, Derward W. Deere, and Carlyle Bennett (not pictured).

precarious existence for many years but in the seventies got its own property and prospects became much brighter.

Many personnel needs came to the fore as the seminary occupied the new campus. Maintenance required a larger work crew and additional supervision, but it was only a guess as to how much. It seemed logical to have a superintendent of buildings and a similar person for grounds, but this proved to be impractical. After a year Mr. Mason became superintendent of buildings and grounds, with the assistant business manager, Clyde Beasley, becoming comptroller.

Several changes in the teaching force reflected the growing curriculum along with an effort to distribute administration responsibility. Dean Carleton, with an increasing load in administration, could give less time to the classroom. J. W. Manning, who had been assisting in church history, was relieved of the field work supervision to give full time to teaching evangelism and church history. There was concern about the time when Dobbins would have to relinquish his teaching of church administration. Elmer Gray, longtime California pastor and seminary trustee, appeared to be just the man to assume the field work and prepare to teach church administration. He had been serving churches in California for more than a decade and was at the time pastor of the First Southern Baptist Church of San Diego. Gray joined the seminary family as it moved to Marin County.

School opened September 1 with an enrollment of 318, considerably below expectations. Texas, with 61 students, was ahead of California.

The week of September 29, 1959 included the celebration of laying the cornerstone. The account of the passing of this milestone was reported in the October issue of the *Golden Gate*:

> In July this year, the school saw a long-cherished dream come true when it moved to its spanking new . . . campus at Strawberry Point, Mill Valley, from cramped quarters in Berkeley.
>
> The significance of the move, which seminary leadership

Workmen seal a time capsule in the cornerstone of the seminary's new administration building on the Mill Valley campus on September 29, 1959, while, from left, President Harold K. Graves and former presidents Isam B. Hodges and B. O. Herring watch.

believes will herald a new era of rapid expansion for the seminary, was duly recognized in a series of functions in September and October. On September 29, a cornerstone laying service was held to mark completion of the first stage of construction. . . .

Dr. E. H. Westmoreland was the principal speaker . . . and challenged the faculty and students to turn the beautiful campus into a spiritual temple interested in spiritual goals.

Other speakers were Rev. Isam B. Hodges, the founding president, who reviewed the humble beginnings of the institution; Dr. B. O. Herring, who described the period of growth and transition into the care of the Southern Baptist Convention; Jack Craemer, managing editor of the San Rafael *Independent-Journal,* who brought greetings from the people of Marin County; and Dr. William A. Carleton, Golden Gate vice-president, who presented the history of Baptist beginnings in Marin.

Toward the climax of the program, Dr. Graves led the audience to the northeast corner of the administration building where the service was concluded. A prayer of dedication was offered by Dr. John Raley, president of Oklahoma Baptist University and seminary trustee.

The copper box in the cornerstone contained the following items, along with the names of the persons who placed them:

> First charter—Hodges
> Second charter—Herring
> Third charter—Breazeale
> Picture of first site
> Picture of second site
> Picture of third site—Rutland
> Picture of three presidents—Harwell
> First catalog and current catalog—Brantley
> Abstract of Principles or Confession of Faith—Posey
> Pages from SBC minutes of 1950, showing action of
>   Convention accepting Golden Gate—Gregory
> First issue of the *Golden Gate*
> July issue of the *Golden Gate,* containing history of the

       seminary, pictures of seminary scenes, . . . and story
       of cornerstone laying—Dye
       Current issue of student paper—Welch
       Student-faculty directory and faculty picture—Carleton

Graves reported to the trustee executive committee that "it now appears that we shall lack $100,000 or less being able to pay all building and furnishing costs by December 31, 1959. . . . in spite of the fact that we will lack $50,000 realizing all of our investment out of the old campus in Berkeley at this time."

With the October issue, the *Golden Gate* became the *Span*. It carried the report of the ceremonies in connection with laying the cornerstone and many pictures. In that issue Graves wrote:

> It is beautiful today in Marin County as I sit looking out my window toward a mountain peak. I hear the distant noise of traffic on the Redwood Highway . . . some one-half mile away. An occasional airplane flies overhead—mostly transports from Travis Air Force Base going and coming from Pacific regions. As I stand at my window, I do not look at the traffic for beyond it on the hillsides and in valleys are homes, and nearer are the villages in which our students live. . . .
>
> Wherever one looks—mountain, sea, housing, streets or landscape—it is beautiful; I am glad to be alive and enjoying it all. Besides this personal gladness within, there is gratitude for Southern Baptists, their vision, and their loyalty as they have made this campus possible.
>
> As I walked across the mall to chapel, I looked through a glass-walled lobby and saw San Francisco Bay, and on its horizon the Bay Bridge and the majestic skyline of San Francisco. Here, also, stretched out before me, is more beauty; but that is not all. In the arc of my vision, if I could see for 75 miles, there live more than three million people. . . . Their needs . . . are in the heart and mind of God. That is why Christ came, why we have churches, why we have been called to serve Him. If we can see this, if we can keep this fact prominent in our thoughts as we study and serve, then we shall justify the development of this beautiful campus. In all of its natural setting of beauty and its symmetry of design,

these buildings and grounds are but tools. They provide the mechanics, the environment in which to work. With thanksgiving to God and to Southern Baptists, we at Golden Gate Seminary seek to measure up to the high calling which is ours in Christ Jesus.

In his first report of activities of students in the churches, Elmer Gray reported in the November *Span*: "Students at Golden Gate are serving in many capacities in 103 Baptist churches and several non-Baptist churches in the greater San Francisco Bay area." The December *Span* reported,

> An overflow audience estimated at more than 600 sat spellbound through a superb rendition of excerpts from Handel's *Messiah* by the seminary oratorio choir in Broadus Hall, December 8. . . . The worshipful spirit, engendered by an excellent interpretation of the masterpiece, so prevailed during the one and a half hours of presentation that one could, figuratively, hear the drop of a pin.

The second semester began with the accumulative enrollment for the year just four above the last year in Berkeley. It was apparent there would not be the dramatic upturn many had predicted. And yet, it was those very predictions that affected the formula structure for distribution of funds to the six seminaries and doomed Golden Gate to a marginal financial operation for years to come.

Not many associated with the seminary knew of its financial struggles in detail. Of course, the faculty and staff had some indication when they were told that annual raises in salary would not keep up with inflation.

The first banquet on the new campus for the seminary family was held January 28, 1960. The theme was "Melody 'n Portrait" and was a fun evening with a takeoff on faculty and staff. As arrangements were being made for this affair, one concern was the care of children whose parents attended the banquet. State regulations required that all children be cared for under the same roof as their parents. Could there be a temporary child-care room in the maintenance area below the cafeteria? Should the banquet be held in the fellowship hall? Things began in the fellowship hall near the children then moved to the cafeteria for food and fun. The license was not lifted.

An interesting problem developed as plans were being made for the child-care program on the new campus. Such a program had been a part of seminary life almost from the beginning. The administration was anxious for student wives to benefit from seminary life—classes, chapel, and other experiences. With families scattered over a wide area, without this effort some wives would have had little contact with the seminary. Growing up like Topsy as it did, the child-care program was thought to be similar to those in the churches. No thought was given to checking about special regulations.

As word spread about this new development in Marin County, state officials, concerned with child care, began to inquire about provisions being made on the new campus and for licensing. The authorities studied the plans for the proposed space. Nearly everything was wrong, and some of it had already been built. They wasted no time in spelling out what had to be done. The required changes were expensive. In the end, the minimum requirements were met to accommodate thirty-four children.

Fortunately, that limit did not materially affect the operation of the center because seminary enrollment did not reach expected numbers and the birth rate was declining. Even though the long planned for child-care building was not constructed after twenty years on the new campus, the program has been a tremendous aid to seminary families. It has made class attendance possible for scores of seminary wives; it made it possible for others to work so husbands could concentrate on studying. It has also provided excellent training for the children who attended.

The architect had checked with many state agencies and their requirements were incorporated into the design for the seminary. When checking with the state fire marshal, the architect was asked numerous questions. "How many do you expect to enroll at your school?" the marshal asked.

"We do not know," was the reply.

"How large is your largest seminary?"

"That would be at Fort Worth where in excess of two thousand study."

"Then the halls must be twelve feet wide in the classroom buildings," was his reply. That's why there is so much space in halls, space that not only had to be built but also has to be cleaned, heated, and lighted. Other regulations that required large outlays of funds had to be met because of the possibility of earthquakes. Few people have ever been killed by earthquakes in California, but the fact that it can happen affects the pocketbook of everyone who builds.

Golden Gate has always been closely allied with the mission forces at work in the Western US and in the world. The state convention and the HMB staffs are in almost weekly communication with the seminary in a variety of cooperative efforts. One of the ways these efforts are coordinated is by holding conferences with HMB and state convention staff on the seminary campus. Students, faculty, and pastors are invited. The first such major conference was held in January, 1960. The conference added fuel to the fires of evangelistic concern that has characterized the seminary from its beginning.

The February, 1960 *Span* noted that R. O. Cawker of Louisiana had passed away. As a trustee for several years, he always added wit and wisdom to the sessions. He and Floyd Golden carried on a running feud, all in good humor, for many years after an incident which occurred in the first meeting Cawker attended. Golden, as vice-chairman, opened one session and took the occasion to tell of his own school in New Mexico. Later, when Cawker arose to discuss some issue, Golden picked up a newspaper as if to read rather than listen to him. "Put down that paper," Cawker shouted, bringing a startled look to every face. "We all listened to you brag about your work and now you are going to listen to me." Needless to say, Golden folded the paper and listened. Ever afterwards, in referring to Cawker, Golden would fail just a little in getting his name right and the exchange in the "battle of words" continued.

Three special days of emphasis were planned for dedication week, beginning March 7, 1960 with the trustees holding their sessions between public programs. Tuesday, the eighth, was Community Day with Guy Rutland, Jr., as the principal speaker. Sharing the program with him were John Carl Warnecke, architect; Walter Castro, Sr., chairman of the Marin County Board of Supervisors; Virgil Hollis, superintendent, Marin County Schools; and Jerald Traeger, president, Marin County Ministerial Association. Many from the Marin community were present.

Wednesday was Academic Day, featuring President Walter Pope Binns, William Jewell College, Liberty, Missouri. Representatives of thirty-six institutions of higher learning across America were present to join the faculty and trustees in colorful regalia to emphasize the academic significance of the seminary. Dean W. A. Carleton presided.

Thursday was Denominational Day, featuring Ramsey Pollard, president of the SBC and just chosen as pastor of the Bellevue Baptist Church in Memphis. This was the day of the actual dedication led by E. H. Westmoreland, chairman of the trustees. Also sharing in the program were Porter Routh, executive secretary of the SBC Executive Committee, and J. W. Storer, executive secretary of the SBC Foundation. Vice-chairman of the trustees, Floyd Golden, represented the campus, and Westmoreland made the response. President Graves led in the Act of Dedication. Hundreds of visitors inspected the campus during these days. The total investment on that date was $5,500,000, and the seminary was dedicated practically debt free.

In the March issue of the *Span*, Graves wrote:

Dedication means many things. It is a time for thanksgiving to God for his marvelous provision. It is a time to express appreciation to our churches for their loyal support through the Cooperative Program. For me, it is a time to say thanks to those fine-laborers—trustees, faculty, staff, and students—

whose patience went beyond mine, whose love for Christ and his Kingdom is not measured except in service and devotion. . . .

Dedication also means commitment. Why all these sticks and stones? Why this organization of staff and students? It all has a spiritual meaning or none at all. The true value of our material efforts will be reflected in our spiritual aims and accomplishments. . . .

With these fine facilities we can care for many others—men and women who dare to face the matchless challenge of the millions of the Far West without a Saviour. . . . We dedicate these buildings and grounds to the service of God in leadership training. We dedicate our best efforts as faculty and staff to the kind of labor that will accomplish His purpose in and through us.

In the next issue of the *Span* (April), there were continued echoes of the week of dedication. Sue Williams, a student in Dobbins's writing class, wrote an article entitled, "Seminary Dedication Symbolizes Conquest Through Cooperation." Her first sentence proclaimed, "The 'day of March' has come for Golden Gate Baptist Theological Seminary." She quoted Ramsey Pollard, "This is a monument pointing men to God. You cannot explain Golden Gate Seminary and California if you leave God out. We are held not with ecclesiastical chains but with tender ties of love."

Williams quoted W. P. Binns, "The battle is on for the minds of men. The function of education is not only to train in technical skills for our economy and war possibilities but to develop an integrity and moral fiber that is necessary for ideological leadership." In commenting on Routh's reference to the Cooperative Program of the SBC providing the dollars that "transformed barren hillsides into purposeful beauty," she wrote:

Suddenly these dollars were vibrant and dedicated—an army of Christ's people who had joined hands to conquer for him! I saw my Godly parents who gave me a Christian heritage and taught me by their lives the meaning of stewardship. . . . I saw a young girl in Girls' Auxiliary learning . . . the meaning of tithing . . . I saw also a snowy-haired saintly deacon making a sacrificial gift from his small means . . . a consecrated family in a small church in the peach-growing land of South Carolina managing somehow to fulfill their commitment despite a frost-blighted peach season. . . . I saw the dear faces of the people on 'Victory Sunday' . . . to sign pledge cards together and then brought their gifts systematically Sunday after Sunday. . . . What mean these stones? The answer is clear. This is God's work. You and I share in a wondrous warfare to conquer pagan, materialistic, cultured California for Christ. The seminary here is the key. From this teeming metropolitan crossroads of the world, the gospel message will go out to encircle the globe.

In his report to the trustees meeting during dedication week, Graves spoke about enrollment as it related to the move to the new campus:

We had gained four over a year ago, but had more degree students than ever. Comparison with other seminaries helped us to see that the same number of students as the year before were simply re-distributed. . . . We were heartened by the report from every quarter that jobs were more plentiful than ever and housing was much more abundant in reasonable price range than had been expected.

He suggested that the improvement in the library was perhaps the most dramatic change, with now more than 28,000 items in use. The greatest material need that remained was 100 additional units of family housing. Two new faculty members were being sought, but the largest need in that area was to increase faculty compensation. "This is a critical matter for us if we are to maintain our fine faculty morale and keep them on the job without anxiety and the giving of too much attention to outside earnings," the president said.

Graves also reported that the schedules were in hand to be prepared in an effort to seek accreditation by the American Association of Theological Schools (AATS). In closing the report, he said:

What we have of material plant and equipment has caused much attention locally and among educators over a wide area. We have wrought well as Baptists. . . . Now it remains for us to build such a program academically and spiritually that we may prove to be good stewards of our material holdings. We must enlarge our faculty, provide opportunities for their own personal growth, and free them to do a good job at their task of teaching and writing. Then we must provide the students for them to teach. This vast area needs more churches and more workers. These campus facilities can care for an enrollment twice our present size—the day in which we live demands our best to meet these needs.

In another effort to meet the needs of pastors and other church staff members in the area, an elaborate program of evening classes and special, day classes was approved on recommendation of the faculty (as worked out by Field Director Gray). As in other instances where need does not necessarily guarantee response, this program did not get off the ground that fall for lack of interest. Trustees also approved an effort to reduce the number of noncollege students in regular classes to the level of the 10 percent of enrollment required by AATS standards. With all their action, however, the seminary never refused admission to a qualified Baptist student who gave evidence of being able to profit from the seminary or to any student wife who wanted to take advantage of the opportunity.

The trustees voted to authorize the production of some kind of plantings on the hillsides that would spell out the name or initials of the seminary to identify it for travelers on Highway 101. However, the seminary was unable to get a sign on the highway for many years. When the required road had been built along the west side of the campus (renamed Seminary Drive) a sign with the seminary's name did appear on the highway on June 17, 1965. The plantings were never developed.

An arrangement with the state convention and the HMB of the SBC had been worked out so that financial help could be given to students in new and struggling church situations in California. In his annual report, Elmer Gray cited the fact that 125 churches were served by students as staff members during the year. These reported 504 conversions and 462 additions.

One of the most interesting graduates to complete his work and receive his Master of Religious Education degree at the first spring commencement at the new campus was Augustus Marwieh of Liberia. Gus did some of his college work at the University of California at Berkeley before receiving his Bachelor of Arts degree from Simpson Bible College in San Francisco. President Graves asked him to attend the Mill Valley Rotary Club to tell about his life and experiences. After playing the African drums for them, Gus told his story.

He was born in a field in Liberia where his mother was working. There was no record of the day or even of the year. As Gus grew, he had a feeling that there was more to life than what he saw about him. An older brother told him that he had heard of a school on the coast. Gus went looking for that school, found it, and was accepted. They said that he looked like he might be about ten years old, so they assigned him a birthday. He was bright and learned rapidly. He also became a Christian. In the passing of the years he came to America and ultimately to U.C., Berkeley. There, among thousands of students he stood out, not because he was black but because of his constant smile and happy, optimistic view of life.

He enrolled in a philosophy class and again came to the attention of fellow students and the professor. The professor was heard to say, "That young man is so enthusiastic about life, I hate to be the one to puncture his balloon." Someone reported that comment to Gus, and he went to see the professor. The teacher expressed concern for what would be happening to Gus in his class. Gus replied, "Oh, Sir, you need not worry. You don't understand for you don't know Jesus."

Gus was well received by the Mill Valley Rotary Club. Many spoke to him with deep appreciation. One man, a self-styled "most wicked man in town," told Gus, "When I see what you have done with your life in the past sixteen years, from a barefoot, naked boy in Africa to a gentleman with a master degree, I'm so ashamed of my life I don't know what to do."

The graduating class of 1960 with eighty students was the largest ever. A. Hope Owen, president of Wayland Baptist College in Texas, was the baccalaureate preacher. Just before that service, the graduates and their families were received by President and Mrs. Graves in their home—the first of many such happy occasions in that setting.

Perhaps the most memorable happening of the ceremonies that year occurred as the last graduate was receiving his Master of Theology degree. My custom was to confer degrees on a group receiving the same award, then to award the certificate and congratulations as each graduate crossed the platform. However, in awarding the highest degree, the Master of Theology, each man came to the platform where the degree was conferred. I said something like, "William _____, upon the recommendation of the faculty and by the authority of the Board of Trustees, I confer . . . " On that day, as I took the last candidate by the hand, my mind played a trick on me. I said instead, "John Sargent, upon a profession of your faith. . . . " The audience exploded in laughter. I was about to baptize a candidate.

I was not allowed to forget that break in all the remaining seventeen commencements over which I presided. Faculty members were always asking me just before they marched into the chapel, "Whom are you going to baptize today?" With all that taunting in my mind, it is no wonder that it happened again—exactly ten years later. The candidate was John Hughes, son of Robert D. Hughes, executive secretary of the Southern Baptist General Convention of California.

After one year on the new campus, it was time to take stock with regard to financial support from the SBC. The Convention had been generous in providing a beautiful and usable campus. Economy of operation and easy maintenance had been basic in planning and construction. Yet sheer size and expansion of service cost more than had the operation on a portion of one city block in Berkeley. That first year took $56,000 of the reserve funds. But because of the seminaries' formula regarding Cooperative Program funds, Golden Gate received an increase of less than $9,000.

Application of the formula had proved to be a tedious operation for the six presidents. It took much detailed reporting to each other and considerable time together to iron out details. This, along with other concerns, led the presidents to decide in 1959 that they needed a week-long workshop. There they could discuss and decide pressing issues, especially the formula application. So, the six men and their wives met in Edgewater Park, Mississippi, November 30 to December 3, 1959, the first of what has become an annual occurrence. They have continued to meet at Conventions and in connection with SBC Executive Committee meetings, but the annual workshop has become the time to discuss and determine basic policies of cooperation. Travel expense is pooled, thus eliminating concern for the meeting place.

Just at this time, another major concern was the operation of the SED. Two pressures motivated this effort on the part of the seminaries. One was the concern the presidents had for those serving as pastors and other church staff members who lacked seminary preparation for their responsibilities, yet could not get to a seminary for lack of the academic prerequisites. The other pressure came from certain of the SBC leadership and constituency who were urging SBC support of Bible schools and institutes. It was and is the conviction of the seminaries that the vast majority of the potential students on this level would not attend an institution of higher learning if one were provided near them. They are bivocational and have only limited time for study. The SED, recently changed to the Seminary External Education Division (SEED), has proven to be the most effective program yet devised to meet their needs.

Many questions about the SED presented themselves. Where should its office be located? What staff would be needed? Would field men, dispersed in geographical territories, be the best way to operate? How would the operation be kept to its central purpose and not evolve into another seminary or seek to appeal to seminary-level constituency? It took many years and the best thoughts of three fine directors, Lee Gallman, Ralph Herring, and Raymond Rigdon, and a long line of seminary presidents to develop what the SEED is today.

The 1960 Miami Beach gathering of the trustees at the SBC brought back memories. Just eight years earlier in Miami Graves had been elected to serve Golden Gate. The major concern in 1960 was how to operate and develop a program on the new campus within available resources and how to increase those resources. In confirming the mail ballot election of Golden Gate alumnus Carl Halvarson as assistant to the president, the trustees felt they were helping solve the matter of increasing resources—both new students and endowment. Halvarson knew Golden Gate Seminary and the West and had a missionary zeal that was essential in inspiring young men and women to look to GGBTS for training and service.

Graves told the trustees of David Appleby's impending departure and that there were no immediate plans to replace him. Appleby had made a fine contribution in the four years he was at Golden Gate. He was a superb pianist and a brilliant musician with what might be called a high-church emphasis. He and the Bennetts got along beautifully and enjoyed each other's company, but musically they were on two separate wave lengths. Bennett harmonized well with most of the people in the churches. Appleby was perhaps ten years ahead of the time for Golden Gate and did not attract as many students as he might now. He went to Southwestern Seminary where his talents were very much needed as they moved into a program of graduate education in music.

New trustees elected in Miami Beach included the first Golden Gate alumnus, Robert Stapp of California.

Fifty-four alumni met in Miami Beach, remarkable in light of the location being so far from California. The primary business discussed was the effort to complete the alumni project, the rock entrance sign for the campus. Alumni president E. W. Hunke, Jr., reported that $1,325 had been raised, that construction was underway, and that it was to be dedicated in the fall. Several SBC leaders appeared at the luncheon for brief comments, including Westmoreland, Storer, and SBC president, Ramsey Pollard. Graves reported on "Our First Year on Strawberry Point."

The fall semester opened August 30 with Lyn Elder bringing the convocation address. The enrollment was down ten from the previous year. Graves noted that there were twenty fewer students in the group without college degrees, so a net gain was posted for college graduates.

The first Missionary Day featured reports by Dobbins and Brown from their recent tours. Greetings were read from four couples who were serving outside the United States. These greetings from alumni focused attention on the completion of the alumni project to build the entrance sign for the new campus. Following the addresses, the sign was dedicated as part of the Missionary Day celebration. Alumni president John Hines was on hand to lead in the dedication. In his message, reported in the October, 1960 *Span*, he said:

> The name of the school, "Golden Gate," links it with its dramatic location near the famous Golden Gate Bridge and with San Francisco, "the city of the Golden Gate." . . . The name "Baptist" links it with our historic past, and reminds us of our Godly heritage as well as glorious responsibility to perpetuate New Testament principles. . . . The designation "Theological" links us to our great God and aligns us with his redemptive purpose in the world. It reminds us that all truth ultimately finds its source in God. . . . The designation "Seminary" links us with our Divine purpose for existence, the planting of the seeds of divine truth that will transform lives.

Professor Gray instituted a practice in the fall of 1960 of inviting the area missionaries of the Southern Baptist General Convention of California, who served in the northern part of the state, to spend a day as guests of the seminary for consultation with students. These conferences have helped missionaries to learn of the students available for service in their areas and helped the students to learn of service needs and opportunities. Students were now serving in more than 120 churches in twenty associations. Fifteen were receiving pastoral aid.

Seeing the names of Daryl Heath, Walter Thompson, Byron Todd, and H. O. Black among the area missionaries present that day calls to mind the service Golden Gate graduates have rendered in this role across the years. Add to this list of associational directors of missions, Allen Barnes, William East, Ralph Gardner, Paul Smith, Joe Smith, Wayne Eurich, Wayne Willcoxon, James Warren, Bert Langdon, T. J. DuBose, Arthur Nunn, Geriel De Oliveria, and Dan Coker. James Forrest and Don Jackson also took advanced work while serving as missionaries.

Dobbins described the West as a "Call to Courage" in the October *Span*. Quoting 2 Timothy 2:3 from J. B. Phillips' *The New Testament in Modern English* "Put up with your share of hardship as a loyal soldier in Christ's army," Dobbins wrote:

> It was no fault of Timothy's that life had been easier for him than his great teacher, but Paul knew that this young man he loved would miss something of vital importance if he did not learn the lessons that hardships teach.
>
> The student who comes from the East to attend Golden Gate Seminary has on arrival passed the test for the D.D. degree—distance and desert! Those who come are like Gideon's three hundred. They have to be "men of valor" who do not hesitate to make the venture, . . .
>
> Those of us who are giving our lives to establishing the cause of Christ as represented by Southern Baptists on the West Coast, know that it takes courage. We have no illusions as to the kind of courage required. It is not the courage engendered by prospect of dramatic success. . . .
>
> Golden Gate Seminary . . . has the facilities and training demanded for this difficult field. . . . We need more students, but we do not need "softies."

The annual Bible Teaching Clinic held on the campus in October, 1960 proved to be most significant. It had as one of the program personnel, Grady Cothen, pastor, First Baptist Church, Birmingham, Alabama, whose topic was, "A Christian Teacher Facing His Task." His was to be the final message of the clinic but the announced subject was set aside. Someone had driven Cothen around the San Francisco Bay Area during the day, and he was overwhelmed with what he saw. No one who heard him that night could ever forget how his heart overflowed as he spoke on Southern Baptists in California facing the task of reaching millions for Christ. It revealed the heart of a concerned Baptist preacher.

California Southern Baptists were introduced to the one who many felt instinctively to be the man to succeed S. G. Posey as state executive secretary. Cothen responded to an invitation to visit with state leadership in Fresno and in due time was elected and accepted. He spent five great years of service in California. The new headquarters building in Fresno and the annual pastors' retreat are but two of the things he sponsored. Other out-of-state men sharing in that teaching clinic were Dean Allen Graves of Southern Seminary and Crawford Howell of the BSSB. More than eight hundred attended the four-day conference.

Golden Gate joined Southern Baptists throughout the state in celebration of the twentieth anniversary of the organization of the Southern Baptist General Convention of California in November, 1960. In expressing his congratulations, Graves wrote in the November *Span*:

> When the history of Southern Baptist work in California has been considered one hundred years from now, perhaps one of the most significant relationships will be that between the Southern Baptist General Convention of California and Golden Gate Seminary. It is obvious that one will see the contribution that the Seminary has made to Baptist life in California. It will perhaps be less obvious, though nonetheless important, to observe the part California Baptists have played in the seminary program and progress.

We are happy to be associated with the fine area missionaries, pastors, and convention administrators who are a part
of the training program for those who study in our halls. We
are proud of the fine students who come from California
homes and churches to be a part of our seminary family. We
rejoice in the way you think and speak of Golden Gate as
"our seminary."

Secretary S. G. Posey sounded the same note when he
wrote in that same issue of the *Span*:

The Convention and the Seminary have grown up together
as comrades amid the hardships of pioneer work and
inadequate support for their ministry in a field of unlimited
opportunity and need. . . . It was obvious that we would
have to train our leadership for the work of those early
pioneer days, and Golden Gate Seminary has had a great
part in doing just that. . . . Just as the Seminary was
necessary for the life and growth of our Convention across
the years, so was the Convention necessary to the progress
and well being of the Seminary. . . . National Convention
ownership and operation of the Seminary have not in any
sense lessened the interest of Southern Baptists in California
in the Seminary and her progress.

Dean Carleton took note of the convention's anniversary
celebration when he also wrote in the *Span*:

In 1944, Southern Baptist work in California was so weak
that many in the older states were certain that it would soon
cease to exist. They were confident that when the "war
boom" was ended, the "Okies" and "Arkies" would leave
California, and the weak, struggling churches would disap-
pear. How preposterous it was under such circumstances to
presume to found a Southern Baptist theological seminary in
California! Almost any man who gauges strength by natural
standards would have pointed out numbers of obvious
reasons why the venture was doomed to failure.
But there were those who like Caleb and Joshua saw a
Power greater than the giants and those giants seemed by

comparison as grasshoppers. . . . How insignificant seemed the beginning in the little frame building of the Golden Gate Baptist Church with a volunteer faculty and a handful of students!

The same *Span* also carried stories of the work of two students whose efforts and progress demonstrated the variety of the challenges existing in the area. One of these men, James Roamer, a lawyer-turned-preacher, a graduate of Golden Gate, was giving full time trying to penetrate the San Francisco scene, while his wife made the living. He wrote 13,000 letters of invitation to people in one section of the city. Twenty people came, and the Roamers kept visiting them. Six months later a series of films was shown, having been advertised through 12,000 letters. Crowds reached a peak of seventy on one Sunday, making it necessary to have double services due to the small room in which they met. Later, a series of messages by Professor James McClendon was advertised through three separate mailings of 5,000 each. These brought a record attendance of forty-nine, well beyond the legal capacity of the room. They began seeking a permanent home for the church.

The other story reported the progress of Bethel Baptist Church in Concord, forty miles east of the campus. Clyde Skidmore arrived from Baylor to enter the seminary in June 1954 and was called to pastor this church three weeks later. After six years, it had grown from 125 members with seventy-five in attendance to 525 members with over three hundred in Sunday School. Two buildings had been built. The average baptisms per year were sixty, with fifty-eight joining by letter. It had taken Skidmore five years to get his B.D. degree because he was doing double duty. He said of the effort:

Although the work is harder in California than in the Midwest or South, the challenge of the unreached people here and the joy of being in the Lord's will make the effort worthwhile. . . . Our people must visit and witness as in the early days of Christianity. The mere presence of a church will not attract the people. . . . For challenge and pioneer work, there is no better mission field in the world than California. A Christian must be willing to work; victories do not come easy, but each day is a challenge.

These stories were included in an enlarged edition of the *Span* issued to send not only to the regular mailing list but to a host of potential students in colleges across America. The center spread of pictures and appeals, entitled, "Opportunity Unlimited," sought to capitalize on these mission opportunities. This challenge, as much or more than the appeal of Golden Gate itself, attracted many young people to the West.

Graves met with the other seminary presidents in their second annual workshop in late November in Phoenix, Arizona. They voted to move the administrative offices of the SED from Jackson, Mississippi, to the new SBC office building in Nashville when it was completed. In the meantime, Dr. Gallman resigned as the director. Before the move was accomplished, they elected Ralph Herring as his successor. In a most significant action, the presidents voted to add $25,000 to the base appropriation for Golden Gate since it was not gaining in allocation through growth. They voted to hold the 1961 workshop in Florida at a place to be selected by Millard Berquist, who chose Key Biscayne near Miami.

The Golden Gate faculty inaugurated a program offering a workshop for the January Bible Study emphasis on Friday and Saturday, December 16-17, 1960. The study was organized by Fred Fisher, and the format was set to begin at one o'clock on Friday and to end Saturday noon. Across the years, this has proved to be a helpful exercise for pastors. Attendance has run from 100 to 160, more when a less familiar Old Testament book is under study.

When the second semester opened in January, 1961, the accumulative enrollment for the session was down three from the year before. Particularly noticeable was the small enrollment of music students. One reason that the music program did not grow at this time was that there were no full-time music jobs in California churches. All music jobs were in combination with other tasks. This led the administration to deemphasize music until need caught up with supply.

The January, 1961 issue of the *Span* announced the first Student Missions Conference to be held on the Golden Gate campus the first weekend in March. Jesse Fletcher, FMB personnel secretary, was the featured speaker. The target group was college students and high school seniors. Other FMB personnel included David Lockard of Africa, Catherine Walker of Indonesia, and Ervin Hastey of Mexico. HMB personnel were led by Edmond Walker, missions director from Fresno, aided by Peter Chen of San Francisco and Don Kim of Los Angeles. The keynote speaker for Friday night was Elwin Skiles, seminary trustee and pastor of the First Baptist Church of Abilene, Texas. The banquet speaker on Saturday evening was Eugene Patterson, president of Grand Canyon College.

The churches in the area—led by Wallace Hough, pastor in San Rafael—assisted in providing homes for the students. The women of the Redwood Empire Baptist Association provided the Saturday noon meal. The basic work of preparation for the conference was done by fifty seminary students. Attendance was far beyond expectations, reaching 314. The conference gave a boost to the whole seminary family and to Southern Baptist life in the area.

Each month the *Span* featured the opportunities for service at Golden Gate and in the West, seeking to influence more students to join the western march. The January, 1961 issue used the center spread to publicize student services, proclaiming "Full Employment—Adequate Housing." Pictured was an apartment complex in San Rafael, eight miles away, which had been leased by the seminary in an effort to provide additional housing. The apartment leasing project proved to be a failure. Try as they would, the seminary was not able to fill the units and the project was abandoned.

Mission fires were burning on the Golden Gate campus during this period, and there was concern for academic excellence as well. I was giving much thought to this in light of the self-study underway, using the AATS guidelines for accreditation. As I prepared to report to the trustees in their first annual meeting since the dedication of the campus, I would not be talking of permits, building schedules, and so forth. I was free to plan for and lead in a major effort to enlarge and improve the program of theological education and to make the seminary family a more effective mission force. I closed my column in the March, 1961 *Span* by writing:

> In all of these considerations, one of our major concerns is the financing of a program on this highly developed campus, so far away from the major portion of our Baptist constituency. We are aware that additional student family housing is desperately needed. . . . This will bring additional students and will improve the economic picture materially, but more to the point of our being here, it will bring people to the area for training and service to reach the multitudes.
>
> Surely Southern Baptists, their leaders, and all who know our program will be joining us in prayer for wisdom in solving these matters which have never really been faced on such a scale by any other institution as it is faced here. We are in a sense in a pioneer territory, yet trying to promote the kind of program that would be carried on in the midst of a tremendous Baptist population.

I continued to sound this note in my report to the trustees at their annual meeting in March, 1961, saying in part:

> We were able to dedicate our wonderful campus just a year ago this month. A major milestone has been reached. There are energies to be placed in other concerns. Too long a period dealing with materials could be damaging to our sense of direction if not to our sense of values. A seminary is not really a campus, anymore than a church is its building. Buildings and equipment are necessary in either case, but they do not guarantee the reality either of the seminary or the church.
>
> A seminary . . . needs, besides a campus and adequate equipment, a faculty, a student body and a holy urge to excellence in its endeavor. These essential ingredients are

not obtained through money alone, while this is certainly a continuing consideration. The philosophy of a school must be developed—a spirit that is worthy to inspire and strengthen. . . .

. . . After we have used the adjectives "most beautiful," "most unique," or even "largest" or "oldest," or even most "evangelistic" or "intellectual," what have we said? Maybe very little if we cannot also say, "measured by all the normal accepted standards our seminary is doing a good job in training for the Master's service." This means faculty and books and equipment, and it also means good students with a serious purpose who have caught the vision of the opportunity of service offered in God's call to the West.

. . . Most of us seemed to feel that once we moved to Strawberry Point enrollment problems were solved. Two years' experience has proven the falsity of this assumption. . . . The inertia of distance, the pull of family and church opposition, the drag of old "seminary loyalties" for pastors and other leaders of youth—these have taken their toll, and we do not have the 500 or 600 students that we and the West needs to be in training now . . .

. . . The task here in the West demands the best and you can be proud of what more than 500 graduates are doing. . . . They are making their mark. . . . Yet our graduates can never be of better quality than our entrants. We shall take all who qualify and do what we can with each, but we have a larger place for more of the best.

In his report to the trustees, Dean Carleton stressed the effort to improve the quality of instruction. A recent faculty seminar on methods of instruction had been offered by Dr. Swanson of the U. C., Berkeley. Carleton also spoke of a need for additional faculty as resources are available. With twenty-seven students from CBC and eighteen from Grand Canyon, along with some from a few other schools, the seminary was above the allowed 10 percent from unaccredited colleges. Golden Gate did not accept non-Baptist students from unaccredited schools but did receive Baptist students from such schools in spite of a possible notation. The expected accreditation of CBC and Grand Canyon soon solved the problem.

The trustees granted Professor Elder a sabbatical leave for the summer and fall of 1961 and Professor Insko 1962-1963. Insko had been offering courses in both ethics and preaching. During his sabbatical he was to take advanced work in the field of Christian ethics. The trustees also voted approval for the addition of another professional in the library where holdings now exceeded 33,000 volumes.

The properties committee presented a recommendation to accept the low bid for building the road required by Marin County on the west side of the campus. Cost estimate was $88,000; but because the moving of fill was set at a price per unit, the final figure would depend on the amount moved. The actual cost of the road proved to be much higher. The officers of the corporation were authorized to deed the road and right-of-way to the county when completed. The trustees also authorized the addition of several units of family housing in villages #2 and #3 when funds from the new capital needs allocations were assured.

The budget for 1961-1962 was adopted with the "understanding that it was based on an anticipated enrollment of 350 in the fall." If that were not realized, the executive committee of the trustees could revise as might be necessary.

During the time the trustees were on campus for the 1961 meeting, a dedication ceremony was held for a set of Deagan chimes. Donated by Mr. and Mrs. G. Heyward Mahon of South Carolina, the chimes memorialized their late daughter Mary Mahon Ellis. The trustees took notice of the upcoming tenth anniversary of President Graves in 1962 and the twentieth of the seminary in 1964 by appointing committees to arrange appropriate observations for each. The small preaching chapel was designated as the William Conover Chapel in honor of the man whose estate assisted the school in 1952.

They also approved a recommendation from Carl Halvarson that a committee on public relations be formed. In due time this committee has become a major unit of the trustees. With the combining of properties and finance, the board continued to have three major committees, in addition to the executive committee. The next annual meeting was set for June, 1962, following sessions of the Southern Baptist Convention in San Francisco.

In anticipation of inviting him to become a member of the faculty, J. Winston Pearce was asked to spend some days on the campus in March. He gave a series of lectures on "The Preacher." Out of the week's fellowship came an enthusiastic invitation for Pearce to join the faculty as professor of preaching.

The 1961 commencement exercises were held April 27-28. The baccalaureate preacher was Grady Cothen, executive secretary of the Southern Baptist General Convention of California. Graves addressed the graduates the next day and presented the degrees and diplomas to eighty-eight graduates.

When the trustees met in Saint Louis during sessions of the SBC, they elected J. Winston Pearce to the faculty. A native of North Carolina, he was graduated from Wake Forest and had studied at Southern Seminary, University of Chicago, Yale, Union, and Edinburgh. As pastor, preacher, writer, and denominational leader, he was qualified both by training and experience to give maximum service to Golden Gate.

The trustees heard of the completion of furnishing the Conover Chapel with pews and carpets from the old chapel in Berkeley. Recording equipment had been secured for use in the preaching classes. The president also reported the receipt of two significant gifts. Roy Brown of the *Independent-Journal* had sent $200 and Lowell Berry of Oakland had sent $1,500 for student aid. Both were but the first of many such gifts from these men. Wishard Brown and Jack Craemer of the *I-J* continued the practice begun by their fathers until they sold the paper. Many student families have been blessed by the gifts, the assistance often making it possible for them to continue in school.

The Golden Gate faculty and staff were busy during the summer of 1961 in activities all over the world. One day Graves had a conference with a former student (three hours' credit earned), who wanted to straighten him and the faculty out on the meaning of inspiration. The student was convinced that Graves and the faculty were liberal. In that conference in the presence of Dean Carleton, Graves said that he did not believe in the verbal inspiration of the King James Version of the Bible. The student went from that meeting to prepare and publish a thirty-five page book, condemning the seminary in general and Graves in particular.

Ironically, some fifteen years later not having had any other personal contact, that young man and the president appeared on the same program at a Good Friday service in San Francisco. When he arose to speak, following Graves, he took several minutes expressing his regrets for his foolish action earlier and proclaiming his belief in the president. Unfortunately, students sometimes enter a seminary, not to learn and grow as interpreters of truth, but to confirm their views, gain a degree, or in some sad circumstances, deliberately seek to discredit the seminary and its faculty. Sadly not all change!

The seminaries were going through another round of attacks from those who considered their faculties liberal, primarily on the basis of views of inspiration. I spoke to this in my column in the October, 1961 *Span*:

> Southern Baptists can miss their chance—fumble the ball—be passed by. All we have to do is to get divided—go on a witch hunt—solidify our expressions of belief to the point that no room is left for individual differences. This can come about in many ways.
>
> One who disagrees with any one policy or program can over-emphasize failures he would ascribe to these mistaken efforts. Another who holds a strict view on the ordinances or some other doctrine can redouble his efforts to make all stand with him. While yet another would call for a departure from regimentation to the freedoms others seem to have.

These are the pressures that could divide and destroy us. Yet all these efforts could be made in the name of "the faith," "orthodoxy," and dedication to the "old-time Baptist beliefs."

The seminaries of our convention are both a part of the problem and of the solution. Whether through simple semantics or deliberate purpose, professors are misunderstood. They are not infallible men nor do they claim to be. They are sincere students of God's word and the world who function within the framework of an abstract of principles. . . .

They are a part of the problem in that they would move us along the path of deepened understanding of God's truth and his will. . . . They are a large share of the answer in that they would earnestly give themselves to building the kingdom of God. They believe in simple New Testament Christianity and would seek to challenge their students to proclaim such to the minds and hearts of men.

Looking back to the "searching sixties," one is struck by the kind of students attending the seminaries during that decade. Those students produced by the homes and communities of America in a decade absorbed with violence, protest, and division over an unpopular war in Asia were to change the face of education for the whole nation. Berkeley was just twenty-two miles away, and planes and ships were plying the air and sea bearing soldiers and arms to Vietnam. How could Golden Gate Seminary escape the effects of such a time? It didn't—though it was to be some time before these forces would affect it in a major way.

When the executive committee of the trustees met in September, 1961, enrollment had fallen seventy short of the anticipated 350. The budget was revised in an effort to bring expenditures in line with income. Graves had discussed this enrollment problem with the other seminary presidents, and they had voted to ask Oren Cornett and his associates to restudy the formula.

The long-awaited visit of an inspection team from the AATS came in October. Presidents Colwell of Southern

California School of Theology and Moss of Lancaster Seminary in Pennsylvania were the team. The experience was encouraging, as the seminary shared its philosophy and program with these experienced educators.

In the November, 1961 *Span*, J. W. Pearce wrote of his impressions after three months in Marin County:

> From my office window in W. T. Conner Hall, I have a fabulous view: the bay with white sails gliding swan-like over the blue water, the Bay Bridge, stretching like ribbons of steel, "The City" rising gracefully through the fog in the distance, tall green eucalyptus trees keeping silent watch, the golden hills of Marin County standing like silent sentries. It is peaceful and indescribably beautiful.
>
> Yet, from my office window, right in the middle of that beauty and peace, I see "The Rock," Alcatraz Prison. Its ominous silence and in-accessibility, says, "Do not be misled by all this beauty and peacefulness; there is sin and wickedness here that is second to none on earth. That is why you, and the institution you represent, are in the midst of this place. The Lord Jesus Christ and a great denomination felt impelled to get involved." . . .
>
> The need of the world is very real to those of us in the Golden Gate Seminary. San Francisco is not only the "Gateway to the Orient." In a very real sense, it is the Orient and the world. Our students are in touch with 50 nationalities. . . .
>
> . . . We have a warm and creative fellowship here at the seminary. . . . It is an atmosphere of learning and an atmosphere of good will and Christian concern. The students, the faculty, the administration know a close and mutually respectful relationship.
>
> When the lady of the Welcome Wagon learned that we were affiliated with Golden Gate Baptist Seminary she dropped her usual line of talk and said, "I am not a Baptist; I am a Catholic, but may I bear a word of sincere appreciation for the young couples who are students in your seminary? I have visited dozens of them. I have never called on one that would not be a credit to any Christian institution. These

young people of yours are on small budgets and I have yet to hear the first word of complaint. There is a joy and a sense of purpose with them that I only wish all homes might know."

The first meeting of the local arrangements committee preparing for the SBC sessions in San Francisco in June, 1962 was held at the seminary in November. Grady Cothen and Graves served as cochairmen. An anticipated attendance of more than 10,000 was a challenge for Southern Baptists of the Bay Area and the state. It was also seen as an opportunity to show firsthand what God had wrought both in the state and at the seminary.

The December, 1961 *Span* had an article about student-chaplain Kenneth Glenn and his work at San Quentin prison. His experiences there and at Soledad prison near Salinas had helped him mature as a Christian and develop sympathy for all suffering humanity. His deepest impression came as he "gripped the metal railing outside the green gas chamber to witness the execution of a sex-slayer." Some left the room in a jovial mood, but he went to his car and wept. Men like Glenn were seeing life as it was beyond the campus.

There was great rejoicing on campus and far beyond, when word came in mid-December that Golden Gate had been accredited by the AATS. It was a public acknowledgment of what those associated with the seminary had grown to feel was true. Golden Gate was offering a quality of work commensurate with the quality of its facilities. In the January, 1962 *Span*, I wrote:

This is an accomplishment that can be measured. It is the result of long years of effort on the part of so many. The denomination gave us funds for our fine facilities including library books, and funds for operation that make possible our superb faculty. The faculty has contributed through dedicated lives of study, teaching and counseling. The staff has supported the teaching program without reservation. The students have come from across America and around the world to add their share of sacrificial effort in study, service, and total dedicated effort to the cause.

. . . This crowns ten years of effort on my part. . . . I thank you all for every support. With this statement, I would remind you that there is so much yet to be done.

We need to double our holdings in the library. We are now eligible for some outside assistance with this, but such assistance calls for matching funds beyond our previous generous annual expenditure.

We need to greatly enlarge the student body of qualified young people for training and service in this vast western area. . . . Additional family housing on campus will be needed. . . .

We need endowment. We now have something to endow. . . . We now have less than $4,000 in endowment. . . .

Hitherto has the Lord led us! Let us go in his strength.

On September 1, 1961, after determining the fall enrollment, I wrote the other SBC seminary presidents, saying in part:

The enrollment picture is not good . . . it is 5 to 7% below last year. . . . Even with the same adjustment as last year, Golden Gate cannot live within the formula. We were $15,000 short on income for the year ending July 31 in spite of strictest economies. . . .

We must discuss this matter . . . in Nashville. The Program Committee will be meeting Tuesday and Wednesday, and I must take up the matter with them; and I have already requested an appearance through Dr. Routh. I want to stay with you and have in the past, but this is something we cannot live with. When the formula was adopted, Dr. Cornett said we would be hurt here at Golden Gate if our enrollment did not increase 75 over the 1957 figures. Instead, it is . . . less. I agreed with the formula with this protest and was assured that consideration would be given.

Can we discuss this with the prospect for some positive answers on Monday, the 18th?

Suffice it to say, the presidents did discuss the problem and took two actions. First, they voted that "we make provision for Golden Gate as we did last year, the method to be determined at the December meeting." Second, "that a formula committee be selected to restudy the formula," and then, "that we invite the former committee, composed of Cornett, Haswell, and Campbell, to make the study." Midwestern Seminary was having some of the same problems, though not on the same scale. The presidents arranged to meet with Cornett and associates in Washington, in January, 1962.

A decline in enrollment was facing each of the seminaries. This seemed to reflect attitudes in many church families. In light of scientific progress as demonstrated by conquests in space and in light of the social struggles claiming so much attention, how could one best affect the world? The signs of the times indicated that troubles were just beginning for the seminaries. There would be fewer students and those who enrolled would approach the offered curriculum from a different perspective. Some would perhaps be in school to avoid the military draft.

When the presidents met for their workshop in December, 1961, they were faced with how to distribute funds according to the formula in light of the plight of the two smaller schools. With the enrollment figures in hand, the formula was applied and the results noted. Golden Gate could expect $60,000 less than the minimum Graves believed necessary for a bare existence. The situation was similar at Midwestern. After a long and grueling period covering several sessions of their meeting, the four larger schools agreed to surrender funds to a common pool to aid the smaller schools. Golden Gate was to get $55,000. They did not change the formula but rather applied it and then adjusted the results to make this distribution possible.

Thinking back on that meeting in Miami, Graves remembers the tensions and difficulties involved in obtaining sufficient funds to keep Golden Gate alive. He is also very grateful for the continued generosity of the men as shown in this action and that of a year earlier, when $25,000 was added to the basic allocation for Golden Gate.

A special service was held on the Golden Gate campus

December 14, 1961 in connection with the presentation of an automobile and some groceries to alumnus LaVerne Inzer. The chapel choir had learned of his labors in Nevada while on a tour and returned to campus to enlist the seminary family in giving him a lift. A front page editorial in the January, 1962 *Span* said:

> The courage and witness of Alumnus LaVerne Inzer at Winnemucca, Nevada, is writing a new chapter in the annals and life of Golden Gate Seminary. . . . His one-man stand against a deep-rooted Nevada vice and his sacrificial service in a 40,000 square-mile area reminds us once again of the true spirit of Golden Gate Seminary. . . . Tangible goals of a brand-new Strawberry Point campus and now full accreditation in the American Association of Theological Schools are milestones in the life of a young school. But more than stones and standards is the inner spirit of the seminary itself.

Now that Golden Gate was accredited, a major project was to gain support in an effort to qualify for matching funds for library improvement. The Selantic Fund, through AATS, was offering to match up to $3,000 per year for three years above the normal budget allocation for library materials. This meant spending an additional $6,000 each year, besides the $9,000 already budgeted. With present holdings of nearly 38,000 volumes, totals might exceed 50,000 in three years.

A good library is an essential part of each theological seminary. As Golden Gate's library began to take on the proportions of a truly fine collection of resource materials, tribute was called for to those who had paid the price for that achievement. Many people had a share in that growth through contributions of either books or money to purchase them. Among these was a man whose efforts outdistanced any others, G. W. Keaster of Oakland. As a Baptist layman, busy in his own church from its beginning, he found time during his travels to discover and secure thousands of valuable books for the collection.

Keaster was an auditor with the Southern Pacific Railway Company. This required his spending a major portion of his time away from home in the various offices of that company. When not on duty in those cities, he visited used book stores. Armed with an appropriate list of titles and authors, he searched for much needed volumes for Golden Gate Seminary. He bought priceless books for twenty-five, forty, or seventy-five cents. Only rarely did he pay more than a dollar or two for volumes, some long since out of print though still classics in the field.

He loaded these books in his car and brought them to the campus every few weeks for years. Sometimes he would accept enough money to recover his investment, but often would not. Professors' libraries benefited from his labors as well. Carleton's library had been lost in a fire a few years before he joined the Golden Gate faculty. With the aid of Keaster, he was able to gather a library which was the envy of every church historian that saw it.

As the Golden Gate library began to take shape, Keaster turned his interest toward California Baptist College. Before his death, he was able to give valuable assistance to their collection as well.

Cooperative efforts among Bay Area seminaries had taken on a more formal appearance with the beginning of the Graduate Theological Union (GTU), based in Berkeley. This development grew out of the desire of several schools in Berkeley in the late fifties to reduce costs by working together. Golden Gate shared in the original discussions but did not actually participate in the cooperative effort. This was partly due to the fact that Golden Gate was not accredited at the time and partly to the fact that there was little time for the Golden Gate faculty to be involved in other ways.

When Golden Gate became accredited, pressure developed to enlist it as a full partner. The president was invited to be an observer in the GTU board meetings. Several Golden Gate professors having close associations with their counterparts in the other seminaries urged participation. Some trustees were also interested in the school's involvement. It was studied from every angle, but it was finally determined that the purpose of the GTU was "graduate education in religion," rather than preparation for ministry. Cooperation called for a serious surrender of individual school autonomy, even to giving up ownership of library resources. Ultimately Golden Gate became involved only in the library cooperative effort by contributing to the budget required to maintain a common catalog.

The history of the GTU has proven that the right decision was made. There is a friendly cooperation with the GTU on the part of the Golden Gate faculty and administration, but the president is no longer involved with their board or other official activities.

The theme for the second annual student mission conference in March, 1962 was "Encounter." Leaders emphasized "Positive Discipleship—not Spectatorship." C. O. Johnson was the banquet speaker Saturday evening. Student departments of the Washington-Oregon, Arizona, and California Baptist conventions assisted in promotion. One carload each came from Moscow, Idaho, and Las Cruces, New Mexico, both 1,300 miles away. Over 450 were registered for the conference.

The week beginning Sunday June 3 will long be remembered by the Golden Gate family and Southern Baptists of the area. SBC messengers began arriving days before and many visited the campus. More than 100 foreign missionaries were on the campus for a pre-Convention conference with FMB personnel. The SBC Church Music Conference met there. On the evening of Tuesday, the fifth, from ten to midnight, following the evening session of the SBC, President and Mrs. Graves were hosts to more than 350 at their home. Invitations had been sent to trustees, members of the SBC Executive Committee, SBC agency heads, state convention executive secretaries, presidents of Southern Baptist colleges, and heads of their departments of religion. It was a perfect evening, warmer than usual, and the outside patio areas around the house were put to good use. It was a high hour as the Golden Gate family shared their hospitality with Baptist leadership from across the nation.

The next afternoon, June 6, was open house at the seminary since there were no meetings of the Convention. The number who visited the campus is not known but estimates range from 6,000 to 8,000. Some, driving their own cars, but strangers to the area, were surprised to have a highway patrol motorcycle draw along side and hear the patrolman ask, "Looking for Golden Gate Seminary?" Replying in the affirmative, they heard, "Follow me." They were led off at the next ramp and back to the campus entrance. A Baptist patrolman and his associate were doing this on approval of a gracious captain. The cars bearing Southern state license plates gave the patrolmen a clue in identifying the Baptists.

The alumni luncheon was held on campus that day, with John Hines presiding. The climax of the afternoon came at four o'clock, when a special convocation service was held recognizing the ten years of service given by President and Mrs. Graves. Brooks Hays, former SBC president and then special assistant to President Kennedy, was the featured speaker. The chapel was packed with Golden Gate family, trustees, Convention leaders, and other friends.

The annual trustees meeting began Friday afternoon, June 8. Elwin Skiles was chosen as chairman; Westmoreland had served for twelve years. Ernest Guy was elected vice-chairman. The 1962-1963 budget of $514,940 was adopted, including a revised salary scale for the faculty if funds became available.

In passing, it may be noted that the funds did come but were inadequate to make these adjustments when the trustee executive committee met in August. However, when they met in December, there was enough improvement in the financial picture to implement the revised scale.

An interesting development came from a large spread in a local paper concerning the seminary in connection with the meeting of the SBC in San Francisco. In the article there were several references to "the 125 acre" campus. An assistant assessor for Marin County, must have come up out of his chair when it dawned on him what was being said. Golden Gate had 125 acres of land which had been tax free since it was occupied in 1959. Taxes had been paid as by any other owner until the seminary occupied the campus. What the assessor realized was that there were twenty-five acres in excess of the 100 acres allowed to be tax free for educational institutions by the California constitution, Leland Stanford University excepted.

That assessor was in the seminary offices the week following the SBC meetings sharing the bad news. He soon produced a tax bill based on the value of the most expensive land the seminary owned. After some discussions and considerable adjustment, agreement was reached designating a sixteen-acre parcel of firm land and the twenty-three acres of tide lots as being the excess. The tax levied that year was $4,880.

A proposition on the California state ballot in November 1962 was approved by the voters, lifting the 100 acre limitation so the tax was paid only once. However, some years later, that same assistant assessor proposed that the tide lots and the five-acre portion of the firm land, cut off from the campus by a public road, were surplus to the institution's needs and should be taxed. Appeals failed to alter this decision, and it was determined that only court action could change it. The trustees decided against this move, so taxes are being paid on this portion of the property, amounting to more than $5,000 annually.

When the trustee executive committee met in August, Graves reported on some financial matters, including the trading of some small parcels of land. He also outlined his upcoming trip to the Orient for the United States Air Force. Plans called for him to visit mission work in Korea, Japan, Taiwan, Hong Kong, and the Philippines, in addition to preaching on air bases in Japan, the Philippines, and Guam. He would also attend the Hawaii Baptist Convention. The trustees voted to care for such expense as was not otherwise provided. Trustees also approved the idea of Golden Gate offering a doctorate, the Doctor of Sacred Theology (STD).

Carl Halvarson was authorized to spend two months with the Japan convention to prepare for the New Life Movement to be held in 1963. They also approved the capital needs

The 1962 faculty and staff included, standing from left, R. F. Royal, J. B. Nichols, A. J. Hyatt, Jack Manning, J. Lyn Elder, Kyle Yates, Fred L. Fisher, Clayton K. Harrop, Elmer Gray, Carlyle Bennett, J. Winston Pearce, L. A. Brown, Derward W. Deere, and Carl Halvarson. Seated from left, Orine Suffern, Elma Bennett, Gaines S. Dobbins, Harold K. Graves, W. A. Carleton, Geil Davis, and Isma Martin.

request in the 1963-1968 program, setting priorities as (1) fifteen units of housing, completing villages #2 and #3, (2) forty-two units, village #1, (3) child-care building, and (4) the library. The request was to be presented in September. The trustees postponed the 1963 annual meeting to May in Kansas City during the SBC sessions in order to cut expenses.

When the fall semester opened in September, 1962, enrollment was down, but California now provided fifty-two students.

Graves wrote from the Orient to share with readers of the *Span*, his joy in having fellowship with more than two hundred missionaries, many of them graduates of Golden Gate. He had participated in the annual mission meeting in Japan and visited five of the seminaries supported by the FMB.

R. F. Royal instituted the first "G" day observance in Sacramento and Sierra Foothills associations on November 17. Twenty-five men participated. This had the dual purpose of giving the students an opportunity to preach in the churches and for the churches to have contact with seminary students.

The SBC seminary presidents met for their annual workshop in Jackson, Mississippi, in December, 1962. They agreed to increase the request for allocation to the seminaries by $400,000. They discussed "Seminary Day" on college campuses and asked Chairman Graves to write to Baptist colleges encouraging the practice. This led to a heated discussion concerning "competitive recruiting," a built-in result of the use of a formula with the enrollment factor so prominent. In meetings with Ralph Herring, director of SED, they made the final decisions about moving the offices to Nashville.

When the 1963 spring semester at Golden Gate began in January, the accumulative enrollment was down thirty. The problem of distance was highlighted by a study of the origin of students which revealed some amazing facts. Sixty percent had traveled in excess of 1,000 miles from their homes to reach Golden Gate. This compared with 50 percent or more in each of the other five SBC seminaries who traveled less than 400 miles to attend seminary.

The opening session of the State Evangelism Conference for the northern part of the state, was held on the seminary campus in January, 1963 with R. G. Lee as the preacher. Other sessions were held in Richmond, California. Speakers included Winfred Moore of Amarillo and C. E. Autrey, director of evangelism for the HMB.

The Eleventh Annual Church Music Workshop broke all previous records with fifty-three choirs attending and sharing in the festival. More than 1,000 people attended one or more sessions, 700 as participating choir members. The music emphasis of the seminary during these years was largely geared to work with the churches and their part-time music leadership. The whole student body was being used in every way possible to help emphasize music as a very important part of worship. Carlyle Bennett, with his concept of music never being an end within itself but as a part of the whole, was the right person to give leadership at the time.

With the mission emphasis week in 1963, a new plan was instituted as a substitute for the old missionary days. The week immediately preceding the Student Missions Conference emphasized missions for the seminary family. This gave them an opportunity to have more intimate contact with program personnel. Four of the men in the conference appeared in chapel services.

Many different people have appeared in the chapel at Golden Gate. A wide variety of viewpoints has been presented. It would have to be said of many, "These views do not represent the beliefs of the seminary." It has been the conviction of the faculty and administration that exposure, with the counsel of trusted teachers near at hand, is a good way for students to learn about what they will encounter where they are to serve.

Being guided by this principle, a variety of theologians and church leaders, as well as social workers and others have been invited to speak. One of the most interesting and surprising representatives of this group appeared in chapel on March 28, in the person of James Pike, Episcopal Bishop of Northern California. Some weeks earlier J. Winston Pearce, chairman of the chapel committee, had called the president to inquire if he felt that the bishop could be asked to speak. Graves replied in the affirmative. The president had often thought of asking him to come but had not done so to this point.

Bishop Pike was invited and accepted. Contrary to the usual pattern, chapel was well attended that day, but nobody expected what they heard. Pike was in high spirits. He enjoyed the music and entered into the singing, commenting later on how well the Baptists sang. Then came the sermon. It was on the atonement. His basic illustration pictured sin as garbage. He said that garbage can be called anything, but it is still garbage. Someone could wrap it in beautiful paper and tie it with a bow and place it in a prominent place. Soon its true nature would become apparent and it would have to be moved. Another could try to hide it in a closet, but again, it would make itself known. The only thing to do with garbage is to get rid of it.

Pike said that sin is like that. Dress it up or try as you will to hide it, it still remains sin and abides with us. We can't even get rid of it by ourselves, but there is One who can. Placing his left hand above his head, Pike said that it represented sin as the burden hanging over every person. Then placing his right hand beneath his left hand, he said, "Christ comes in between you and your sin and lifts it away. It is the only way man can be rid of it, let Christ remove it."

Dean Carleton and I had coffee with the bishop in my office and talked with him about the very strong influence one of the Episcopal rectors at a nearby church was having on some Golden Gate students. The pastor was holding Thursday night prayer meetings, dominated by practices associated with the so-called "charismatic movement." It was learned later that Pike wrote a pastoral letter to the pastors in his diocese about the matter, and the emphasis of the local pastor was somewhat tempered.

An article appeared about this time in the campus paper about the involvement of students with the local Episcopal Church. It reported that "twenty-five students have received the 'baptism of the Holy Spirit' " and indicated the marvelous effects. Graves talked with the student editor and the president of the student body about the matter, pointing out principles of good journalism. A phrase like, "It is reported that" or that certain people "claim to have received" would be proper. No question was raised about the fact that students might have been blessed. The question was how they should interpret this to others. The charismatic emphasis was passing through one of its cycles and soon subsided, not to recur in the seminary for another eight or ten years.

Commencement exercises for 1963 were held May 2 and 3, with Cecil Hyatt of CBC as the baccalaureate speaker. Graves conferred degrees or awards on fifty-six graduates. He and Mrs. Graves then rushed to the airport to catch a flight to Houston for the twenty-fifth anniversary celebration of the pastorate of E. H. Westmoreland at South Main Baptist Church. They arrived in Houston just in time to enter the stage and participate in a "This Is Your Life" program for Westmoreland. They went on to Kansas City to attend the Southern Baptist Convention.

When the trustees met in Kansas City, Graves shared the news of accreditation by the American Association of Schools of Religious Education (AASRE), a group later to be merged with the AATS. He quoted Royal in saying that 60 percent of the students were in some staff position with churches. The president also noted that Elmer Gray had been asked to serve as chairman of the religious education division of the seminary. This was an effort to emphasize the program and enlist additional students. The library development program was doing wonders with holdings, now including 44,000 books, 458 current periodicals, and hundreds of slides, films, and filmstrips.

Among actions taken by the trustees was the adoption of a resolution providing for representation of new state conventions on the board. They voted to hold a Founders' Day in the fall of 1964, marking the twentieth anniversary of the seminary, and that this become an annual observance thereafter. They also adopted an improvement in the retirement program, providing for a contribution of 8 percent of the salary of each faculty and administrative staff member.

Before the six seminary presidents met in February, Graves, chairman that year, sought to get an agreement on how the formula was to function in light of the probable SBC appropriation. Prior to his presentation, they voted to raise the formula base to $200,000, with Golden Gate at $225,000. There was dissatisfaction with the decision, however. Some even wondered if Graves had presented the true picture to the program committee. There was general agreement that the presidents would have further discussions when they met in July with the program committee in Dallas. As the time for that meeting approached, Graves wrote them expressing his doubts about the possibility of a workable formula.

He suggested that there were several extreme variables that militated against it, such as differences in enrollment, size of endowment, and location. He stated his belief that formula considerations in the past, however, had undoubtedly produced increased allocations for theological education. He pleaded for continued efforts to produce a formula for both allocation and distribution which did not require a plan so rigid that there was no possibility for adjustment. Surely Southern Baptists wanted a quality program at each of its seminaries.

When the seminary presidents met in Dallas, in attendance for the first time was the newly-elected president of Southeastern, Olin Binkley, along with Sydnor Stealey, the retiring president. Several basic issues were discussed relative to the formula, and each was asked to study various alternatives in redesigning the formula to bring to a meeting in September.

The presidents met in September as agreed and decided one issue at once: enrollment for the whole year should be considered instead of just one day in the fall. Then Naylor suggested that they get outside help or work at it themselves with the introduction of some new concepts like a three-year rolling average on enrollment, a limit on the number of years graduate students might be counted, and so forth. The presidents agreed to use these ideas when they met in the December workshop.

Graves was never very creative in suggesting how various factors might be worked into a formula, perhaps partly because he felt that a rigid formula could be fatal to a school. The larger schools wanted a fixed formula for a minimum of three years, but Graves could not agree in light of history. Graves felt that after a formula had been applied, there ought to be room for adjustments to prevent hardship. The presidents kept at work on a year-to-year basis, making such adjustments as seemed necessary, some of them quite arbitrary. In due time, of course, this all but destroyed the formula and outside help was again required. In the meantime the tensions remained and division of the allocation continued to be a traumatic experience for all of them.

When the fall semester began at Golden Gate in September 1963, enrollment was up by thirty-one students. The most hopeful sign was the 30 percent increase in new students. CBC was making a difference now, with forty-five alumni enrolled. There were nineteen from Grand Canyon. Also to be noted, there were sixty-two students from California and only forty-seven from Texas. The growth of the churches in the West was now being reflected in the seminary enrollment. While seventy-two of the 1957 enrollment were non-college, in 1963 only sixteen were. College graduates were almost equal for the two years.

As the trustee executive committee met in October, the president could report that for the first time in four years, income had exceeded expenditures for the year. He reported that additions to villages #2 and #3 on campus were ready for contract negotiations. The trustees approved, in outline, a ten-year development program with details to be worked out by the president and his staff for the board to consider in March, 1964. They also authorized the borrowing of up to

$25,000 for operations before December 31.

On November 21 the faculty and administration of Golden Gate were again hosts for a dinner involving their counterparts at the Berkeley Baptist Divinity School. Special tribute was paid to President Ralph Johnson of BBDS, who had resigned to accept a pastorate in Washington state.

The next day, November 22, was to become a day burned into the memory of most living people. President Kennedy was assassinated. In my column in the December *Span*, I wrote:

> Disagreement has been expressed in violence. A nation has been shamed. Then, to compound our shame, another of our citizens takes upon himself the role of judge and jury to pass sentence and proceed to execute the defendant. . . .
>
> . . . It's beyond belief that others among us saw some sort of justice in either deed. Can it be true that we in America are so lacking in moral judgment and a commitment to law and the right? . . . Can we in America see that patriotism is not a sentimentalism. . .? Has our debunking of the past gone too far? . . . As Christians and Baptists, can we be content to seek to reach only our own kind and to avoid the one that is different or difficult? . . . Can we love those with whom we disagree? . . . May our love for Him be reflected in attitude, word, and deed, that men may see and know that He makes a difference.

It is interesting to note the many ways God uses to direct men and women to their fields of service. In the spring of 1963, the Marin Visitors Bureau sponsored a photo contest for pictures taken of beauty spots in the county. First prize was a week for two in Hawaii. A seminary student, Bob Duffer, won the prize for a photo of Mount Tamalpais from the seminary campus with an acacia tree in full bloom in the foreground. Bob and his wife went to the Islands that summer and fell in love with the people. After Bob's graduation, they took a church in Hawaii and have continued to serve there. He has been elected president of that convention.

There were signs of a changing emphasis for many students and faculty members during these days. Disturbing things were happening in the United States, and serious students were groping for answers. An example of developments is illustrated by an article Dr. McClendon wrote for the November *Span*, in which he discussed influences he felt in England and Europe during his sabbatical. He suggested that if he were seeking to serve God in England, he might be more effective as a journalist. There was need for a strong Christian voice at the center of the great human problems—moral, spiritual, and economic. What was really needed was an ability to meet the intellectual leadership and outthink them in the name of Jesus Christ. McClendon went on to say, "My mind has also changed, or begun to change, about how this work can effectively be done. I believe that contemporary philosophy, for example, has put into our hands conceptual tools of enormous usefulness."

The urge to get involved in life and to affect change in the world was reflected in the theme adopted by the student body council for the year 1963-1964, "Not Tomorrow, Today." Bob Wells was student body chairman for the year.

The program committee of the SBC Executive Committee decided in February, 1964 to require the seminaries to pay certain costs for campus maintenance out of operational instead of capital funds. In adjusting for this, the presidents added $18,000 to the base allocation for each school. In response to the plea from the presidents for funds to raise faculty salaries, the program committee also designated $100,000 additional to be used specifically for that purpose. Wow! How do they divide it? The presidents agreed to do it by head count of faculty. That helped to push the formula further out of shape. It was becoming increasingly difficult to use the formula with all these factors. Divisions of funds began to be affected more by the past year's plan than almost anything else.

During the weeks prior to the meeting of the Golden Gate trustees, Graves was making contact with men whom trustees had proposed as potential members of a development council in the new program under consideration. On his way home from Nashville in February, he visited in Abilene, Texas. Elwin Skiles introduced him to Ed Connally, an oil man whose wife, Virginia, is a physician. Ed and Virginia actively supported the seminary across the years. Ed served as chairman of the council for a number of years before his death in 1976. Virginia gave the beautiful Baldwin piano in honor of Ed, which was dedicated in May, 1979.

When the trustees met in March, 1964, five state conventions were represented for the first time: Washington-Oregon, Colorado, Indiana, Kansas, and Ohio. It was reported that Clarence Kennedy—longtime trustee, secretary, and building committee member—had died in January. News was also shared that former chairman E. H. Westmoreland had suffered a serious heart attack and that Guy Rutland, Jr., had suffered a stroke.

In his report, Graves reminded the trustees that the seminary was in its twentieth year and that since the first graduating class in 1949, more than 700 had been awarded degrees or diplomas. Of this number 27 percent were in service through one of the mission boards, counting the military chaplaincy. More than 60 percent of the graduates were in service in the western part of the United States. The current student body consisted of students from thirty-four states and seven other countries. Baptist colleges produced 65 percent and 25 percent came to the seminary from east of the Mississippi River.

He reported a probable capital needs allocation to Golden Gate of $500,000 in 1966-1967, to be used for housing. The Berkeley property still had not been sold, a balance remained of some $85,000 due on the Wells Fargo Bank loan.

Pastor E. J. Wood expressed the appreciation of the Tiburon Boulevard Baptist Church for the use of seminary facilities during the years since its founding. The church anticipated moving to its new building in early fall. He also voiced gratitude for the contributions of several trustees in securing the building site.

The "Projection '74" development program was presented

by Carl Halvarson. The new logo of the double G and the cross was introduced and a sample of the materials proposed. The ten-year program was approved, and several men were elected to the council. These included Guy Rutland, Jr., Atlanta, Georgia; George Mitchell, Mobile, Alabama; Charles Green, Lawton, Oklahoma; Floyd Golden, Amarillo, Texas; Preston Johnston, Lubbock, Texas; J. E. Connally, Abilene, Texas; and C. F. Harwell, Tucson, Arizona; along with trustees, Horn, Guy, Koonce, and Gregory.

Graves pointed out that the faculty had only one man in the area of theology and philosophy for the past eleven years. Another should be added when resources were available. The trustees gave general approval to seeking someone in this area, to be definitely decided in Atlantic City, in light of finances at that time. They urged that the missions area be strengthened through addition of missionaries on furlough each year. They also voted to consider a combination of evangelism and missions under one professor.

The personnel committee planned other efforts to strengthen the missions area. The committee, the dean, and mission professor L. A. Brown met to consider a sabbatical that would allow Brown further study. It was then brought to the trustees for their consideration.

The following motion was voted unanimously by the trustees:

"That Dr. Brown be awarded a sabbatical this next year, at salary of $6,000, for study in comparative religions, then in 1965 return to seminary, at salary of $6,000, to teach comparative religions and possibly in foreign language fields."

This action brings up what continues to be a major concern in a school like Golden Gate. When committed, warmhearted people become members of a seminary faculty, the seminary has a responsibility and an opportunity to help them develop their potential. Sabbaticals allow time for intense study that help professors stay abreast of their disciplines and abreast of their students' needs. As better prepared and more intellectually curious students enter Golden Gate in larger numbers, it is important for them to know they will study under professors who are able both intellectually and spiritually.

Students vary too, of course. One extreme is the student who considers the seminary a perpetual revival meeting— with but few demands for work, testing times, and grades. Such a student seems surprised that any class requirement would take precedence over a revival meeting or any other "spiritual" activity. To him, the longer the devotional period and the more direct help for next Sunday the better the class.

The other extreme is the student who has been bitten by the academic bug. History, philosophy, and other so-called "heavy" courses are his meat—looking for top grades in pursuit of higher degrees. He may be enamored with new ideas, especially those that might shock a less "mature" person. He picks up on two Isaiahs or an author of some Bible book, different from tradition, and flaunts such ideas as the height of intellectual attainment.

Actually, there is both an academic and a devotional side to theological education. Fortunately, the two are not mutually exclusive. In the Roman Catholic tradition, "formation" seeks to produce a theologically prepared man who has grown spiritually as well. As Baptists, we have the academic side developed to a high degree, but the spiritual side has not claimed so much attention. Lacking the authority or power to require prayers and other devotional exercises, we have to make-do with chapel services and conferences, plus urgings for voluntary programs of spiritual growth. What surprises most students in a seminary is that they have to work at maintaining spiritual health and growth during their semi- nary careers.

A professor may or may not be a spiritually exciting person, regardless of his academic field. An archeology professor may excite students, a history or theology profes- sor bore them or vice versa. Professors and students must work at maintaining spiritual warmth and health. Not all do, nor do they all grow intellectually. They are human and in this fact lies the problem. Growth in either realm is not automatic.

The Board of Trustees of Golden Gate Seminary for the year 1964-1965

James Landes, then president of Hardin-Simmons University, was baccalaureate speaker for the 1964 seminary commencement. President Graves spoke, then awarded degrees and diplomas to sixty-eight graduates.

As consideration was being given to the addition of a faculty member, Professor McClendon suggested that LeRoy Moore, a Golden Gate graduate, be considered. A graduate of Baylor, Moore had been an excellent seminary student. He was then studying at the Claremont Graduate School. Dean Carleton shared this enthusiasm for Moore as a scholar but wanted to interview Moore about his development since seminary days. Both Carleton and the president had conferences with Moore before the trustees' meeting in Atlantic City in May. They agreed that they could recommend him for consideration.

When the trustees met, two actions were taken. One decision was "that we elect LeRoy Moore as a member of the teaching staff, effective July 1; that his rank, salary, and fringe benefits be that of Assistant Professor (1st yr.) as soon as work on the Ph.D. degree is completed." The other action was "that we continue the (ATLA) library program for two more years." This meant an additional grant of $12,000 for books to be matched by gifts from seminary friends.

The fall semester opened September 1, with J. Winston Pearce as the convocation speaker. The enrollment was disappointing, with another drop. New students numbered eleven below the previous year. All the other SBC seminaries, except Southern, were down as well.

The first Founders' Day was observed on October 7, with the founding president, Isam B. Hodges, as speaker, using as his subject, "A Dream Come True." The recurring theme of his message was, "California for Christ; Christ for California!" The truly inspiring service was attended by a large group, including trustees, development council, and other interested friends.

When the executive committee of the trustees met the next day, the president indicated that the faculty had shown considerable interest in attending meetings of academic societies. He suggested that a specific plan for allocation of assistance in this area was needed. The trustees agreed and asked that such be provided for their consideration at the annual meeting in 1965. The trustees acknowledged receipt of a George DeMont Otis painting and expressed their gratitude to his widow for the gift. Entitled *Corte Madera Grade*, the painting is of a scene in Marin County near the seminary campus. His work is of such note that posthumous showings have honored him as no other Marin artist.

With the launching of the development program, Graves reminded the executive committee that all of Golden Gate's resources had come from the churches through the Cooperative Program. In the October, 1964 issue of the seminary publication, now to be called *Gateway*, he wrote in a front page editorial:

> To speak of the Cooperative Program and Golden Gate Seminary is like speaking of the relationship of cotton farming to the clothing industry, of the petroleum market to the automobile. It is hard to conceive that Golden Gate would exist apart from the support of the cooperative efforts of Southern Baptists.
>
> The lovely campus—grounds, buildings and equipment— is a trophy of the Cooperative Program. Less than $50,000 of the $5,500,000 invested in this development came from any other source.
>
> A new seminary like Golden Gate also has its operations budget almost as dependent on the support of the denomination. 86.6 percent of the income for the year 1963-64 for Golden Gate was provided by the appropriation to the Seminary from these mission funds.

The associated student body leaders, with Glenn Saul as president, held a fall planning conference and announced goals for the year. Saul suggested that there was a "need to emphasize moral responsibility to the community." Activities were to include service to the handicapped people in the county. Campus concerns would emphasize political trends in the election year.

These social concerns had been coming to the fore in many ways. The 1964 Student Missions Conference had, as part of its program, several seminars on social involvement including the Peace Corps. When Doyle Burke was selected to be chairman of the 1965 conference, in the absence of Dr. Brown or any other professor directly related to it, the students largely shaped the program. They announced in the October, 1964 *Gateway* that the "emphasis of the conference will be on the contemporary student recognizing and accepting his responsibility in the communication of the Christian faith." With the announced speakers, it appeared at the time that home and foreign missions would have the central emphasis. Actually, other options were presented in a most attractive fashion.

A new president of Berkeley Baptist Divinity School was inaugurated in October, 1964. With this, there was a turning of the tide in theological education in the area. Influences of the president of the San Francisco Theological Seminary and a professor brought by him to that school, on his way to becoming the dean of the GTU, were already being felt. Now to join them, the president of BBDS is reported to have said that he would make BBDS the liberal seminary of American Baptists. The fellowship dinners between GGBTS and BBDS were over. It was BBDS's time to serve as host, but no invitation was extended.

America was in turmoil as we set about to elect a new President in the fall of 1964. This was very apparent in California. With all its glorious attributes, it had many problems. Its people were, indeed, in a land of plenty: climate, economics, education, and in *insecurity*. I addressed these issues in my column in the *Gateway* for December, 1964.

I heard Dean Samuel Miller of Harvard Divinity School a few days ago, speaking on the subject "Training for Insecurity." Since it was on the occasion of the inauguration of a seminary president, it might well be considered a philosophy of theological education in our day. Certainly our modern day theological student has plenty of insecurity.

Indeed, he is a part of an insecure age, yet is called of God to minister in and to this age.

One who thus serves should know all that he can about his world—its heritage, its sureties, its doubts and its fears. He must go beyond the men of this day, however, in his experience with and knowledge of the "things that remain." His security must rest on solid ground if he is to speak to an insecure age.

Such training for a minister must take for granted that a man has a sure knowledge of God in Christ. . . . Doubt here undermines faith elsewhere.

Next, one must know God's will for his life as to calling and area of service. If he could be happy in any one of a number of callings, then he lacks an essential ingredient for one who would serve with the confident "this one thing I do."

. . . These sureties will be questioned, reexamined and restated, but they remain as sure footing along the pathway of preparation for service. Testings will come in many ways. Security for one's family may be a real problem. The loneliness of a strange environment may try one's sense of mission. Add to this the struggle required of one whose understanding of God grows and expands. . . .

. . . Yet, out of this crucible comes stamina, confidence, and faith that will stand the test of contrary winds and circumstances.

The SBC seminary presidents held their workshop in Miami, beginning November 30, 1964. The major problem was to work into the formula base the additions that came from the two SBC Executive Committee actions in February. This produced a rather odd-looking structure. The presidents then voted to request the percent of increase in allocation equal to the increase in 1964 gifts through the Cooperative Program.

Brougher Maddox, pastor, First Southern Baptist Church, Hollywood, had requested that the presidents consider offering seminary level work in the Los Angeles area. Graves reported conversations with Maddox and that the Golden

Gate faculty would consider some offerings in addition to work by the SED. The presidents approved this effort.

In their February, 1965 meeting, the presidents authorized placing a SED man in the Los Angeles area to work with Golden Gate, or lacking that, a part-time person from Golden Gate might be used. They discussed also a joint effort to raise endowment funds, but decided to work on it further in Dallas at the SBC.

The funds granted through the AATS for library improvement included assistance on a personal level for schools requesting it. President Alvin Rogness of Luther Theological Seminary in St. Paul and Raymond Morris, librarian of Yale Divinity School, visited Golden Gate in February, 1965. Morris wrote the report, which was predominantly favorable but with several specific suggestions for improvement.

The Seminary Conference and Chaplains Retreat was held in February with Grady Cothen, executive secretary of the Southern Baptist General Convention of California, and Colonel William Clark, USAF Chief of Chaplains' office leading. Cothen challenged the seminary family to help the churches and state convention to "chart new courses, develop urban strategies, and train the minds of Southern Baptist young people for church leadership in California and the West. The task of Golden Gate Seminary in these areas cannot be overestimated."

On March 1 bids were opened for construction of additional student family housing left out of the original construction program. The newly formed development council and the trustees were arriving for their annual session. The week coincided with the missions emphasis time for the seminary family and preceded the missions conference. Against this backdrop and the social tumult that was raging, I decided to bring a more formal address than usual to the trustees and development council. I sought to give a theological and philosophical base for what the seminary was attempting to do. Speaking of the ministry and the seminaries, I said:

The function of a seminary is primarily *education*, to

provide a trained ministry for the churches. A secondary function is *leadership through creative study* of the life of the churches and the denomination. Another secondary function is *study and research*; the continuing creative relating of revealed truth to contemporary man.

As Christians we are simply not being realistic if we think we can perpetuate the old patterns of life in the preatomic age with its simple ways of life. We must, as representatives of the Lord Jesus Christ in this age, accept the world as it is in our efforts to make it aware of Him whom we serve. . . .

While repudiating the world's standards for success and its relative ideals and denial of absolutes—the thoroughly furnished servant of God in our day must see in every man this rough image of God—this candidate for the kingdom of God. Our task here in the West does not end with the gathering of "our kind" from back home into little cells of isolation and fellowship. It is, rather, that out of our fellowship of Christ we shall go forth to communicate the love of God with compassion and concern to the end that man may be drawn to Him.

The development council met on Tuesday morning, elected Jerry Wheat as its chairman, made plans, adopted goals, and recommended Stanton Nash as the person to give leadership to the development program. He flew from Atlanta to appear before the trustees, was elected by them to serve, and stayed on to go to work as assistant to the president for development. The trustees approved a contract with the Crown Development Company for construction of fifteen units of two bedroom housing for married students, completing villages #2 and #3. They were to be ready by September.

G. S. Dobbins was elected for his tenth and final year as Distinguished Professor. Upon recommendation of the development council, the trustees voted to raise funds individually for the development program, a goal of $2,000 for laymen and $1,000 for ministers. They also voted that all income from regular endowment funds be added to the principal until $50,000 was attained.

More than 600 young people and their leaders attended the student missions conference in March. It taxed everything about the seminary—space, resources, and temperaments. Program leaders challenged the youth to be involved in service to humanity. Nathan Porter of the HMB introduced the new US-2 missionary program in the United States for college graduates. The new overseas Missionary Journeyman Program for college graduates was introduced by Bill Marshall of the FMB. Students were also informed concerning Secular Careers Overseas by James Cobban of U. C., Berkeley placement center. Thus they were offered many options in service at home and overseas.

Action by the United States Supreme Court in 1954 with regard to school segregation was just the beginning of an open struggle that went on for more than a decade, picking up intensity and force as it moved. It was at its height when Martin Luther King was planning the Selma march—in mid-March, 1965. Many people from across America were gathering to participate in the event. A bus load of students went from the neighboring school in Marin County, the San Francisco Theological Seminary. Their president flew to join them. One Golden Gate student from Louisiana, Anthony Vos, expressed a conviction that he should go. Several teachers and students gave funds to assist with his trip.

Ironically, Tony seems to have been so tired upon his arrival that he went to sleep and actually had very little to report upon his return. Most of the seminary family knew more than he, having seen TV and read the newspapers. The effort to assist Vos in making the trip, however, aided in bringing the whole matter into focus for the seminary family. The question began to be asked as to whether there were other actions they could take to reflect their support.

Before chapel time, Tuesday, March 16, Glenn Saul, chairman of the student body, came to my office to report the rising insistence that the students be allowed to express themselves about the actions in Selma. I cautioned about taking any hasty moves, but Saul felt that one way or another the students would act. Sending telegrams seemed the best way. Saul and his associates had prepared messages to be sent to Governor Wallace and to King. I went over these with Saul, suggesting substitutions for a few volatile words. I proposed a process to get them before the seminary family, sending Saul to J. Winston Pearce, who was in charge of chapel. He suggested that they tell the audience about the telegrams, have them read, then have them voted on. If there were any desire for discussion, the process should be delayed until after the service; if not, they could be voted on at once. The telegrams were read, nobody asked for discussion, so the vote was taken. No negative vote was indicated. After the service, a few raised a question with me about the lack of discussion. I felt that ample opportunity had been given for such a request and that since no one had so indicated, the matter was closed. But that was not the end of it.

Someone took it upon himself to send a report to the Baptist Press (BP). Such action had not been discussed with the administration. Perhaps the one who sent it did not feel that was necessary. The BP sent out a supplement to a previous story which indicated the text of the telegrams. When the BP story reached Baptist leaders in the South, the reaction was swift and, for a few, heavy. A seminary classmate of mine received the release and wrote on March 23:

> I received a copy of the *Baptist Press* report of the telegrams which were sent, of all things, to Martin Luther King and to Governor Wallace by the student body of the GGBTS. . . .
> I am confident that this official action of your student body was conscientiously motivated, but regret the fact that greater wisdom was not exercised on the part of the faculty and administration in guiding your students into an appreciation of the fact that it is exceedingly difficult to pass judgment upon states, people, organizations and conditions, without having *all* of the information, and having lived under the pressures that can be exerted in such circumstances. . . .
> It is real strange to us who live in Alabama and who are

dedicated and consecrated to the cause of Christ and live under the authority of the Scripture, to see our brethren, and particularly our youth taking sides, determining positions and exercising pressure without consideration to the effect of such action upon those who are struggling to maintain fellowship and financial support of the institutions that represent us in Southern Baptist life. I recognize that there is a difference of opinion, and yet feel that in justification, both sides of an issue should be considered before expression and support is given to one side. . . .

My quick reply to this friend was also sent to those who had received copies of the letter to me:

I have your letter of March 23, and must say it was not unexpected and I can understand the reaction. You are right in saying that many people outside the South do not understand the situation. However, I believe that I have a pretty good understanding of it.

Do you understand our situation as well? We are the only Southern Baptist institution outside the sharply defined Southern tradition. By its location, the Golden Gate Seminary family is in the midst of the cosmopolitan atmosphere of the North and West. Many Christians feel that the Scriptures have much to say concerning the worth of individual people in God's sight. In the light of this truth, it is easy for people in this area to feel that a great host of people are being denied their rights and to want to speak out against it.

You can know that discussions have been lively for weeks. There are students here from all across America and, as you know, many from the deep South. The student body is by no means unanimous in its position, but it would be fair to say that their vote represented the opinion of the great majority of them, including those from southern states.

Note what they expressed to the Governor and to King—that they deplore the fact that so many are denied the right to vote and that violence was used to break up the peaceful protest rather than their being protected in that peaceful protest. Perhaps the additional word of encouragement to

King was stated in an unfortunate way. They did not mean a blanket approval of all of his program, I'm sure.

I'm simply saying . . . that we, too, live in a community that needs some understanding. A witness to basic principles of rights to American citizens, as seen by people here, was called for as the students saw it. As a matter of fact, they felt their witness in an effective way to much of the California scene was at stake. It was in that regard, of course, a judgment of a situation that it has been impossible for them to explain or justify.

Perhaps, and I say *perhaps*, if I had refused them the opportunity to express themselves, the telegrams might not have been sent. But I have real serious questions about the results here of such an action on my part—both in the seminary family and in the community. I beg an effort on your part to understand this.

There had been an implication in the critical letter that Golden Gate students had been irresponsible in their action in light of the fact that Golden Gate is a Southern institution, supported by Southern dollars. In light of this and other factors, I sent copies of the telegrams and the exchange of letters to the trustees.

LeRoy Moore was not on campus the day the students voted to send the telegrams. When he heard of their action, he wrote a letter of appreciation to the student body president.

The Selma incident caused no further discussion in official circles either in the seminary family or among the trustees. It seemed not to affect the attitudes of Southern leadership in the SBC toward the seminary in any way.

The Golden Gate family was becoming increasingly aware of its task on the "Urban Frontier," as it was called in a *Gateway* article in April, 1965:

In an emerging urban America, California is fast becoming a society of great cities with the challenge and problems of rapid urbanization. . . . Los Angeles, called a "prototype of the supercity" by Fortune Magazine, is larger than all but seven states.

Southern Baptists living in California and the West are not unaware of the enormity of their evangelical task. Seminary President Harold K. Graves states the case for Christian Mission today:

"Can patterns of church life and growth Southern Baptists have developed in the South be duplicated in the urban North and far West? There may be many kinds of answers to the question, but at Golden Gate the faculty is rephrasing the question: How can we best communicate the gospel and reach the urban cosmopolitan multitudes?

"Now through the cooperation of pastors, California convention leaders, and Southern Baptist Convention agency personnel, the seminary launches a study in depth on urban evangelism and church growth."

In the same April, 1965 *Gateway*, R. F. Royal reported on a recent survey, revealing a growing need for church staff personnel. Letters from 150 churches in California, Arizona, Washington, and Oregon, indicated a probable need for 210 new staff members in the next five years. J. B. Nichols reported in the same issue that employment continued to be plentiful in the secular fields near the campus. The faculty had arranged the course of study in such a way that a student could choose to earn his Bachelor of Divinity degree not only in the normal three years but also on a three-year-two-summer schedule or one that took four years.

Commencement was held for seventy-seven graduates on April 28-29, 1965. Herbert Howard, pastor of Park Cities Baptist Church, Dallas, Texas, was the baccalaureate preacher. Of these graduates, a significant number received the Master of Theology degree who have proved themselves to be unusually effective servants. These included Henry Blackaby of Canada; Kenneth Glenn in Europe; Charles Hancock with the HMB; Cliff Hoff and Carl Kinoshita in Hawaii; and William Hunter in counseling work in Southern California.

The summer workers enlisted by the Baptist Student Union and directed by the HMB and the state convention to work in California met for their orientation on the Golden

Gate campus, June 13-15. Having these young people on campus each year, for most of the years since, has proved to be helpful to the seminary and the state convention. It is another way in which the two have been mutually supportive.

On Thursday, June 17, Graves gave up his Rotary Club presidency. He had missed only seven meetings during the year, in spite of his heavy travel schedule. On one occasion, he had spent a Monday night in Jackson, Mississippi, but arrived home just in time to preside at his club luncheon Tuesday noon. It had been a rich experience and extremely profitable to the seminary in public relations. When five years later he was asked to serve as district governor, there was no question in his mind, or that of the trustees, that he should do it.

The fall semester began August 31, 1965, with R. F. Royal bringing the convocation address. The enrollment increased only three from the year before. Assisting Dobbins in the Survey of Missions course was Francis DuBose, superintendent of missions for Detroit since 1960. His general theme for his ten day visit was "Christian Mission in Crisis." He returned to the campus in November for another series of lectures on the theme, "The Crisis in Urbanization." It was from these contacts that attention was called to DuBose as a possible faculty member. He seemed fully qualified to fill the role designated by the trustees in the area of evangelism and urban church.

The second Founders' Day celebration was held September 29, with Floyd Looney, former editor of *The California Southern Baptist*, as speaker. In his message Looney paid special tribute to Isam Hodges and other pioneers in the beginnings of the seminary.

In the December, 1965 *Gateway*, under a picture of Sproul Court on the campus of U. C., Berkeley, Graves wrote concerning the role of theological education:

> "I am a human being; do not fold, bend or mutilate." Thus read a sign held by a marching, protesting student in the Free Speech Movement disturbances of the University of California campus. . . . This cry was but one expression of

protest against the restrictions imposed on the students who demanded freedom. . . .

. . . Education is suffering from a lack of clearly defined goals. With such rapid growth in the mass of knowledge and swift change in the world, it could hardly be otherwise.

Specialization in education is another contemporary problem. . . .

In the light of our world today, what kind of education must we seek to offer in our theological schools? In brief, four suggestions seem to me to be pertinent to our day and to these growing implications.

First of all, . . . we must recognize this growing, changing society, and the world of knowledge. We cannot bury our heads in the sand and live in this world as if no new books had been written since 1900, or even 1960. . . .

In the second place, we must . . . seek truth. But, . . . we must not reject the past as unrelated to today's world; the past continues to be new to the uninstructed. . . .

Furthermore, we must provide an explanation, an interpretation of life in terms of human experience. . . .

Finally, we must provide, . . . an understanding of and the skill to use organization in making the message of redemption vital, relevant and effective for changing men and a changing world.

The seminary presidents and their wives met for their annual workshop November 29, 1965 in Sarasota, Florida. When the fall enrollments were shared it was discovered that Southern was up thirty-seven and Golden Gate three, while others were down. It was agreed to ask the SBC for $4,250,000 in 1967. McCall planned to use the information gained from a survey of salaries among AATS schools to push up the total. In light of the plight of the two smaller schools, if the allocation was as much as $4,000,000, they agreed to go back to an equal base for the four larger schools at $260,000 with $285,000 for the two smaller ones. This would provide an increase of near $20,000 for Golden Gate.

The second semester opened at Golden Gate on January 4, 1966 with Elmer Gray serving as active dean. Dean Carleton was at Oxford for six months. Dobbins brought the convocation address. It was his final address as a seminary faculty member. With that semester, he ended forty-five years of teaching, the last ten at Golden Gate. His message was missionary to the core, reflecting in part his years of service and wide travels as chairman of the BWA Commission on Bible Study and Training, as well as his current responsibility in directing the research project concerning the work of the urban church. He had closed the current phase of the study, stating that his efforts had done little more than uncover the enormous proportions of the task.

The mission conference was held in February, 1966. Winston Crawley, secretary for the Orient of the FMB, and Hugo Culpepper, former foreign missionary and seminary professor, then director of Missions Division of the HMB, were the missions headliners. The other featured speaker was John Killinger, professor at Vanderbilt. The theme of the conference was One World/One Mission.

The missions conference registered 597 but, with many local people attending but not registered, there were certainly more than 700 in attendance. The Washington-Oregon group of 172, sponsored by Gene Bolin, BSU secretary, came in 4 buses. Other program personnel were Cecil Etheridge of the HMB and Louis Cobbs of the FMB who led seminars along with several from the Bay Area who presented alternate service opportunities.

The four days preceding the conference were used by the seminary family for a missions emphasis. John Killinger spoke Friday morning and again at the opening session of the conference that evening. His keen mind was apparent to all and his wide acquaintance with modern literature unmistakable. His audience was enthralled, at least those who understood him, or thought they did. The evening message left something to be desired, however, as a keynote address for a "missions" conference. Whatever the purpose of the message was, the effect was negative and reflected negatively on denominational efforts. The social emphasis lacked the complement of the missions emphasis.

Needless to say, there was much discussion in many circles after the service that night. Culpepper, Crawley, Cobbs, and Etheridge spent the night at the Graves's home. Culpepper was the principal speaker Saturday night. Perhaps from impressions gained in that fellowship, or perhaps simply reflecting his own strong convictions, Culpepper changed his message. The report in the *Gateway* read:

> Dr. Hugo Culpepper provided a high point of the conference when he disregarded his manuscript and spoke extemporaneously at the Saturday night session. He told of the growth of his Christian maturity during three years as a Japanese war prisoner and challenged the young people to consider their own lives in view of the Christian mission.

Sunday morning Killinger brought the closing message and gave an invitation. He chose an excellent subject for young people living in America and in college in the mid-sixties, "Christianity Is a Revolution." He got their attention at once with a story about a modern British poet who visited an empty church and wondered:

> When churches fall completely out of use
> What we shall turn them into, if we shall keep
> A few cathedrals chronically on show,
> Their parchment, plate and pyx in locked cases,
> And let the rest rent-free to rain and sheep.[1]

Killinger continued by pointing to the New Testament church and the way in which the early disciples were willing to break with the dead past, to establish new paths of service to meet human need. His points were well taken, to be sure, but many felt he overstated his case. The contrast between the church making waves to change the social structure, as over against personal salvation was forcefully drawn. Again, regardless of the intended purpose, the effect was negative. The message seemingly left no room for an organized statement of theological truth, which implied a theological anarchy. The invitation came and went without response.

Graves had heard Killinger on Friday and on Sunday morning. While there was great value in much that had been said, he felt the negative had dominated and that this could not be left standing as the conference ended. He got Chairman James Orrell's eye, indicating that he wanted to make some remarks before the benediction. In due time he was given the chance and said:

> I think in many ways that the experience of these days has been one of the most stimulating, if perhaps, not one of the most provocative that many of us have ever had. Certainly you have had many things said to stimulate and raise many questions. Many of the things that you have stirred within your own hearts have led you, particularly the mature ones of you, out to the other side.
>
> We appreciate the fact that you have been stimulated. We would not have wanted you to come here, to have listened to clichés and to have a sort of emotional revival that would have sent you along thinking . . . the rather narrow interpretation that would not stand the test of much that you're learning in school. But I think I must say a word in closing here this morning, . . . I agree that the Christian faith is a revolutionary faith. I believe also that in that revolutionary presentation of it, it is presented in a form, an organized form, that reflects the beliefs and the convictions of a great majority of people.
>
> I believe the Word of God to be understood by individuals as the Holy Spirit directs them. Yes, there will be many interpretations of why we did not respond this morning. I pray that as you go you will go with the conviction that Whom we know in the Lord Jesus Christ is the Lord of ordered life and that our institutions reflect that and an institution like this reflects a great body of belief, of truth. . . . I believe that a great denomination like ours has existed and has its evangelistic impact because we have shared what we believe.

Graves spoke for several minutes, making a positive stand for a body of basic beliefs and for the place of a church and its fellowship in the maturing of Christians. While paying due credit to the speaker for his stimulating thoughts, the president felt that the missions conference should end on a high note of conviction rather than with the discord of doubt. His conclusion spoke for the seminary.

Graves received many letters, most of them favorable to his response. Two paragraphs from Gene Bolin's letter illustrate the comments:

> Your closing remarks were the thread of hope many had been looking for and grasping for during the entire conference. . . . I do not mean to imply that our students have, on the basis of this one experience, become embittered. There are some, without doubt, who have been forced to begin a first-time evaluation of their faith; others were reinforced in their negativism and skepticism. On the other hand, there are those who were diligent in their analysis of what was said and were thus able to find the vulnerable conclusions based upon questionable logic. These students seem to have been strengthened in their insistence upon the personal relationship with Jesus as the object of their mission.
>
> We will be looking forward to next year anticipating the honoring of Christ and the challenge to become more fully involved in sharing Him with the world.

With the strong statements made and actions taken, Graves thought the missions conference would be turned back to its central purpose—missions. But that did not happen at once. Because of space and to assure a more mature clientele, attendance became restricted to college and college-age young people. The particular "social" bent of students, not necessarily the majority though certainly the most vocal group, still controlled the conference, however, and gave it this turn rather than a more "spiritual" or mission tone. If this group were in student government, they worked that way; if not, they ran a parallel course. But the conference was finally turned about.

The *Gateway*, during these months, was filled with an emphasis on the "Projection '74" development program. In the April/May, 1966 issue, Graves had a front-page article, "Do You Want to Know Why?" In it he pointed out the disparity between Golden Gate faculty salaries and those of neighboring seminaries, where, in one case, those at Golden Gate were exactly one half. The Consumer Price Index showed that the cost of living in the San Francisco area was 23 percent higher than in Fort Worth; 17½ percent higher than in New Orleans, and 14 percent higher than in Louisville. He appealed for more dollars for theological education and a larger share of that allocation for Golden Gate.

At the SBC Executive Committee meeting in February, the program committee announced an allocation to theological education that was more than $400,000 short of expectations. Graves knew immediately that the presidents would use the 1966 allocation formula to distribute the 1967 allocation and that would be tragic for Golden Gate. It happened that way.

Wednesday of that February week in Nashville was a full day, including a conference that Graves had arranged with James L. Sullivan and some of the BSU workers from the BSSB. He left that meeting to eat alone and then go to his room for a few minutes before going to the SBC Building for the seven PM Executive Committee session. He felt weak and exhausted from the activities of these meetings, the crowded schedule of the past several weeks, the emotional experience of the missions conference, and now the prospects of another austere budget allocation.

When Graves went to the SBC building that evening, he sat in an end seat on one of the back rows in the Austin Crouch Room with President Berquist. As the evening wore on, Graves became dizzy and disoriented. About nine o'clock, he told Berquist he would have to leave but would need help. They went to the lounge where he lay down. The

California member of the Executive Committee, Dr. David
Page, a physician, was summoned. He was not sure but felt
that it was a heart attack. He sent for medicine and called an
ambulance.

The ambulance came as the meeting was breaking up, and
everyone seemed to be in the lobby as Graves went through.
At Baptist Hospital another physician checked him thoroughly and ordered an electrocardiogram. The results did
not indicate a heart attack. He spent the night and was
examined again the next morning and, being assured that it
was not a heart attack, was dismissed. Terry Young accompanied him to San Francisco and saw him to the helicopter for
Marin County. Dr. John Lee was called the next morning and
came to Graves's home. After other examinations and an
electrocardiogram a few days later, he said it was a case of
total exhaustion.

Trustee chairman Elwin Skiles was called. The annual
trustee meeting was postponed, and Fred Fisher was appointed acting president. Graves was out of the office for
seven weeks, his only illness in the twenty-five years he
served the seminary. He spent one week at home, another in
Southern California, then took a leisurely trip East, attending
a few meetings as he felt like it, and finally spent the first
week of April at the China Lake Naval installation in a
preaching mission. He had to miss a week of hearing C. Roy
Angell preach in chapel and several other activities, but he
could not escape the decisions about personnel that had to be
faced.

The week preceding the missions conference at the seminary, E. J. Wood, pastor at Tiburon Baptist Church, resigned
suddenly at a Sunday evening service, effective immediately.
After the faculty meeting the next day, the president pleaded
with those who were members at Tiburon not to help
precipitate a further crisis in the church. However, several
were involved in a move to lead the church in refusing the
resignation. At the church business meeting on Wednesday
evening the resignation was voted down two to one.

Ironically, the next action was to designate a committee to seek a successor.

There was considerable division in the faculty about the many happenings of these days. They were affected by several things: the missions conference, the Tiburon church difficulty, and the rumor that an instructor would not be continued. All were part of the same issue—that of where the central emphasis was to be. Was it to be on social change or evangelism? A kind of freedom that was anarchy or an ordered church and denominational life? It was a time when many people were debunking the church and the denomination. Not all agreed on any particular view but groups formed for or against various concepts.

During these troubled times, Moore and McClendon left the seminary faculty. McClendon later became a professor at CDSP, the Episcopal seminary in Berkeley, where he continues to serve.

Carl Halvarson had given the president a letter of resignation in December, but it had not been publicized. They had agreed that he was to give his main attention to promotion of the missions conference, then be free to depart. He left the campus after the conference and later moved his family to Nashville, then to Jackson, Tennessee, where he became associated with Union University. His older daughter had increasing difficulty in the Bay Area climate, and the move was advised by their physician.

Commencement exercises were held April 28-29 with Elwin Skiles, chairman of the trustees, as the baccalaureate preacher. This was his final year as a seminary trustee. Sixty-one students received their degrees or diplomas. The senior breakfast was held off campus and was largely unstructured.

Many of the students were upset about Moore's leaving. Commencement morning was more like a funeral than a happy graduation time. The executive committee of the trustees had met the day before, and there was widespread interest in their action. Just before the service began, Moore approached Graves to inquire about the trustees' decision.

Moore was told that the recommendation of the administration not to continue him had been adopted unanimously. The faculty was so informed as they gathered to march into the chapel.

The record of the trustee action reads:

> It was moved by Mr. Purser Hewitt that the services of Mr. Moore as an instructor on the seminary teaching staff be discontinued following this school year as of July 31, 1966, and that President Graves give him appropriate notice of this action. . . . After full discussion the motion was approved unanimously.

The full board unanimously confirmed this action in their Detroit meeting in May. Later in the summer, by a mail ballot, they approved a recommendation by the president that Moore's salary be continued to October 31, a full six months following the official action in April.

Immediately following the commencement exercises, President Graves left for Arizona, to participate in a student retreat. He was away when, that afternoon, the *Independent-Journal* (April 29, 1966) appeared with its front-page headline, SEMINARY FIRES RIGHTS ACTIVIST. An article, written by Ellen Bry, said:

> LeRoy Moore, a teacher at Golden Gate Baptist Theological Seminary at Strawberry, has been fired by seminary trustees because of his civil rights views. . . . The ouster came as a result of his taking the lead last year in backing a student from the seminary who walked in the civil rights march to Selma, Alabama, faculty members said. . . . Other faculty members active in the rights move have tenure. Moore did not. . . . Another seminary employee sympathetic to the rights work was Carl M. Halvarson, assistant to Graves since 1960, who was replaced in January by Stanton Nash.

Since Fred Fisher was quoted in the article, he moved at once to deny some statements made to the reporter. As a result, the *I-J* headlines on Saturday, April 30, were BAPTIST OFFICIALS CLAIM TEACHER NOT REALLY FIRED. The subtitle was, "Moore says 'Ecumenical' Stand Brings Dismissal." Fisher was quoted in the article as saying that "no reason for the trustee decision would be announced." Fisher went on to say, "His service has been of a probationary nature . . . the seminary is not obligated to state cause why an instructor is not continued in service." Fisher added, in denying that Moore was dismissed for his civil rights views, that "so far as they are known, [Moore's views] are in general accord with those of the entire seminary, faculty and student body."

Apparently Moore had been unavailable to the reporter before her first story, so was quoted at length in the second article. He said,

"I regard myself as a loyal Southern Baptist. . . . But I am very much concerned about the future of the denomination. I would be most concerned to see the denomination move in an isolationist, fundamentalist, racist, provincial direction." . . . Moore is quoted as saying that "he had known since February 28, when he had a private talk with seminary president Graves, that his job was 'in danger.'" He added, "In fairness to the seminary, I should say that they were disappointed that I did not finish up my doctoral studies as quickly as had been anticipated by the faculty and myself."

Moore told his story to faculty members at the GTU in Berkeley. Many of them believed his account and carried it to the staff and executive committee of the AATS. The biennial meeting of the AATS was held in June at the Episcopal Seminary in Alexandria, Virginia. There, President Graves was lectured by the executive director, was quizzed by a member of the Accrediting Commission for two hours, and was notified that the commission was investigating further. Graves met with the special committee set up for the investigation in Dayton, Ohio. Later the committee visited Golden Gate, talked freely with many people, and wrote their report. They gave the Golden Gate administration a clean bill of health and the report was approved by the Accrediting Commission.

The trustee executive committee considered other matters at their meeting on April 28. Dobbins had completed his preliminary study on the urban church and copies were being prepared for distribution. The major thing learned in the study was that it is a big subject and needs to be studied for a long period of time. That has proved to be true. DuBose has been hard at it ever since but still keeps stirring up more questions than answers. Whatever else comes from his efforts, he has helped Southern Baptists to become more urban conscious in all areas of their work. DuBose has also been widely used by the FMB in urban studies and workshops in the major cities of the world.

The president informed the trustees of the sale of the Berkeley property and payment of the Wells Fargo note. Since that loan was at such a low interest, they had been using capital funds to build more housing. They approved a recommendation to invite the president of the alumni association to attend trustee meetings. One of the most significant discussions had to do with securing funds for the Chair of Evangelism and Missions, as living endowment. Nine thousand dollars of the necessary $12,000 annually had been pledged. It appeared that someone could be elected to the post in the Detroit meeting. The trustees acknowledged the fact that Dobbins was ending his ten years of service with Golden Gate.

The trustees met May 23 in Detroit with twenty-four trustees and Henry Blackaby, alumni president, present. They authorized borrowing up to $100,000 to build faculty/staff housing on campus. They confirmed the action of the president in accepting the resignation of Professor James McClendon and voted that a letter of "commendation for his twelve years of service and a prayerful concern for his future" be written to him. Again, what a loss. McClendon was one of the brightest minds ever to touch Golden Gate Seminary. His studies led him away from his earlier involvement with a Baptist institution. He seemed to no longer feel comfortable within the confines of that relationship.

The trustees also ratified the president's action in accepting the resignation of Carl Halvarson as assistant to the president and asked that a word of commendation be sent to him for his six years of service. Ernest Guy, chairman of the personnel committee, brought a report concerning a new statement on "Academic Freedom and Tenure," and it was approved in principle. Orine Suffern was elected as "instructor in keyboard instruments," without tenure but considered a permanent employee. While away from teaching a while, she had earned another music degree. The minutes record:

> Next they voted "That a Chair of Missions and Evangelism" be established at Golden Gate Seminary with an emphasis on reaching men in the urban community. That we set a goal of $300,000 to be secured in five years or less to fund this chair. That the chair be named by the time it has been funded. In this connection an Institute of Urban Church Life should be established to offer special training for short periods of time for those who are engaged in Urban Missions either as pastor or other worker. That the occupant of this chair be the Director of the Institute. He would seek the cooperation of the faculty, the Mission boards, the state conventions and any other sources of aid which might be available in development of this program of urban emphasis.

The trustees acted immediately to elect Francis DuBose to fill the post. They expressed appreciation for Fisher's service as acting president and for Elmer Gray's service as dean in the absence of Carleton during his semester leave. Appreciation was expressed for the service of Elwin Skiles on the board from 1950-1953 and then 1957-1966, the last two years as chairman. Ernest Guy of Tiburon was elected chairman. On his way home from Detroit, Graves went by Louisville to visit with Edward Humphrey, missionary to Nigeria for eighteen years, who was in the United States due to the illness of his wife. He agreed to teach theology. He and his wife and three children moved into one of the new three-bedroom units just completed for students during the summer, and he was on hand to teach that fall.

With the coming of DuBose to the faculty, the minds of the

seminary family were focused anew on the urban task. He would help determine the dimensions of the task and hopefully some of the challenges it presented. He had written in the *Gateway* (April/May, 1966):

> Urbanization, the process, brings people closer together physically—but, paradoxically enough, urbanism, the way of life, which result inevitably from urbanization, tends to cause greater separation of people socially.
>
> The tendency toward impersonalization and anonymity which is a by-product of the urban process compounds the already complicated problem of communicating the gospel in the heterogeneous urban culture.
>
> . . . We face the challenge of developing an evangelistic methodology which will be designed to penetrate the secular mind of urban man with the dynamic of the gospel.

The 1966 fall semester opened August 30 and Derward Deere gave the convocation address. Enrollment was just short of the previous year. Some notable enrollment trends were developing, however, with less than 20 percent of the students from east of the Mississippi River and only 50 percent from Baptist colleges. One-third of the students were from the far West. A record thirty-two foreign students were enrolled, and this trend has continued above any other SBC seminary.

When the executive committee of the trustees met in October, Graves stated that his two main concerns were increasing enrollment and financial support. In the seven years since occupying the new campus, expenditures had exceeded income by more than $150,000 and all reserves were depleted, in spite of constant efforts to reduce expenses. He said,

> Barring an occasional obvious mistake in judgment on our part, I consider these expenditures as having been necessary to remain operating. The trustees have been verifying that judgment regularly. I have sought in many ways to expand the income. Recently our burden was so dramat-

ically presented to the Executive Committee of the SBC that they began serious studies of our plight. This led to an invitation for each president to present his situation to the Program Committee of the Executive Committee of the Southern Baptist Convention on September 20 and 21.

He then outlined what he had reported to them. The campus was planned for 500 students but a maximum of 300 had enrolled. The small enrollment affected operational costs and recruitment by graduates. The location away from the main body of Southern Baptists magnified the problems of promotion and travel costs. The higher cost of almost everything in California affected the budget, as did the outlay for taxes and public services not paid elsewhere. Deficits for six of the seven years were the result. The faculty and staff had really paid the difference in their willingness to live and serve in this high cost area.

The president had closed his report to the SBC Executive Committee by listing the evidences of an effective program at Golden Gate. It had enrolled nearly 2,300 in its twenty-two years. Two-thirds of these remained in service in the West. Eight hundred and eighty-three had graduated and a third of these were in mission service. More than one-half of the churches and missions related to Southern Baptist work in California were begun by Golden Gate students and graduates.

The November/December, 1966 *Gateway* announced the program personalities for the seventh annual student missions conference to be held in February, 1967. The theme chosen was "God's Action/My Response." David Lockard of the FMB and Glendon McCullough of the HMB were to speak along with Bill Lawson, black pastor in Houston and prominent Texas Youth leader.

DuBose was making his presence felt in other ways besides the classrooms. In October he led a group of thirty-five students in a survey of a portion of San Francisco. He called San Francisco "the greatest evangelism laboratory in the western hemisphere." These "Missions in Action" programs were planned to recur several times throughout the year.

In November Dean Carleton was elected president of the Southern Baptist General Convention of California. This was the third such state convention that he had headed, having served in Illinois and Oklahoma. Carleton was the third member of the Golden Gate faculty to be chosen in California. Dr. Posey was elected in 1948 and Dr. Aulick in 1952.

The *Gateway* also listed the names of thirty-seven couples and nine single persons from Golden Gate who were known to be serving on foreign mission fields. There was also a report of the largest "G" day ever, when thirty-six students shared with churches in the Central Valley Association on November 13. Dr. Yates had written the book for the study of Amos for the January Bible Study, and the workshop for pastors was held in December. Dr. George Harrison of New Orleans Seminary, who was living on campus as he studied at Berkeley, shared in the study.

The Graveses' son, Harold K., Jr., had departed from Travis Air Force base for Vietnam on Tuesday evening, September 20, 1966. He was assigned to the 25th Division based at Chu Chi. He was given a squad and was on patrol duty by Friday night and was involved in combat almost immediately. His group engaged the enemy often in the weeks that followed. Reports concerning the 25th Division appeared often in the press and on television. The *Today* show had a "Vietnam Report" about eight o'clock each morning that often gave rather specific details.

On Monday morning, November 7, Mrs. Graves was at home alone watching this report. It concerned the action of a company from the 25th Division, and there was no doubt that it was Graves's group. The report ended with the statement, "All commissioned officers were killed or injured." I was in Abilene, Texas, attending the inauguration ceremonies of Elwin Skiles as president of Hardin-Simmons University.

Mrs. Graves called our daughter, Nancy McLaughlin, in Sacramento, and our daughter-in-law, Eileen, in Millbrae. The McLaughlins headed for Mill Valley but bought a newspaper along the way. It carried a story about the battle in Vietnam, quoting the Graves's son by name and address as he described the battle. When I arrived in San Francisco that evening, the whole family met me and told me the story. No word had been received from the Army, so we were encouraged.

The Graveses were in Hawaii on Wednesday for the Hawaii Baptist Convention. The home base for the 25th Division was there, so many wives and friends attended the meetings. Chaplains for the Pacific area checked through military channels open to them and could not find Graves's name on any casualty list, so there was further encouragement.

On Monday, the wife of a chaplain with the 25th called to tell the Graveses that a letter from her husband told of their son being in the Sunday service. They later learned that his wounds were superficial and that he was soon back at his post. A few weeks later he was selected as an aide to a brigadier general and spent the rest of his year in that capacity. The Graveses were relieved until they learned that he spent much of the time in a helicopter. Lieutenant Graves's write up of his captain and his sergeant gained for each of them the Congressional Medal of Honor. He himself received the Silver Star. After his discharge, he was flown to Washington to be present at the White House when the President awarded the medals to his comrades.

When the six seminary presidents met for their workshop in late November and shared enrollment, the total was down more than a hundred. All schools had lost except Southern. Representatives of the program committee of the SBC Executive Committee invited themselves to talk formula with the presidents for a whole day. Four questions were discussed: (1) Is a formula desirable? (2) Who should administer it? (3) Can it be modified? (4) When and by whom can it be reworked? The presidents agreed that a formula was desirable and needed to be administered by them, but perhaps they needed to seek the counsel of outsiders to study and revise it. Lawrence Wilsey of the Booz, Allen, and Hamilton firm met with them in January, 1967 and was asked to propose a plan. The SBC Executive Committee agreed to finance the study.

The spring semester at Golden Gate opened January 3, 1967. I delivered the convocation address at the request of the faculty. It occurred to me that since it had been almost fifteen years since I was inaugurated, I decided to look at my first address to see if it was still relevant. It proved to be a profitable experience, at least for me. Essentially, I repeated much of the 1952 inaugural address, updating the statistics, then sought to draw helpful comparisons:

> Reading over these words after nearly fifteen years has been a sobering experience. First of all, I am moved with gratitude when I think of the goodness of God in providing what we have—in faculty and staff—in buildings and grounds—in library and other materials of study. But above all, I am grateful for the most priceless gift of all—dedicated men and women who have been prepared and gone forth to serve around the world. . . .
>
> . . . My major concerns of fifteen years ago have not been changed. God's word is basic to our message. Evangelistic concern is the heart of our task for man's basic need is spiritual, whether he lives in the favored United States, in war-torn Asia, or the jungles of South America or Africa. This is not to deny that men have other needs and that as Christian men and women we have obligations toward them. It is to say, however, that unless the Christian's message carries this redemptive quality there is no group on earth with the answer to the basic need of mankind. . . .
>
> Finally, I am even more convinced that our message must be relevant to man's felt needs. . . .
>
> I believe that I have come to a new insight into the underlying drive of our generation. I have quoted Dr. Carmichael as saying that men lack commitment. If that was true fifteen years ago, I am sure that it has made a striking change for many lives today. Students, if not their professors, want something to live for and even to die for.

. . . Men want to believe in something that demands, that costs something, that may even demand death.

I have seen these youth. . . . In many respects they are youth and energy in search of a cause. . . . We have the answer to their search.

I sought to reemphasize the historic characteristic of Golden Gate—evangelism and missions—in light of a constantly changing community. I was still pleading for a combination of a disciplined mind and a warm heart. When enrollment was completed, there was a drop of ten from the year before. It had varied only twenty-three in five years.

At the end of convocation week, I flew to Wichita, Kansas, to lead the January Bible Study at the Metropolitan Baptist Church and serve as the Bible teacher for the state evangelistic conference. On the following Friday, just before I was to leave my room I received a call from my wife. Coming at a peculiar time, I knew something was wrong. Was it about our son in Vietnam? She spoke calmly and with amazing composure as she reported that our home had been burglarized. Silver, jewelry, cameras, TV, and the like were gone—taken in broad daylight. She was calm because, by comparison, it was not the worst news she could be sharing. These things could be replaced, but our son could not.

In the loss of the silver, much of it given by loving parishioners and other friends during our pastorates, we lost our tools for entertainment which had to be replaced. The loss was estimated in dollar value to be near four thousand dollars at 1967 prices but in sentiment—priceless, but again, not as valuable as persons. She could have returned home while the thieves were there, to her own hurt. Anxiety for our son relaxed in September of that year, when he called from Travis Air Base to say, "Come and get me. I'm home," a week early.

The Student Missions Conference was held in February with more than 600 in attendance, even though restricted to college and college-age youth. In addition to those already mentioned, the program included Walter Delamarter who spoke on the world of the seventies and eighties, saying of love, "It is easier to say the word than to be the word." David Lockard said, "A God who cares can never be represented by persons who don't care." It was definitely a missions conference. Even though much of the thrust of the conference was to vocational mission work, more emphasis was placed on the individual's need to share his Christian witness.

Isam Hodges was memorialized in a service held March 7, 1967. A week later, during the meeting of the trustees, a memorial service was held on campus with Floyd Looney delivering the address. God had called to his reward a soldier of the cross who had labored long and hard in the Master's service.

In the opening session of the annual trustee meeting, Graves repeated much of his convocation address, along with appropriate remarks concerning the current situation. Significant actions by the trustees included electing J. B. Nichols as dean of students, with a job description that included the field work Royal had been directing. Nichols was to work with the students on and off campus, administer student aid, assist with jobs and off-campus housing, and so forth. This was a continuation of the effort to use Nichols in the best way possible. He was concerned for people and very approachable by the students.

Edward Humphrey was elected to the faculty as associate professor of historical theology and reference librarian. A native of North Carolina, Humphrey held degrees from Wake Forest University and Southern Seminary. He had taught in the Nigerian Baptist Seminary for eighteen years. Trustees also raised the allocation for faculty retirement from 8 to 10 percent of faculty and administrative staff salaries.

In a chapel talk, Geil Davis reacted to the situation she had found on the USC campus while on her study leave during the previous session:

> Today's youth seek to champion causes designed to have Social Shock Value—evidenced by dress, grooming or absence of it, sex attitudes and slogans. All of these are

negatively expressed and . . . are adopted because of their ability to shock the established generation. . . .

Among the interesting attitudes I observed among the youth . . . was one of admiration for the "intellectual" by their definition. . . . An intellectual could talk forever in generalities, raising questions, talking in a vague world of philosophic double-talk. . . . The admired "intellectual" stated his outlooks concerning life without ever committing himself on anything. . . . The "intellectual" by student definition . . . committed to noncommitment.

Let me invite you to take a trip to the "we know" land of 1 John in the New Testament. For this trip you need no LSD but you will have a spiritual experience. By this I mean that I am challenging you to trade the "NO" attitude of your youth toward those values already established for the "KNOW" attitude of 1 John.

Baccalaureate preacher for commencement exercises was Robert Hughes, executive secretary of the state convention, whose son John received his Bachelor of Divinity degree. The senior breakfast was addressed by Ernest Guy, trustee chairman. Mrs. Graves awarded the PHT's (Put Hubby Through degrees) to the wives of graduates, and Ken Bolinger welcomed the graduates into the alumni association. President Graves awarded degrees and diplomas to fifty-nine in the service that followed.

Changes in the faculty came with the resignation of Elmer Gray to go to the Baptist Sunday School Board (BSSB) in Nashville and the retirement of Brown. In the June, 1967 meeting in Miami at the SBC, the trustees elected Richard Cunningham as assistant professor of systematic theology and philosophy of religion and Roger Skelton as professor of religious education. Cunningham was a graduate of Baylor and Southern Seminary. He was then serving as Baptist student director at the University of New Mexico. Skelton had been on the staff of the Baptist Sunday School Board for nine years after several years on church staffs. He was a graduate of Mississippi College and Southwestern Baptist Seminary.

The trustees approved the construction of a ten-unit faculty/staff housing village, Platt Court, and a plan to convert the cafeteria into a full-fledged student center. The administration was asked to study the possibility of a pedestrian bridge between the student center and the dormitories to encourage use of the center by the single students—part of the effort to improve morale.

The fall semester opened August 29 with C. A. Insko as the convocation speaker. While enrollment was again down, growth was being recorded in the number of students from the Western states, as well as from state university graduates. CBC provided thirty-eight students but Grand Canyon only nine. It is noticeable that Bethany College (Assembly of God) provided six and Simpson Bible College (CMA) provided eight. There was a significant upward trend for non-Baptists and foreign students. Several of the brightest students were among these and their influence was being felt.

Physical improvements on the campus were significant as the students returned. The children's playground had appeared where the old "Fort Mason" corporation yard had been. A commuter room and faculty lounge had been added in Conner Hall. The student center conversion was soon to be finished. The pedestrian bridge would be completed before the end of the semester due to the generosity of Mr. and Mrs. Guy Rutland, Jr.

The executive committee of the trustees met in October with the remaining members of the campus building committee. E. H. Westmoreland brought the Founders' Day address. He and John Raley were the only members of the building committee who could attend. Graves suggested that Golden Gate seek accreditation by the Western Association of Schools and Colleges, the regional agency for California. In this regard, he spoke at length about the trends he saw in theological education in America:

> Theological education continues to be a complex operation and, with all education in America, seems to be presently in a most confusing stage. . . . The degree name is the

least of the problems, in my judgment. The M.Div. may or
may not win acceptance.

The basic questions in theological education have to do
with curriculum content, cooperative use of resources for
basic content construction, and the relation of this whole
process to liberal arts education.

Most attention is now being given to the matter of
cooperative efforts between seminaries, usually located
near a university. The GTU in Berkeley was one of the first in
this latest wave of such efforts.

It is interesting to note how the GTU had developed in the
years since 1967. It had definitely taken on the image of
graduate studies in religion, rather than training for ministry.
The San Francisco Seminary tried to offer their first two years
of work in Berkeley and almost lost their identity in San
Anselmo. They changed the program to offer the first year in
San Anselmo as well as the third. Berkeley Baptist almost
went out of existence and remains on shaky ground. A
common library has developed, housed at CDSP, but the
Pacific School of Religion has never surrendered its books. A
new library building, in the planning stage for many years,
has just been completed and occupied.

Graves reported the serious illness of A. J. Hyatt, librarian.
In light of his condition, the trustees approved the search for
an acting librarian to be employed by March 1, 1968. Hyatt
died on November 7, 1967, and a memorial service was held
for him in the seminary chapel on the tenth. He had served
as librarian since 1956, after having taught New Testament
1947 to 1951.

In the presidents workshop in late November, the central
topic was again "revision of the formula." There was general
agreement on chapters 1—3 of the document presented by
the consultants, Wilsey and Harness. Revisions were proposed for chapter 4, and the presidents approved it in
December. They agreed to ask for a sharp increase in the
allocations for 1969, based on these new studies. Wilsey
stated that if the allocation varied more than 10 percent from

the request called for in the formula, it would not work. When they met with the special committee in January, 1968, even though some committee members expressed doubts that the formula could be funded 100 percent the first year, they accepted the proposed formula in principle.

When the presidents learned in February that the allocation was not nearly enough to fund the formula, they set it aside for the year and decided to distribute the allocation arbitrarially. Golden Gate's allocation was up only slightly. The struggle for existence continued.

The missions conference held in February, 1968 had as the theme: "Before You—An Open Door." Bill Sherman, Woodmont Baptist Church, Nashville; Glendon McCullough, HMB; Frances Dawkins, FMB; and E. J. Combs, California convention were featured. More than 500 were in attendance. Still concerned about the emphasis, the faculty voted in March: "That Dr. Yates meet with the student council for conference concerning the missions conference (what can be done to be more effective in future conferences, clarification of certain problems, etc., and to provide some guidelines)."

Preliminary guidelines for the missions conference, presented to the faculty in April, placed responsibility with a joint faculty and student committee.

President Graves and Dean Carleton attended their first meeting of the Western Association of Schools and Colleges (WASC) in Sacramento, March 7-8, 1968. They made contacts that were to prove valuable in preparation for accreditation.

When the trustees gathered in March for their annual meeting, Graves took considerable time to explain the proposed new formula. As he talked of purpose, objectives, goals, and a philsophy of theological education, he closed by saying:

> What, then, is the Southern Baptist pattern of theological education? First of all, we have done our theological education in separate schools—separate from the university . . . and separate from other denominations. . . . the *second* thing I would say . . . is that it is to be biblically and

theologically based . . . and the *third* . . . is that theological education is definitely to be church-oriented.

Other matters reported by the president included the fact that Golden Gate had been accepted as a candidate for accreditation by the WASC. The seminary had received a notation from AATS for having too many students without college degrees (13.6 percent), most of these being wives of students. In the SBC capital needs budget being proposed, the library was not funded, but $150,000 was allocated for completion of village #1. This was only half of the housing request but with it came the suggestion that the trustees borrow to complete the project, to be repaid out of rentals. Members of the SBC Executive Committee felt that 50 percent might be borrowed. The president was convinced that no more than 30 percent should be borrowed in light of high costs, high interest rates, and low rents. This has proven to be true.

Paul Hamm had been employed as librarian and was in U.C., Berkeley to earn his Master of Library Science degree. The library had 66,000 items, and the circulation for the year was up. In other personnel changes, Royal was to retire July 31 after twenty-two years of service to Golden Gate. Both he and Mrs. Royal had served well in the classroom, in the churches, and in their community. Clyde Beasley continued to suffer the effects of his second bad automobile accident and asked to be relieved as business manager by July 31.

The trustees voted to authorize up to $5,000 to be spent in observing the twenty-fifth anniversary of the seminary during the 1968-1969 session. Harrop was promoted to full professor and DuBose given tenure. They improved the insurance program for the faculty and staff. In the new budget, a valiant effort was being made to stay near the salary level of the other SBC seminaries, holding out the hope of even exceeding it because of being in the highest cost-of-living area in the country.

At the faculty-trustee dinner, tribute was paid to Edward Landels, the seminary attorney for more than fifteen years, and personnel from the Wells Fargo Bank. Bank officers present included James Dobey, vice-president, who was so helpful in securing the construction loan.

Graves was often heard to say during these days that he didn't miss the pastorate as much as he had anticipated. Students and graduates had replaced parishioners. He saw graduates almost everywhere he went and, for many of them, there was a whole series of incidents to remember. In the January/February, 1968 issue of *Gateway*, he wrote of what he had witnessed in the past fifteen years:

> One of the joys I have is to be reminded often of the part the seminary is playing in this work. At a conference or convention in the West, our graduates lead, make judgments, give themselves wholeheartedly to the task of advance. As I see them, I remember from where they came— one from Georgia, another from Illinois, a couple from Kentucky, and another from Tennessee. I read of a couple going to Africa and I remember seeing them at a college in Texas, at the seminary, then at a church at work here in the West—now to service overseas.
>
> I visit with a young oil company executive on Long Island, see him next in the seminary across America working as a janitor to buy groceries, then see him and his family off to the Orient where God called with a need his experience could meet.

Commencement exercises were held April 19, earlier than usual because many of the seminary family were involved in the Crusade of the Americas evangelistic campaign. Milton DuPriest, pastor of the Beech Street Baptist Church, Texarkana, Arkansas, was the commencement speaker. By faculty action, no baccalaureate was held the night before. President Graves awarded degrees to fifty-nine graduates and then gave a charge to them.

When the trustees met in Houston in June, 1968 at the SBC, Graves reported on several items of business. Dr. and Mrs. H. I. Hester of Liberty, Missouri, had endowed a lectureship in preaching to begin spring, 1969. The survey of music needs in California was moving ahead and would climax with a conference in September. The Library of Congress cataloging system was being studied as a way to reduce costs and to better correlate with the GTU libraries. The AATS would meet that month and the resources planning report would be of extreme interest, as it might set new guidelines of cooperation.

The AATS met at Concordia Seminary in Clayton, Missouri, June 11, 1968. They adopted the resources planning report that almost mandated the association of each school with a university. The Roman Catholic seminary representatives were present in force for the first time. They represented schools that were mostly associate members. Had their status been properly clarified by President Moss, many believe they would have voted on the above issue and it would not have carried. As it turned out, no one paid any attention to the action anyway. All the Southern Baptist seminary presidents opposed it.

On July 15 Eugene V. England began service as the business manager of the seminary. He came from Costa Mesa, having served also at Compton and Hawthorne since being graduated from the seminary in 1956.

A new program was inaugurated for the Golden Gate faculty when a pre-school retreat was arranged on campus, beginning on Friday, August 30. The wives were not included, but the idea caught on and it was decided that such a retreat including the spouses should be held annually off campus. This has been the policy since.

The fall semester opened Tuesday, September 3, with the enrollment up nearly 23 percent over the previous year, at 295, the highest since 1960. There were some notable reasons for the increase. The number of international students doubled to total 56. Seventeen of the 38 in the Tuesday evening class on the "Urban Church in the Racially Changing Community" were new and taking only that class. An additional 19 (12 army chaplains and 7 pastors) were added through a

Master of Theology seminar at Fort Ord. However, the number of regular seminary students was increasing in all of the SBC seminaries.

The opening convocation address was delivered by J. Ithel Jones, principal of Wales Baptist College, and president of the Baptist Union of Great Britain and Ireland. Lecturers for the Missions 103 (Urban Church in a Racially Changing Community) included Raymond Harvey of Tuskegee, Alabama; Paul Gillespie, pastor, Takoma Park Baptist Church, Washington, D.C.; and Victor Glass and Paul Adkins of the HMB.

The Fort Ord seminar grew out of a desire of the post chaplain, Colonel William R. Hett, and his associates to take advantage of an opportunity for continuing education. The cooperative effort was opened with much fanfare on September 29 with the post commander attending the convocation. Graves spoke at what was announced in a printed program as the "First Annual Convocation." What was the first proved to be the last, however. Hett was reassigned, and his successor did not continue the program. The seminars were moved elsewhere, some of them to the Golden Gate campus. Eight or ten of the men who began did complete work for the Master of Theology degree, one of them a Roman Catholic chaplain.

On September 26 Derward Deere suffered a coronary attack and was placed in the intensive care unit of Marin General Hospital where he remained for three weeks.

October 16 was Founders' Day. B. O. Herring, the second president, spoke. He and Mrs. Herring came from Waco, Texas, for a day of renewed fellowship with the institution he had served for six years, 1946-1952. He spoke of the happenings of his term of service, including the move to Berkeley and the adoption of the seminary by the SBC.

Mrs. Howard V. Platt of Ventura participated in the ribboncutting ceremony opening Platt Court. This complex of faculty/staff housing was made possible through her generous support, though most of the cost would be paid for through rentals. Cecil Pearson of the California Baptist

Foundation was present and told the trustee executive committee of Mrs. Platt's establishment of a trust in favor of the
seminary. She had been encouraged in this action by C. F.
Harwell, longtime friend and trustee of the seminary.

Graves began his report to the trustees by stating that the
seminary was in its twenty-fifth year of operation. He then
reported the completion of the new Faculty/Staff Manual
which codified the rules, regulations, and customs affecting
those employed in the operation of the seminary. The study
of the need for a music program in the seminary had been
completed, and there seemed to be a developing need for
full-time music directors in California churches. Also with a
new rule in AATS calling for each visiting team to have a
NASM representative for schools offering a music degree,
the entire accreditation of the seminary could be affected.

After much discussion, the trustees voted that:

> In order that the president may be guided to put a
> proposition together and to talk to prospective candidates
> . . . that the music program of the seminary be modified by
> eliminating the BCM degree, as such, and that there be such
> appropriate changes in the MCM degree as will adequately
> meet NASM standards, and that we bring Dr. Bennett's
> successor as soon as possible (1) to assure the highest
> quality MCM degree, (2) to offer public relations benefits,
> and (3) to provide a smoother transition of personnel when
> Dr. and Mrs. Bennett retire.

The November/December, 1968 *Gateway* announced the
program for the ninth annual student missions conference to
be held in January, 1969. The theme was, "Mission in a
Revolutionary Age." Program personalities included Nathan
Porter, HMB; Baker J. Cauthen, FMB; Ron Willis, pastor of
Golden Gate Baptist Church, Oakland, and HMB worker in
Haight-Ashbury, San Francisco; and E. V. Hill, pastor of
Mount Zion Baptist Church in south central Los Angeles.
Theme interpretations were written and produced by Mike
England and Larry Storer, seminary students. All seminars
to be offered had *revolution* in their titles. Some of the

seminary family saw in the plans much of diagnosis but wondered what cures might be offered.

Derward Deere died on November 11. Graves learned of his death while attending the South Carolina convention and returned home to participate in the memorial service on the thirteenth. Deere had served Golden Gate Seminary for eighteen years, making the Old Testament live for hundreds of people in the classroom and in the churches. J. W. Watts was enlisted to assist in Old Testament for the spring semester.

The annual workshop for the SBC seminary presidents in December, 1968 was delayed in opening due to the late arrival of Leo Eddleman because of illness and Duke McCall due to an unplanned excursion to Havana, Cuba, when his plane was hijacked. Once all the presidents arrived, they faced the task of selecting a new director for the SED. They sought to determine the future direction the department should take. The pattern of scattered field men was changed to provide for a smaller staff in the Nashville office.

The presidents voted to use chapter 4 of the Booz, Allen, and Hamilton study as a basis for the 1970 request for allocation of Cooperative Program funds. Had the formula been funded Golden Gate would have received nearly $600,000, but the figure was only $535,000 in February decisions. This represented an increase of only $50,000 in three years.

With the opening of the spring semester in January, 1969, the enrollment for the year climbed to 361, the highest since moving to the new campus and second highest in the twenty-five-year history of the seminary. Foreign students accounted for sixty-two, and forty-six students (some of them internationals) were other than Southern Baptist, representing twenty-six denominations. There was much excitement as the twenty-fifth year developed. Even though 1969 was the final year of the searching sixties, many still had doubts about the place of the church in those revolutionary times.

That spirit continued to be highlighted in the student

missions conference. The theme interpretation for the opening session consisted of a slide show depicting the life of Abraham Lincoln, Martin Luther King, and John F. Kennedy while a popular song, "Abraham, Martin, and John" was being played. At the conclusion of the song and in total darkness, a gunshot broke the silence. The second theme interpretation was a combination of an original reading and the playing of another popular hit song, "Peace, Brother, Peace." Revolution and revolt were impressed on the more than four hundred in attendance.

Ron Willis spoke of the failure of the established church, and in spite of all Nathan Porter and Baker J. Cauthen could say, those in attendance were given a strong dose of diagnosis of problems and revolts. Little information was given to direct them regarding positive action they could take. Many felt that the Student Missions Conference was still not entirely back on track as a missions conference.

Later in February, Graves reported to the other seminary presidents on the progress toward offering additional training for pastors in Los Angeles, especially for blacks. A program was being arranged to offer courses on three levels at the Calvary Baptist Church in the fall: (1) Extension materials of the American Baptist Seminary, (2) SED materials, and (3) seminary level work. The presidents agreed that Golden Gate needed to investigate and act at its discretion in light of previous decisions with reference to work in Los Angeles. Raymond Rigdon became the new director of SED, launching the department in a new direction of truly effective service.

The official celebration of the twenty-fifth anniversary of the Golden Gate Seminary was held the week of March 10, 1969. The trustees and members of the development council were on hand. W. A. Carleton delivered the historical address on Tuesday. W. A. Criswell, president of the SBC, addressed the dinner for the faculty, trustees, and development council members on Wednesday evening. He also addressed chapel on Thursday.

The silver anniversary theme was central in the report

Graves made to the trustees. In his seventeenth annual report, he stressed progress along many lines: enrollment, property values (now beyond $6,500,000), and library holdings (now at more than 70,000 volumes). Fourteen of the teaching force of twenty-five had been with the seminary more than twelve years. More than one thousand men and women had received degrees or other awards at the twenty commencement exercises.

In discussing the continuing effort on the part of the seminary presidents and others in working out statements of purpose, objectives, and goals, Graves quoted President Pusey of Harvard:

> "Professional education and graduate education never melded completely until the twentieth century and even now exist . . . in uneasy alliance. It is a truism that a professional school that is not a graduate school is always in danger of being little more than a trade school or a school for technicians. On the other hand a professional school that is a graduate school is always being tempted into the pursuit of scholarship to the neglect of the practical needs of the profession it was established to serve; and it rationalizes the neglect by insisting that the profession it serves must be a learned profession. So a question remains as to the proper nature of a graduate professional school, that widely admired and needed hybrid which is required to be two things at once and is continuously in danger of being neither."[2]

Graves then turned to the matter of support for Golden Gate a being of major concern for trustees and council members as they participated in the development workshop. He dramatized the support picture for the six SBC seminaries by use of a chart. The Cooperative Program provided more than 91 percent of Golden Gate's income. For Southern, only 50 percent came from this source.

Trustee actions included the election of Wayne Peterson as associate professor of Old Testament. Peterson, a native of Texas, was graduated from the University of Corpus Christi and Southwestern Seminary and had taught at Ouachita and

Members of the seminary's Administrative Council in 1969 included, seated from left, Dean W. A. Carleton, President Harold K. Graves and Business Manager Eugene V. England. Standing, from left, are Assistant to the President Stanton H. Nash and Dean of Students J. B. Nichols.

at Louisiana College. The trustees also approved the use of student evaluations for faculty improvement.

A special sixteen-page issue of the *Gateway* (January/February, 1969) was produced by Stanton Nash and his office to help celebrate the twenty-fifth anniversary. Pictures of former presidents and faculty, as well as previous buildings, appeared with those of current personalities and present campus. Graves wrote of "Seven Significant Steps in Golden Gate History" and Carleton wrote of "Echoes from the Past," concerning Baptist beginnings in California in the mid-nineteenth century.

The first series of lectures on preaching made possible by the generous gift of Dr. and Mrs. H. I. Hester was held March 24-28. Theodore F. Adams was the preacher. Mrs. Adams accompanied him. Dr. and Mrs. Hester were also present, renewing fellowship with seminary classmates, the J. W. Wattses, who were on campus while Watts assisted in Old Testament.

Commencement exercises were held for the sixty-six graduates on May 9, with W. Eugene Grubbs, executive secretary of the Washington-Oregon convention, as the speaker.

During the SBC meeting in New Orleans, the trustees met and Graves announced the resignation of Kyle Yates, Jr., to go to the department of religion of Oklahoma State University. He had taught at Golden Gate for seventeen years. The trustees expressed appreciation for that service. Graves reminded them that Carleton would retire in 1970. Pearce was also looking toward early retirement then. Including music, this meant four faculty members were being sought. The trustees had to decide if they would seek maturity and experience, requiring that the people take large cuts in income or go after promising younger men. Often a young man on the faculty would urge the administration to seek out men who had already earned a reputation. "Great if they can be found," they were told, and then they were often reminded that it was men of reputation who were being sought when they were added.

Twenty-five years have been completed by Golden Gate

Seminary. What will be her lot in the next twenty-five? The remaining question which is ever present is, how can more support be enlisted? The Golden Gate story must be told, over and over again.

Notes

1. From Philip Larkin, "Church Going."
2. Nathan M. Pusey and Charles L. Taylor, *Ministry for Tomorrow,* Seabury Press, N.Y., 1967, pp. 118-119.

6

Upward to New Heights

Golden Gate Seminary had occupied its permanent campus for ten years as it entered its second quarter century. It was becoming a mature member of the academic community, even though many of its dreams had not been realized. Growth in enrollment and in the music program had not reached expectations. The financial struggle continued, and population growth in Marin County had accentuated the problem of housing for both faculty and students.

The seventies brought significant progress in the realization of hopes for enrollment gains and in the development of the program of church music. It took several years for this to become apparent; but by the middle of the decade, the upward trend was set. Prospects in financial support were brighter as well.

In contrast to the searching sixties, this decade might possibly even be characterized as the settling seventies. Enrollment gains and maturing California Baptist churches brought their own problems, but a solidly structured seminary was set on finding some answers.

Jack Manning was the convocation speaker when the 1969 fall semester opened. Fewer were enrolled in the Fort Ord seminars, but more students—significantly more college graduates—were on campus than the year before. Southern Baptist colleges were now providing 40 percent of the students. Only three were enrolled for music degrees and these were foreign students. Serious thought was being given to discontinuing a degree program in music for a period and providing for that emphasis in combination with the Master of Religious Education degree.

The Earl Martins of Tanzania were the missionaries in residence for the year. Jack Finegan of the Pacific School of Religion offered a course in archaeology. The beginning of a possible major in social work was made with the offering of one course. Royal was the Founders' Day speaker, recalling some exciting events in the Golden Gate/California Baptist history following World War II.

Enrollment for the 1970 spring semester was enough to push the accumulative total for the year up to 366, just 5 above the previous year. This was almost 100 more than two years before, but most of that growth was due to the enrollment of 61 international and 69 non-Baptist students. Eliminating the overlap, these represented 30 percent of the total. In 10 years students from California had grown in number from 20 to 92. The number from Texas and Oklahoma dropped significantly.

The 1970 student missions conference had as its theme "Odessey: Journey into Mission." In speaking to that theme, Ed Seabough of the HMB said, "If Jesus is to be taken to the world, we can't just protest and demonstrate. We as Christians must become sensitive to persons in need." Other personnel participating in the conference included Wimpy Smith, FMB, and Ernest Guy, professor in U.C. Medical School and seminary trustee chairman. More than 600 attended one or more of the sessions of the conference. Graves, who was unable to attend the conference, reported to the trustees in March, "The Missions Conference stirred things up and in general was considered effective, but with some strong negative overtones." There was still concern that the commitment to missions had been somewhat lost in their effort to "Journey into Mission."

Central concerns for the seminary presidents workshop January 12-15, 1970 were, as usual, distribution of funds and matters having to do with accrediting groups. They adopted a request that the SBC Executive Committee attempt to fund the new formula requirements with no more than a 12½ percent shortfall for 1971. A total allocation of $6,000,000 was called for. This was $1,325 per student compared to an average of nearly $3,200 for other AATS schools during the current year.

When the seminary presidents gathered in Nashville a month later, James Mosteller was acting president of New Orleans, following Leo Eddleman's resignation. Naylor asked for sufficient budget from the six schools to prepare an audio-visual presentation of the seminaries' report to the SBC meeting in Denver. When word came from the Executive Committee about the allocation to theological education for 1971, Graves learned that Golden Gate would receive an increase of only $20,000. The struggle continued.

The HMB conducted a Convention-wide Pioneer Missions Colloquium on the Golden Gate campus, February 23-27, 1970. Two hundred and fifty men attended, largely from the Western portion of the US including Alaska and Hawaii. HMB personnel participating included Kenneth Chaffin, recently elected director of evangelism.

Bishop Gerald Kennedy of the Methodist Church from Los Angeles was the speaker for the H. I. Hester Lectureship on Preaching, held March 3-6. Several pastors, as well as a number of Southern Baptist chaplains from the West, attended.

When the trustees gathered for their annual meeting in March 12-13, 1970, Graves began his report by recounting the history of the American Association of Theological Schools. He had attended his first AATS meeting in 1954. He spoke of happenings since:

> That was the first year of the student "trial year" funding and the selection of a staff to direct it. A full-time staff was in the making for AATS with funding from a foundation. In 1956 this became a fact with the election of Charles Taylor as the first director.
>
> New schools were being added yearly as Theological Education launched out to expand in order to meet the promised enrollments and support that seemed guaranteed.

. . . The famous Niebuhr study was completed and its findings published in 1956. Everybody just knew we were in for a great and wonderful new day.

Libraries grew, faculty fellowships were provided on a broad basis, and the whole philosophy was to maintain a small student-to-faculty ratio, on a small isolated campus. Bigness was a sin, and each institution was encouraged to develop its own program.

In 1968 AATS adopted guidelines that called for large schools, or rather the clustering of schools about a large university center. In 1970 they were now talking about the basic degree being the Doctor of Ministry degree.

Graves went on to recount how enrollments began to drop in 1957-1958, just as Southern Baptists were opening a new seminary. Then came the lumping of the six seminaries together by the SBC Executive Committee, forcing the presidents to divide the allocation. One formula came after another, all efforts to do the impossible—divide an inadequate amount of money in an equitable manner. The new formula adopted in 1968 was good only if it had been fully funded; failing that, Golden Gate suffered.

Graves reported to the trustees that the search for a dean was being centered on persons who might also fill a vacancy in the faculty. At the faculty/trustee dinner, special honor was paid to Carleton and Pearce in view of their retirement. Proper resolutions were read which had been prepared by the public relations and development committee.

Graves introduced the problem caused by the heavy load of non-Baptist students. The trustees requested that he approach the executives of denominations represented in large numbers in the student body and ask them for possible assistance. (A negative response was received from each.) They voted also to limit the number of non-Baptists to the present proportions and raised the possibility of a charge to these students.

J. Kenneth Eakins was elected as assistant professor of Old Testament and archaeology. Eakins, also a physician, would give some time to a medical practice in connection with the

Kaiser hospital system. He began service June 1, 1970. A native of Missouri, Eakins had his Bachelor of Science degree from Wheaton, his medical degree from University of Illinois, and his Bachelor of Divinity and Doctor of Theology degrees from Southern Seminary. Carleton was asked to give two-thirds of his time the next school session as director of admissions, some teaching, and service as chairman of the self-study committee for reaffirmation of accreditation.

March 23-28 was a free week on the campus as many students and members of the faculty participated in evangelistic efforts in the churches. Early in April Graves called Elmer Gray and asked him to consider returning to the seminary as dean and to teach religious education. After talks with the faculty and administration, Gray and they became convinced that he should return and it was proposed to the trustees. They voted by mail ballot to elect him.

One of the most interesting student body elections ever held came during the spring of 1970. For the first time a slate was prepared. A campaign by one candidate was launched with many promises of changes in seminary life. Some students on the slate were quite militant. Another candidate for president was a quiet, serious-minded mission volunteer from Indiana. His campaign was carried out through visiting each student on campus.

The result was a landslide in favor of the quiet candidate. That vote was interpreted to mean that students wanted to continue in the central task of preparing to proclaim the gospel. They would seek to change the world through seeking first to change people. This spirit was eventually to change the emphasis of the missions conference as well.

In this connection, action by the faculty on March 9, 1970 is significant:

> Motion made and seconded that we ask the Special Events Committee to draw up a statement of purpose for the Mission Conference, in consultation with representatives from the Student Council . . . , to be adopted by the faculty and thereafter to be binding upon both the faculty and the student body, and that the future of the Mission Conference

be dependent upon the adoption of an acceptable statement of policy by the faculty.—Approved.

The faculty committee prepared the document requested and presented it to the faculty for their consideration in April. In brief, it stated that the "Golden Gate Mission Conference is a Christian conference for seminary and college-age young people which is designed to confront students with the opportunity and challenge of the Christian mission in our time, and to help them seek to know God's will in carrying out this mission." That was the beginning of a long document which spelled out detailed purposes, responsibilities, and emphases. Guidelines approved earlier were revised and updated. A missions conference steering committee was called for. Cunningham was asked to serve as chairman to represent the faculty.

Several interesting personalities appeared in chapel in April. Among them were Dr. and Mrs. Herbert Caudill, who related stories of their long years in Cuba. Caudill and his son-in-law David Fite had spent several years in a Cuban jail. G. W. Anderson of Edinburgh also spoke. Commencement exercises were held for seventy-five graduates on May 1. Roy C. McClain, president of Wayland Baptist College, was the principal speaker at the graduation.

The biennial meeting of AATS was held in Claremont, June 16-19. President Graves, Dean-elect Gray, and Business Manager England attended. At that meeting the Doctor of Ministry degree was approved by AATS, but not as the basic degree some had advocated. When the SBC seminary presidents met, they agreed to confer in the fall for more specific planning. Most were convinced that the Doctor of Ministry degree would be a drawing card for entering Master of Divinity degree students. If that were to be true, no SBC seminary dared not offer it. The Golden Gate faculty was reluctant to begin the Doctor of Ministry program because they felt it would require the elimination of the Master of Theology program. They thought that students would prefer the Doctor of Ministry degree to the Master of Theology degree.

Both the faculty and administration later questioned this assumption. There was a vast difference in the purpose of the two degree programs. In any event, the Golden Gate faculty voted to add the Doctor of Ministry program and drop the Master of Theology program. The Doctor of Ministry program proved not to be popular for current students, and few remained for it after earning their Master of Divinity degrees. It did prove to be a marvelous tool for continuing education. Many experienced pastors have profited greatly from the study required to earn the Doctor of Ministry degree.

The 1970 fall program brought an innovation in the schedule. The session began with a four-week September term with an emphasis on incoming students and short-term classes for upper classmen. Both beginning Hebrew and Greek were offered, the former through the use of the language laboratory, a gift from the 1970 graduating class. The new students also spent considerable time in orientation. Videotape equipment was available for the first time.

Besides the addition of Gray and Eakins, others assisting in instruction included Gordon Green, a recent STD graduate in preaching from Golden Gate and Nobel Brown, visiting professor in New Testament. The faculty retreat held September 10-12 at Asilomar featured Albert McClellan, who spoke on current and future trends of Southern Baptists and how these affect the seminary.

A new evangelism project was begun in October, promoted jointly by the seminary, the California convention, and the HMB. Student evangelism teams were organized and scheduled in the churches. Harry Williams of the state convention, Nathan Porter of the HMB, along with Manning and Peterson of the faculty, assisted in a training period. James McAtee, a student, was principal organizer of the teams. Their aim was to use weekends in the churches to (1) win youth and (2) challenge youth in the churches to a deeper spiritual commitment and involvement in personal witnessing.

The fall quarter opened September 30 with a convocation

address by Edward Humphrey. When the enrollment had been completed, it was learned that there were ninety-six new students on campus. The slight drop in the total was due to the discontinuing of the Tuesday night class on the urban church and the Fort Ord seminars, plus tighter controls used at admission time for non-Baptist and international students.

S. G. Posey was the speaker for Founders' Day, October 14, 1970. The trustee executive committee met on the fifteenth. Graves reported that there was an effort to combine some funds to establish a Derward W. Deere lectureship on biblical and theological studies. He also reported that the twenty-two acres of tide lots and five acres of land, cut off from the central campus by Seminary Drive at the southwest corner, had been placed on the county tax rolls. The trustees voted to pay the taxes under protest until a decision could be made about further action. (It was later decided not to take legal action.) Trustees authorized moving toward establishment of the Doctor of Ministry degree program. They voted to enter a new program of health and life insurance for the faculty and staff being offered by Aetna through the SBC Annuity Board. A charge of fifty dollars per quarter was set as an additional fee for non-Baptists.

J. C. Bennett, former president of Union Seminary, New York, was the speaker on October 23 for the first of the lecture-dialogue days set by the faculty. This innovation has brought men and women to the campus from many areas of life for a lecture and then a period of dialogue with students. It has proved to be a fine addition to seminary life and has introduced many interesting personalities to the seminary family.

Carl Bates, Charlotte, North Carolina, a pastor and president of the SBC, was on campus in November for conferences, a chapel sermon, and a dinner with the faculty. Golden Gate had come a long way in the thirteen years since Bates had been the baccalaureate preacher for the graduating class of 1957.

Representatives of all six SBC seminaries met in Memphis

in November to discuss the proposed Doctor of Ministry degree. It was the first meeting attended by the new president of New Orleans Seminary, Grady Cothen. The opening reports from each campus indicated that many of the schools were projecting the degree as an extension of the Master of Divinity curriculum by a minimum of one year. All were to introduce the new program in the fall of 1972.

When the six SBC seminary presidents met in September 1970, the discussions were held in an atmosphere of the possible failure of the SBC to reach its goal in Cooperative Program receipts. This raised doubts about the full funding of the capital needs budget. There were expressions of concern from those whose agencies had no vital interest in the current capital needs program. These wanted every possible dollar in the operations pool—regardless of what happened to capital needs. Golden Gate was in a dilemma, needing operating funds desperately, yet needing capital funds to provide facilities that would aid in attracting more students. One dared not miss any meeting that was held. Eternal vigilance was considered the price of survival.

The seminary presidents and their wives met in Acapulco, Mexico, for their annual workshop December 7. It was the first such meeting for the Cothens. Much time was taken to determine the cost per student on each campus for each of the past two years, on the basis of completed hours of work. Southwestern was the lowest with $1,009, Midwestern the highest with $2,575, and Golden Gate the next highest at $2,053—the average was $1,333. The presidents agreed to base their unified request to the SBC on an allocation increase for the year of near 5 percent. Should this amount be received, it was to be distributed on the same basis as the current year. They agreed that Golden Gate should charge non-Baptists, if the trustees so desired.

The winter quarter opened January 6, 1971 with the inauguration of Dean Gray, who gave the address. Enrollment was increased by fifteen new students. Bids came in the next day for construction of the pedestrian bridge between the student center and dormitory hill. At $35,500, the cost was less than half of the estimate given a dozen years earlier. Eugene Crawford, the architect, had done a good design job. The balance of the contract, above that accumulated from capital funds, was provided by Mr. and Mrs. Guy Rutland, Jr., after whom the bridge was named.

The week of January 26-29 was one of the finest missions emphasis weeks ever held on the Golden Gate campus. It was largely planned and carried out by students. Gale Fults was student chairman. The speakers included J. P. Allen, John Claypool, Bob Tremaine, and Wimpy Smith, who remained on campus to participate in the annual missions conference.

The program theme for the conference was "My Brother's Brother." More than 500 young people attended. Other program personalities included Ed Seabough and "The Good News Singers" of First Southern Baptist Church, San Diego. This was the first conference after the adoption of guidelines by the faculty. Richard Cunningham matured during that year, as he stood firm again and again on the adopted principles. Due to a joint effort by students and faculty, the missions flavor was being restored and, in spite of doubled fees, attendance increased.

The Hester Lectures were given in February by Howard Thurman, dean emeritus, Marsh Chapel, Boston University and former pastor of the Fellowship of All Peoples, San Francisco. He had been designated by *Life* magazine as one of the twelve great preachers of this century. With a fabulous vocabulary and a keen mind, especially adept at getting to the basis of a matter, he was one of the finest preachers ever to grace the chapel at Golden Gate.

Graves missed several of the Thurman lectures because of service on an examination team for the WASC accreditation of Bethany College, Santa Cruz. Much of what he learned from this experience assisted in preparation for the visit of a similar team to Golden Gate in March. He has served since on a dozen or more other teams for similar visits, both for WASC and AATS.

Mention was made earlier of the beginnings of the lecture/

dialogue days for the students. Other personalities who were in dialogue with students during that session included Ernest Guy, professor at UC Medical School; Harry Hollis, Christian Life Commission, SBC; Rueben Scott, Golden Gate alumnus and pastor of a black church in Fresno; and Kay Arvin, attorney, author, and wife of trustee Lester Arvin of Kansas.

The spring quarter began March 24 with an additional 14 students joining the seminary family. In spite of a loss in total enrollment for the year, that made a total of 125 new students, and that pace would produce the 500 enrollment hoped for. During the same week, Graves appeared before the Marin County Tax Appeals Board but his effort was to no avail, and the property tax remained.

The long-awaited week for the joint visit of the teams from WASC and AATS came March 29. Norvell Young, chancellor of Pepperdine University, was chairman. This was one of the first visits conducted as a joint venture between the two agencies and not all policies had been clarified. It was later agreed that a "free standing" institution like Golden Gate was to be visited by a group chaired by an AATS person. In this instance, however, the WASC representative was chairman, and he did a good job. The self-study, prepared under the guidance of W. A. Carleton, was in excellent shape. It prepared the committee so well that they completed their work in one day. Golden Gate was accredited by WASC in addition to the continuation of accreditation by AATS.

The trustees gathered for their 1971 meeting on Tuesday, April 20. Graves reported that the evangelism teams had witnessed the conversion of sixty-eight persons due to their initial efforts, plus scores of other decisions by young people. This effort had added to the spiritual fervor on campus. There was a definite swing back toward this kind of emphasis—as a matter of fact, extremely so in some instances. There were evidences of a resurgence of charismatic emphasis. This was accompanied by expressions of an extreme fundamentalism that left little room for difference on what inspiration of the Bible means and how God inspired it.

The trustees approved a renewal of the effort to raise funds to endow the evangelism chair ($300,000) and to build the library at an estimated cost of $1,700,000. They set out at once to secure funds to pay for library plans for use in the campaign. The budget was adopted with a new base for faculty salaries providing an increase of $500 each for cost of living. The fee for non-Baptists was increased to $100 per term. Graves reported that the imposition of the $50 fee for the current year had not materially affected enrollment of this group but that it should be noted that before school opened in the fall seven had become Baptists.

The March/April, 1971 issue of *Gateway* carried many interesting news items of students and graduates. One story reported the testimony of Herb Hollinger, a Master of Divinity student, given during the missions emphasis week. Herb was working at a service station with a young man to whom he had been witnessing. The night before, near closing time he was pressing the claims of Christ on his friend and sensed considerable interest. Just then his phone rang, and it was his wife, asking him to rush her to the hospital for the delivery of their child. He took his friend along.

> At approximately 2:30 a.m. today, 15 minutes before God blessed my family with a little girl, in the meditation chapel of the hospital, this 18 year old Jewish boy found Jesus Christ. Fifteen minutes later I saw God's hand again breathe the spirit of life into a little girl. . . . I saw the natural birth and the spiritual birth this morning, about seven or eight hours ago. What a fantastic wonderful blessing it has been to me.
>
> Up until August of last year, newspapering was my life. I didn't think there was anything else in the world.
>
> . . . How God, on the morning that I was to give my testimony, brought me a daughter and let me be used of him to bring a young man to Christ is just more than I can grasp. Praise God!

Since that time, Herb has finished his seminary training,

served a church for some years in the Northwest. Then, to no one's surprise, he was chosen and accepted the editorship of the *Northwest Baptist Witness* of the Northwest Baptist Convention early in 1979. God, indeed, works in wondrous ways his wonders to perform.

That same *Gateway* reported that Golden Gate alumnus chaplain Don Crowley had been awarded the Silver Star "for actions that saved the lives of his fellow soldiers during combat in Vietnam." It was announced that some children of seminary students had taken part in a singing group that had recorded the hit song, "Mill Valley, That's My Home." Rita Abrams, a teacher at Strawberry School, wrote the song and enlisted the students to sing it. Nine seminary children participated.

During the SBC meeting in Saint Louis in June, 1971, the alumni association held their luncheon at the Tower Grove Baptist Church. Warren Rust, trustee chairman, was host pastor. Jack Johnson was elected president of the alumni. Following the luncheon, Rust informed Graves that he was leaving the pastorate to join the HMB staff and would have to relinquish his position on the board. Jack Flanders was automatically elevated to the chairmanship. He was a good chairman and very supportive of all the efforts to advance the seminary, materially and in personal encouragement.

Commencement exercises were held June 8. Charles Pitts, president of Dallas Baptist College, was the speaker as sixty-one received their diplomas.

The Warnecke architectural firm was busy developing the preliminary drawings for the proposed new library. Librarian Hicks of Chabot College was consultant. An excellent design for the new building was produced but no funds were allocated for it in the new capital needs program. In the campaign to procure funds privately, the response didn't justify the effort.

The Golden Gate faculty held their August retreat at Hobergs in Lake County. Dr. and Mrs. Buford Nichols, missionaries in residence for the school year, also attended. Dean William C. Brownell of the Education Department,

U.C., Berkeley, was the conference leader. When the September term opened, the enrollment picture was improved even though there was a noticeable drop in non-Baptist and international students.

On the opening day of school, Gray Allison arrived to spend a few hours with Graves. He came to inform him, as he had the other five SBC seminary presidents, that he was founding Mid-America Seminary in Little Rock. He said he was not fighting the seminaries but wanted to provide a school where students could study with faculty members who believed in "the plenary verbal inspiration of the Bible."

J. B. Nichols left the faculty on August 1, 1971, after having served the seminary for twenty years. There had been many changes in his area of responsibility in an effort to find the most effective place of service. The president and dean discussed with him the possibility of finding a place of service elsewhere in the Lord's vineyard. They offered him a year, with full support, to prepare for another position. He expressed agreement in a letter to the president and all seemed to be understood.

Nichols had second thoughts later and decided that he had been mistreated and engaged an attorney. Many conferences between attorneys, seminary administration, and the AAUP were held. The American Association of University Professors assured the seminary that it had acted in a proper manner. There was a small financial settlement and the matter was closed. Those who were associated with Nichols during his years with the seminary have continued to have fellowship with him. There seems to be no way, even among the most dedicated Christian men and women, to work out a necessary shift in personnel without hurt. No one is infallible.

The executive committee of the trustees met in October 12, 1971, with Jack Flanders serving as the chairman. Graves reported the deficit for the year ending July 31 was just short of $12,000. Prospects for avoiding a similar circumstance for the academic year then in progress depended on the support generated for the "Seminary Advance Fund." The committee approved the agreement worked out between the seminary and Nichols and encouraged the president in his search for a supervisor of field experience, so necessary for the new Doctor of Ministry program. He was also authorized to seek ways of producing income through some use of that part of the campus that had been placed on the tax rolls.

The following day was Founders' Day, and Floyd Golden was the speaker. An educator and college president, he had been most helpful as a trustee, serving as chairman of the personnel and curriculum committee, on the building committee, and in many other ways during the first decade the seminary was operated as a SBC institution. As a member of the development council, he continued to be an effective supporter of the institution.

The first of the lecture-dialogues for the session was held in October with James L. Sullivan of the BSSB as leader. Other speakers during the session were: Charles Schulz, creator of "Peanuts"; Thomas Harris, author of *I'm OK—You're OK*; Foy Valentine, SBC Christian Life Commission; Baker James Cauthen, FMB; Claude Welch, Dean, GTU; Langdon Gilkey, University of Chicago; George Ladd, Fuller Seminary; Culbert Rutenber, California Baptist Seminary, Covina; and Bishop C. Kilmer Myers of the Episcopal Diocese of California.

Wayne E. Ward, professor of Christian theology at Southern, was the speaker for the first series of the Derward W. Deere Lectures on biblical studies, using as his theme "A Theology of Hope."

For the 1971-1972 school year, for the first time in Golden Gate Seminary history, a non-Baptist was elected as student body president. He was Gerald Bruce, a Methodist who later became a US Navy Chaplain. Several other non-Baptists have served since.

The SBC presidents met for their workshop at Key Biscayne, Florida, in December, 1971. As usual, their major concern was the allocation and distribution of funds. Their first action was to vote to ask for an allocation of 21 percent of the total SBC Cooperative Program goal for operations in

1973. They voted to accept and distribute an amount as low as $5,988,500 by the same plan as the 1972 allocation. Golden Gate would receive 9.281 percent of the allocation.

They learned in their February meeting that the allocation was to be $6,575,373. Golden Gate thus received an increase of $54,000 over the last full year (1971). That was considerably more than had been anticipated when the trustees met in October.

The Doctor of Ministry degree program was officially announced at Golden Gate in the 1972-1973 catalog. The January/February, 1972 issue of *Gateway* featured pictures and descriptions of the proposed new library. It also carried a disappointing note that the "Seminary Advance Fund" had reached only $4,000 of the $20,000 goal.

On March 31 Gordon Green came to the president's office to discuss his future with the seminary. The president sought to interpret for him the meaning of faculty and trustee actions that related to him. In effect, he told Green that they felt he needed more in-depth studies in biblical and theological disciplines. Assurances concerning tenure would not likely come until that was done. Green returned the next week with his resignation. It was accepted regretfully since he had been doing well in teaching preaching.

The trustees met on April 12, 1972. Graves, then completing twenty years of service at the seminary, recounted some of the highlights of those years. He commented on personalities, programs, and problems. In closing his report, Graves repeated some paragraphs from an outline of the task described in the Projection '74 program five years earlier. He then listed some of the objectives which had been achieved—over two million dollars added in buildings, equipment, and endowment. He went on to challenge them with what could be done:

We can build and equip the new Library/Learning Resources Center! We can endow it and some chairs of instruction, including Evangelism! We can attract a first rate faculty with proper support! Such a dream challenges my own faith, but it has been tested before! This campus was once only a dream—impossible of realization to the mind of any reasonable person, yet here it is—a reality! Because, little by little, it dawned upon some of us that it *could* be so—it *is* so! We planned—told our story—and it became reality! Such bold thinking is the need now! Our present plans do not stretch our faith as much as did plans in '52, '53, or even '55!

. . . We lack the wealth and status of Southern Seminary, the size and reputation of Southwestern, but the short life of Golden Gate has already proven its place in the framework of Southern Baptist life. Its traditions are being formed and its service acknowledged. Her graduates cover the globe! They serve in needy places without prestige or glamour—but serve they do, and God is honoring their labors!

. . . Let us match their faith and tell their story so well that their number will be multiplied over and over again! A Dan Lambert, Glen Allen, Jack Johnson, Steve Carleton, James Williams, Ken Branton, or a Glen Paden is worth all we can do—to name but a few!

. . . These are the intangibles in our record and they are the hope and inspiration for our future! What Baptists do in the West for the generations before us depends more on what Golden Gate does than on any other single move we make! We'll move as Baptists only as far as our leadership takes us!

Dean Gray reported that the accumulative enrollment for the session was up 11 over the previous year. California was now providing in excess of one-third of the students with 121 this year. Texas had fallen far behind with only 33 and Oklahoma 18. Less than 40 percent of students came from Baptist colleges. He reported also that the evangelism teams had been even more effective this session with a record of 163 professions of faith in the first 7 months.

At the trustee-faculty dinner, special recognition was given to Carlyle and Elma Bennett who were to retire August 1. They had given twenty years of outstanding service to the seminary and the Baptist churches of the West. The twentieth anniversary of the Graveses was also noted. To celebrate the occasion, they gave Mrs. Graves flowers and presented President Graves with a plaque and a beautiful, engraved gold watch. Words of appreciation were spoken by Jack Johnson for the alumni, Robert Hughes for the state convention, W. A. Carleton for the faculty and staff, and Purser Hewitt for the trustees.

Actions in the area of personnel include the naming of Carleton as dean emeritus and the election of John Johnson as assistant professor of church music. Johnson, a native of Florida, was graduated from Stetson and Southern Seminary and had taught at Mississippi College. Faculty status was authorized for Paul Hamm upon receipt of his STD.

In a follow up of the action of the trustee executive committee in October, a plan was approved to work with a group of local business men in the development of a portion of the seminary land as income-producing property. They also authorized the construction of six three-bedroom units of student housing. They voted to sell one acre of land, on which the firehouse sits, to the Alto-Richardson Fire District for $26,000. The base faculty salary for the full professor was raised by $750.

A remodeling and improvement program for the existing library space was approved. It provided for the removal of some 25,000 little used volumes to a room in Carroll Hall for storage, office space for the librarian, other offices and conference rooms on the lower floor, and the addition of study carrels in the main reading room. This helped to alleviate the space problem, provided for more efficient operation, and made possible continued growth both in books and enrollment.

The trustees adopted a detailed request for consideration of the capital needs study committee of the SBC Executive Committee. They asked for $1,500,000 toward the new library and equipment; funds for remodeling the existing library space for faculty offices, and additional student housing. The new library was not funded in subsequent SBC action, but, interestingly enough, the $115,000 for reworking the present library space for offices was. In due time, however, that allocation was diverted by the SBC Executive Committee to meet other needs at Golden Gate.

A plan was authorized by the trustees to enlist local support for the seminary through the beginning of a Community Advisory Council. That group was established and has been a most effective medium for public relations efforts in Marin County.

The Hester Lectures on Preaching were delivered by J. P. Allen of the Radio and Television Commission April 25-28, 1972. His theme was "Preaching in the Mass Media Age." Chaplain William Clark of the Air Force Chief Chaplain's office led the chaplains conference.

The 1972 senior class, under the leadership of their president, Ed Collier, gave some $900 toward playground equipment for the nearby Strawberry School. More than one-third of the students in that school were children of seminary families.

The March/April, 1972 *Gateway* carried a lengthy story by James Young on the beginnings of the Baptist Institute founded by Harvey Gilbert in San Rafael in 1859. The building stood at 4th and E. In that same issue of *Gateway*, it was reported that Dr. Samuel Tang (Master of Theology graduate '61) had been inaugurated president of Hong Kong Baptist Seminary.

Commencement exercises were held May 31 with President James Staples of CBC as the speaker.

After attending the SBC in Philadelphia, the Graveses attended the biennial meeting of AATS in Saint Paul, Minnesota. There, again, the big issue was the Doctor of Ministry degree program. A motion to limit the program to candidates having some years of pastoral experience beyond their basic degree almost carried. This action mattered little since those with such experience have been the ones most often attracted to the program. The following week the Southern Association of Baptist Schools and Colleges met at William Jewell College in Missouri and the Graveses were there.

During the summer Graves visited with Paul Turner of

Louisville, Kentucky, about the possibility of his coming to Golden Gate as professor of ministry and director of professional training in the new Doctor of Ministry program. His training and experience seemed to qualify him superbly for such responsibility. Turner later visited with the faculty, who gave a positive recommendation to the trustees. He was elected to the faculty by mail ballot and began serving October 1. Turner was a graduate of Union University in Tennessee and Southern Seminary. He had served as a pastor in Tennessee for more than twenty years before returning to Southern to earn the STD.

Others assisting in the program of instruction at Golden Gate in the fall session 1972 included Nobel Brown in preaching; Fredrick Norwood of Garrett, church history; Tommy Starkes, HMB, Cults and Christian Deviations; and Allen Graves of Southern, who offered a Doctor of Ministry seminar in church administration. Finlay Graham, visiting professor of missions, on leave from Lebanon, and Charles Hancock in pastoral care assisted all year.

Speaker for the first chapel, September 7, 1972, was Ernst Kassemann of Germany. The convocation speaker on October 10, was assistant professor Richard Cunningham. When the trustee executive committee met on October 16, the heart of the president's report dealt again with the basic problem of support and the related question of enrollment.

> We must somehow get the denomination to give thought to the kind of institution we are to be.
>
> If we are to have 250 or 300 students, largely from the West, the Orient and other denominations, then we have library enough and very nearly enough housing. If, on the other hand, we are to be an institution to train an increasingly larger number of workers for the task to be done in the West, our enrollment must be doubled. To get this done demands help from the whole denomination, including other seminaries.
>
> There is a pool of students committed to enter the six seminaries each year. All our efforts and money spent by the

six schools will not change that pool very much. So, what we're doing is trying to get a larger share for each school. The other five are closer to them and therefore much more able to influence students. . . . So, no matter what we do, we must overcome these pressures along with the many other factors of distance, cost, family, and the many unknowns that multiply for such location.

Southwestern, for example, has 99 more students than last year. It is an all time record. They're excited, and well might they be. But what is the value to Southern Baptists that 99 more chose to go there rather than here? What would a hundred more do for us? Some effort has to be made to better distribute the students.

This is not a new problem. I've talked of it for years. But after 20 years, I'm not convinced that anything will be done unless others see the point and seek ways of making a proper balance.

Dean Gray continued discussions along this line in his report and broadened the concern to include other possible areas of the West where assistance should be given. Concerned with continuing education, he reported that the "faculty elected a committee to consider the possibility of seminary education being provided off campus and also on campus but at other times than in the regular schedule." He went on to report, "In the meantime a pilot project has been started in Los Angeles . . . a course on 'What Makes a Church Grow' . . . is being offered as a part of the fall schedule of the Los Angeles Training Center, a new venture of the Los Angeles Southern Baptist Association."

The dean proposed the offering of both basic and Doctor of Ministry courses in Southern California. This introduced the off-campus concept that was developed in the next six months and resulted in the establishment of the Los Angeles Center of Golden Gate.

The trustees approved having a student attend portions of their annual meeting to share student viewpoints. Having already named one lane in village #1 after Basil Lee Lockett, missionary to Africa, they voted to name a second lane after the late George Green, a missionary doctor in Nigeria. In light of a new IRS ruling, the trustees voted to designate up to one-third of a retiree's annuity for housing. They approved a plan whereby the initial planning group for long-range planning should consist of the board chairman and the three board committee chairmen, along with representatives of the administration and faculty.

Founders' Day was held October 17 with G. S. Dobbins as the speaker. He remained on campus for the week, appearing in classes and leading a lecture-dialogue.

The second annual Deere Lectures were delivered by Reginald H. Fuller of Union Theological Seminary, New York, November 7-10. The first presentation of the *Messiah* under the leadership of John Johnson, was given on December 1. He had opened the chorus to people in the community and nearby churches. That increased the size of the choir considerably and added some superb voices. The performance was excellent, good evidence that the music program was again on the move.

When the six SBC seminary presidents met in September 1972, enrollment figures for each seminary revealed that during the previous three years both Southwestern and Midwestern had marked increases while the others were relatively static. Trustee representatives had joined the presidents at a luncheon with the institutions' work group to discuss "the distribution of funds." A special committee was designated by the work group to meet with the presidents and trustee representatives to produce a new formula or some other allocation plan. Franklin Paschall, Preston Callison, and Rheubin South were selected and hope was expressed that they would meet prior to the presidents' workshop. (They met in New Orleans immediately following the workshop.)

The December seminary presidents workshop welcomed Milton Ferguson as the new president of Midwestern. Chairman Cothen said that the SBC Executive Committee was calling for long-range planning to be completed by each school. The SBC assumptions about seminaries were considered. Among these were questions about the offering of advanced degrees and music programs by all SBC seminaries. After much discussion, the presidents produced a list of assumptions which the seminaries should also keep in mind:

> That biblical and theological understanding is essential to the vocational equipment for pastors, etc.; a continuing capital needs program will be provided; the need for seminary trained personnel will increase; there is a growing demand in the number of faculty members; the SBC will continue to provide equitable support for all seminary students in properly authorized programs; the seminaries will continue to provide and enlarge training for nondegree students through on-campus programs; a structured mission program in the SBC will become increasingly dependent upon an enlarged and adequate education program in the seminaries.

As a part of their discussion, the presidents agreed to advise the SBC Executive Committee that its assumptions on theological education needed updating. Such clarification needed to include:

1) Estimated requirements for:
   —Church extension plans
   —Cooperative ministries
   —Missionaries
   —Denominational workers
   —Resignations, retirements, deaths.
2) Answers about:
   —Training of lay leaders
   —Comparative salaries in all agencies
   —Expansion of mission board objectives.

The presidents agreed that Doctor of Ministry students were to be counted as full students for two years in formula discussions. They set Thursday and Friday aside for formula discussions, but these resulted in no conclusions. Friday night, five plans for division were tried, each seeming to produce problems. The BAH formula fully funded would give Golden Gate $729,000. Other proposals would have provided $75,000 less. Late that night the presidents voted to meet Saturday morning from 8:30 to 11. At that meeting they again failed to reach agreement. They adjourned, to meet with the special committee in New Orleans the following week.

On Monday Graves organized the minutes and had copies made for the presidents. The presidents, several trustees (none from Golden Gate), the special committee, plus Porter Routh and Albert McClellan met in New Orleans on Wednesday. After Chairman Cothen explained their efforts in Miami the previous week, the question was raised about the purpose of the meeting. Which was to be central, a long-range plan for distribution or the 1973-1974 year? E. L. Byrd (Southern trustee) moved and Ralph Smith (Southwestern trustee) seconded that "a plan for allocation and distribution of funds for at least a three year span" be discussed. This carried.

After lunch the same two trustees offered a motion that we agree to allocate by a formula. Three voted against (I and the two from Midwestern), and six voted for the motion. Smith moved and McCall seconded that they use the BAH formula for distribution for three years regardless of the amounts allocated. When the vote was taken, three schools voted for the motion and three against. They then voted to refer the matter of the 1973-1974 allocation to the presidents for presentation to the Executive Committee and to confine present discussions to "a three to five year plan." Two voted against (Golden Gate was one of them). I wanted help now.

McCall moved that we ask the institutions work group to recommend to the SBC Executive Committee the employment of consultants to develop another formula for allocation and distribution of SBC funds to the six seminaries with the following understandings:

1) That the rough draft be discussed with the seminaries and the institutions workgroup.
2) That the SBC Executive Committee accept or reject the formula and, if accepted, indicate the period of time it is to be in force and the method of amendment.
3) That the Executive Committee and the six seminaries

operate on the formula or an amended formula until the Executive Committee votes to dispense with it.

4) That the above formula shall not be predicated in any way on the FYE 1974 distribution among the seminaries.

This carried with Brian, chairman of New Orleans trustees abstaining, saying he was not willing to be bound in advance.

In their meeting in January, 1973, the presidents tried again to reach agreement using the BAH formula with a 10 percent shortfall, with all above the 1971 allocation being divided on a percentage basis as if the formula were fully funded. That would produce for Golden Gate $677,745, by far the best funding yet, but there was no agreement. Then a proposal was adopted to take the totals produced by that plan, determine the percent for each school, and divide *whatever* the allocation was by those percentages. Golden Gate would get 9.219 percent of such an allocation.

When they met in February, the presidents learned that the allocation was to be $7,000,000. Golden Gate received its percentage, almost the lowest figure of all the proposals in Miami. In effect, Naylor's suggestion finally prevailed. The effective budget resources for use by Golden Gate was $30,000 below what the trustees considered to be the absolute minimum with which they could operate. The struggle continued.

The winter quarter began at Golden Gate on January 2, 1973, with Roger Skelton as the convocation speaker. The visiting professor of preaching for that quarter was E. H. Westmoreland, retired pastor of South Main Baptist Church, Houston, and longtime chairman of the Golden Gate trustees. He and Mrs. Westmoreland were the first occupants of one of the new three-bedroom units on campus with furnishings from the home of Mrs. Howard V. Platt.

A memorial service was held at Grace Cathedral in San Francisco on January 5, 1973 for the late President Harry S Truman. I was asked to bring the principal address.

World missions week was held in January. Student chairman for the week was Keith Williams. Speakers included Harry Hollis, Christian Life Commission; Mori Hiratoni, pastor, Pearl City, Hawaii; Sid Smith, HMB, Los Angeles; and William O'Brien, FMB. The theme for the missions conference which followed was "Beauty from Ashes," based on Isaiah 61:1-3 and Luke 4:18. More than thirty young people responded to the call for mission volunteers.

The next week brought visitors to the campus that ushered in a new era for Golden Gate Seminary. Guy and Marie Rutland came to spend the week with the Graveses and Westmorelands. Rutland's primary purpose was to discuss the possibility of opening a satellite center in Los Angeles. He had written to me some weeks earlier, making a plea for a study of the matter. At my insistence, Rutland agreed to discuss it further with the administration and faculty.

In the discussions Rutland asked, "What would you do if you had the money to open a center offering courses for credit in the Los Angeles area and what would it cost to do what you suggest?" After hours of discussion, the faculty gathered for a period with Rutland. When a workable program was decided upon, the cost was projected to be $35,000 the first year and perhaps $30,000 each subsequent year. After calculating all the revenue that would be generated by the effort, it was determined that it would cost between $40,000 and $50,000 in extra money to fund the program for two years. Rutland said he would guarantee that amount. This started the wheels turning.

The six directors of missions for the Baptist associations in the Los Angeles area were enlisted to help determine possible response. Their initial report indicated that about 140 pastors had college training but no seminary degree, and that perhaps 100 pastors with seminary degrees might be interested in the Doctor of Ministry program. The mission directors provided a mailing list of 320 pastors and other staff members. A survey sheet and cover letter was sent from the president's office to each of these. More than 90 people replied, with 70 showing interest in seminary level instruction, some for the Doctor of Ministry degree. This was enough to begin the work. In March, Graves and trustee Levi Price met with the six mission directors, and they agreed on a location and related details.

The first of several series of lectures on evangelism provided by the HMB was held in April. Leonard Sanderson, director of evangelism for the Louisiana Baptist Convention, was the speaker. The exciting week included the 1973 meeting of the seminary trustees. Graves reported to the trustees that enrollment for the year was down in spite of the introduction of the Doctor of Ministry program. Of major concern was the lower number of students in the entering class. The elusive enrollment of 500 still seemed far away. He also reported that the development of a part of the campus site into an apartment complex for income had run into difficulty with new regulations, zoning, and so forth, with no promise that it could ever materialize. (It never has.)

The upcoming capital needs program was being developed, and the SBC Executive Committee had employed a consultant to advise them concerning needs on the seminary campuses. The consultant was to visit Golden Gate in May. In speaking of needs to be presented for the trustees to consider, Graves mentioned instructional help in preaching, music, and religious education. He also outlined the proposed program to start work in Southern California. After speaking of personnel needs there, he said, "Our public relations in Southern California need a boost as well. Many Southwestern men send their youth to Texas for training. Some of these are lost to our Western work. Enlistment of Southwestern and other seminary graduates in courses offered by Golden Gate should turn their loyalties this way."

At the faculty-trustee dinner, H. H. Hobbs, former president of the SBC and visiting professor of preaching that quarter, was the speaker. In subsequent sessions, the trustees handled matters related to personnel. One of the difficult assignments in seminary administration is determining if faculty members have the necessary scholarship and teaching skills. At Golden Gate, matters related to tenure were handled by the personnel and instruction committee and then by the full board of trustees.

The trustees approved reinstating the Master of Church Music degree program with the 1974-1975 school year. They voted to begin offering work in the Los Angeles area "when resources are available." The Wednesday noon meal was shared with the new Community Advisory Council. Eighteen men and women from Marin County were present. Jack Flanders was reelected chairman of the trustees and Glen Paden, vice-chairman.

Graves had been in Nashville in March to make the Golden Gate case for capital needs. While there he discussed with John Parrott the possibility of his coming to serve with Golden Gate. Parrott, a native of Arkansas, was a graduate of Ouachita Baptist University and Southern Seminary. He had served churches in Texas and New Mexico. At the time Graves and Parrott met, he was serving in the First Baptist Church of Roswell, New Mexico. The plan was for him to live in Southern California, direct the center there, and commute to the campus to offer courses in preaching, his major field in graduate study. Following the trustees meeting, Graves went back to Nashville and visited with Parrott again, this time talking in more specific terms, since the trustees had acted favorably on the Los Angeles Center.

Graves returned to Mill Valley by way of Los Angeles to look at a proposed office and academic space which Gene England had located for the center. The location was ideal—in Garden Grove, just south of Disneyland, and near several freeways. Graves approved a lease arrangement and then found an apartment just two blocks away for use by visiting seminary personnel. The trustees voted by mail to elect Parrott as director of the Los Angeles center and professor of preaching.

The Hester Lectures on Preaching were delivered by Ernest T. Campbell, pastor, Riverside Church, New York City, May 1-4. Baptist chaplains met during the week, as well. An interested visitor for part of the week was Charles Carter, a banker and lawyer from Jackson, Mississippi, who was being nominated to succeed Purser Hewitt on the board of trustees. His interest showed that he took his trusteeship seriously.

On Thursday and Friday of that week, the SBC Executive Committee's consultant on capital needs was on campus to study building needs. His report was unrealistic in that he looked at the overall space and then made suggestions for the appropriate division of that space, ignoring the fact that space could not be moved from one building to another. That report, given to the capital needs survey committee, effectively ended the chances for a new library at Golden Gate.

The next week Graves and Turner went to Hume Lake for the state pastors' conference. E. V. Hill, pastor of the Mount Zion Baptist Church in south central Los Angeles, was a speaker. He talked with Graves about the proposed center in Southern California. Hill reported that he could enlist 400 black pastors and other preachers for study. That was an exciting prospect. But after months of developing a program, the preachers did not want to enroll. After another five years and some very patient effort on the part of Fred Fisher, classes were developed that involved a sizable group of black pastors.

Graves spent the first of many weeks in Southern California beginning in May. He visited all the pastors' conferences of the associations involved, seeking to enlist students for the classes to be offered that fall. John Parrott was back on campus for a visit with the faculty and administration in May to get the work organized for the center.

During the same time, another SBC effort was being made to work out a formula for allocation of funds to the seminaries. George Kaludis of Vanderbilt University was on campus to take a preliminary look at the Golden Gate situation.

On Sunday, June 3, 1973, Mrs. Graves and I attended a most inspiring service at the First Baptist Church in San Francisco. The pastor, John Streater, a Doctor of Ministry student at Golden Gate, had invited William Tolbert, the president of Liberia and of the Baptist World Alliance, to preach at the eleven o'clock service. He was in the city to address the graduates at San Francisco State University. Tolbert preached before television cameras, reporters, and so forth. Streater then asked if he would assist with the Lord's Supper. It was a thrilling thing to see this head of state functioning in this observance as a Baptist pastor.

The 1973 commencement service was held Friday, June 8, with William Tanner, president of OBU, as the speaker. He and his wife, Ellen, were guests for the student reception the evening before at the president's home. There were seventy-six men and women in the graduating class.

Mrs. Graves and I were in Portland the following week for the SBC annual meeting. Before the Portland meeting, Southern Seminary had announced plans to begin a new institution, the Boyce Bible School, as a subsidiary of the seminary. Allen W. Graves, my brother, was to head the new school. Allen had not discussed this possibility with me before the announcement. In fact, the matter had not been discussed with any of the other seminary presidents. They saw many problems in such a move, not the least of which was competition for students and thus Cooperative Program funds. The move by Southern was diverted, but feelings were hurt and relations strained.

The Golden Gate trustees met during the SBC, and their only action was to confirm the mail ballot election of John Parrott as director of the Los Angeles Center and professor of preaching. Graves's report was largely concerned with launching the work in Southern California.

The week following the Portland Convention, Dr. and Mrs. Dan Boling of Texas were on campus for a visit. He was looking toward possible service on the faculty with an emphasis on youth. The trustees elected Boling, and he began service August 1. Boling, a native of Texas, had been a director of Baptist student work on college campuses in Texas. He was a graduate of Baylor and Southwestern Seminary.

At the installation of the new officers of the Mill Valley Rotary Club on Tuesday evening, June 26, President Graves was made a Paul Harris Fellow. One thousand dollars had been contributed to the Rotary Foundation in his name. It was a surprise to him, but a greatly appreciated expression of their esteem. The Rotary Foundation of Rotary International is an effort to promote goodwill and friendship between the nations of the world through the exchange of students and others for short periods of study. It is supported through the gifts of Rotary clubs or their members. A contribution of one thousand dollars qualifies one to be named a Fellow in honor of the founder of Rotary, Paul Harris.

The September, 1973 term began on the fourth. Several visiting instructors aided in the short courses offered that month. Ted and Sue Lindwall of Panama were the resident missionaries for the session, the first occupants of the new mission residence provided by Mrs. Howard V. Platt.

The Los Angeles center was dedicated September 9, and an open house was held. Several faculty members were present and preached in nearby churches that morning. On the tenth, Graves and Parrott visited the presidents of three seminaries in the area who agreed to provide library service for students at the center. The schools were Fuller Theological Seminary, Southern California School of Theology, and The American Baptist Seminary of the West. Work offered at the center for the fall quarter included two Master of Divinity level courses: preaching taught by Parrott and pastoral care taught by Elder. A Doctor of Ministry seminar in pastoral care was also offered by Elder, who spent two or three days each week in the area.

The fall quarter opened on campus on October 4, with Elder delivering the convocation address. During this service, the first of the Doctor of Ministry candidates received their degrees. They were William East, Charles Hancock, and George Torney.

The September/October, 1973 *Gateway* announced the death on July 22 of B. O. Herring, the second president of Golden Gate. Eakins' first archeological dig at Tell el-Hesi in Israel was also reported in that issue.

When enrollment was completed for the fall quarter, there

was a slight drop on campus, in spite of a significant increase in new students. With the addition of the Los Angeles center, however, the total was well above the fall of 1972. The L. A. center had twelve students in the Doctor of Ministry program and twenty-three in Master of Divinity courses.

The executive committee of the trustees met October 15, 1973. Graves was able to report that the "Advance Funds" portion of the adopted budget of the SBC for the year before had produced $14,305 for Golden Gate, which was available for use that budget year. He urged consideration of development of village #5 on campus into a complex of sixteen or perhaps twenty-four units for student couples without children. The Strawberry Community Advisory Council had tried to eliminate that village from the campus master plan. Twenty-four one-bedroom units were completed for use in the fall of 1977, despite a costly delay caused by the community advisory group.

Graves proposed some changes in capital funds use to remodel the faculty offices and add some new ones. He closed his report with, "Surely, the greatest days at the seminary lie ahead. Reports from colleges, especially in California, indicate that more students are looking our way than ever before. I'm still hopeful of reporting a fall enrollment of 500 before I turn over the reins to another man!" This did not quite come true, though the accumulative figure for the 1976-1977 year did exceed the 500 mark.

The Deere Lectures were delivered October 30-November 2 by John Bright, professor of Old Testament at Union Seminary, Richmond, Virginia. His topic was "Covenant and Promise in Ancient Israel." Since more of his books were used in Old Testament classes at Golden Gate than any other author, he was well known and well received.

The November/December, 1973 *Gateway* announced a $100,000 goal set by the alumni association for their share in the endowment of the chair of evangelism.

There was also a story about the enrollment of Fred Haynes, Jr., in the seminary. He had succeeded his father as pastor of the 120-year-old Third Baptist Church in San

Francisco, the oldest black Baptist church west of Saint Louis. Haynes, Sr., had died after serving the 3,000 member church for more than forty years. The younger Haynes had approached President Graves fifteen years earlier about attending seminary but did not feel that he could get the necessary college work to prepare for advanced theological studies. He decided to enter as a diploma student (a student without a college degree) and was serious about his studies and did well. Unfortunately, before he finished his course, he died of a heart attack as he stood in his pulpit proclaiming the gospel.

When the SBC seminary presidents met in Nashville in September, 1973, the central subject was the request before the SBC for funding from the Baptist Bible Institute in Graceville, Florida. The presidents discussed the issue and agreed that several historic principles needed to be kept in mind:

> 1) The historic differentiation between responsibility for funding seminaries and colleges is a model for consideration of Bible schools. 2) Bible institutes are regional in character and should be funded accordingly. 3) The nature and purpose of work at BBI is different from what is done at seminaries . . . and 4) If BBI is considered a SBC responsibility, then every region in the nation could expect funding for a Bible school.

The presidents agreed further that the seminaries should "do something more" for those without college degrees. They discussed the role of the Seminary Extension Department and how its work could be enhanced and correlated with existing seminary diploma programs. They led discussions on the matter with the institutions' work group and with the Executive Committee staff. Funding for Bible schools seemed imminent unless an effective case could be made for what the seminaries were doing for noncollege students. Graves reported to the seminary presidents on the inauguration of work by Golden Gate at the Los Angeles center. His colleagues indicated considerable interest in the project and gave general approval to it.

When the seminary presidents met for their annual workshop in December, the first decision was to clarify the "decision-making" process: "All decisions require a unanimous vote with the understanding that any president may have recorded in the minutes any reservations concerning a decision as long as he has, in fact, given agreement to the action taken."

Work with noncollege students was discussed further. The presidents agreed that a strong case could be made for a proper funding of present seminaries before additional institutions were considered. They expressed appreciation for the approach being developed by Raymond Rigdon, director of the SED. Each president then reported what his institution was doing for the noncollege group. These reports were given to assist Chairman Graves in his presentation to the institutions work group. The Southern report included an extensive explanation of the efforts to establish the Boyce Bible School.

There was a growing consensus that the seminaries needed to seek to clarify and dramatically reinforce the historical position that every person who feels called of God to the ministry should have opportunity for appropriate study and training. Their discussions led them to adopt the statement that "the six seminaries establish a structure of correlation using the SED as a central office through which there would be made available an opportunity for theological education for every minister in the Southern Baptist Convention who desires such training."

Graves then outlined his plan for presenting the request for allocation for theological education before the program committee in January. He emphasized the difference in costs at SBC seminaries, in all AATS schools, and in comparable denominational schools. SBC seminaries had increased their enrollment by 17 percent in the past three years while most other schools had declined. He planned to illustrate the effective way SBC seminaries utilized funds in support of the instructional program, in contrast to other AATS institutions.

During that final session of the workshop, a decision was needed about the amount of the request to the program committee and the manner of its distribution. The motion that carried was to request 21 percent of the total Cooperative Program amount for operations—up from 20.66 percent. If received, Midwestern, Southwestern, and Southeastern were to have percentage increases to acknowledge the significant increase in enrollment for these three schools. Again, Golden Gate was to have no increase for the new year, unless their portion of the "Advance" funds would give them a boost, which, in fact, it did.

The winter quarter at Golden Gate opened in January with Wayne Peterson bringing the convocation address, entitled, "From Ritual to Righteousness: Internalization in the Old Testament Faith." The world mission emphasis, held January 22-25, had as its theme "We Beheld His Glory" (John 1:14). The missions conference which followed had the theme, "Declare His Glory." Featured speakers were William Hendricks of Southwestern and David Matthews, pastor, Seventh and James Baptist Church, Waco, Texas. More than 300 young people registered for the conference.

The second series of lectures on evangelism was given in April. John Havlik of the HMB was the speaker. The annual chaplains' conference and Hester lectures on preaching came April 23-25. John Claypool, pastor, Broadway Baptist Church, Fort Worth, was the principal speaker on the theme, "The Preaching Event." Claypool was also the speaker for the trustee-faculty dinner.

In his report to the trustees meeting April 23, 1974, Graves brought a rather detailed analysis of the support of the theological education by Southern Baptists and others. He reported that enrollment at Golden Gate has reached 357 for the year, the fifth time for it to be above 350 in the fifteen years on the new campus. With no radical change in totals, the makeup of the student body had changed significantly in the past decade. The number of California students had doubled, to 126 students; Texas was down from fifty-seven to twenty-five students. The far Western states all gained and California Baptist College provided fifty-four students.

In reporting on his selection to serve on a Citizens Advisory Committee of the City-County Planning Council in Marin County, Graves commented on what he had learned. The average Marin County home was now selling for $51,000, and the prospects were that this would be increased to near $90,000 by 1990. (It will be much higher because that figure was reached before 1980.) How could faculty members expect to buy a house in Marin or anywhere in driving distance of the campus? It was evident that more faculty-staff housing on campus was imperative.

In suggesting personnel needs, the president reported that Dean Gray had resigned to become editor of *The California Southern Baptist*, and Charles Hancock had resigned to go to the HMB. Graves proposed that a director of admissions and student affairs might be a proper position to create in light of the imminent retirement of Isma Martin as registrar.

He reported that the Los Angeles center was off to a good start. Financially, of the $70,000 anticipated needs for two years, $46,000 had been received, with little of it coming from Southern California. Most disappointing was the fact that only 20 of the 140 pastors with college degrees and no seminary had taken advantage of the classes offered. Graves proposed that after one more year Parrott move to Mill Valley and a retired or a part-time person give direction locally, with major direction coming from Mill Valley.

Quoting from recent studies, Graves stated that more than 63 percent of SBC pastors had no seminary degree (12 percent had a college degree only; 53 percent had some work beyond this degree). That presented a big challenge to seminaries. The experience in Los Angeles and in other places taught that many people will not take advantage of training, even when it is "put under their noses." But, the experience also taught Southern Baptists to keep trying because the results for those who continue to study are so dramatic that it is worth the effort.

Graves then referred to the Bible school problem before the SBC at that time:

> Bible institutes have risen up all over the Convention. Far too many of these represent some particular theological bias. Others came for other reasons. Much good has and is being done. Largely regional in character, the ground soon gets grazed over and the institute seeks to enlist from distant areas. All such schools seek to upgrade themselves and would ultimately become seminaries if they could. The good that they do attracts support and produces pressure groups to state conventions and the SBC. This goes in cycles and the effort has peaked again.
>
> The seminaries have answered in the past through diploma programs, the SED, and other efforts like the School of Christian Training at New Orleans. Strong leaders are now telling us that current efforts are not enough. . . . the SBC Executive Committee has now asked us . . . "to answer as fully and as completely as possible the request made in September 1973 for present and future plans for all non-degree students."
>
> Our faculty has taken seriously this charge and has been studying the problem in detail.

Graves then turned to the problem of support for theological education. The following table indicates what major denominations were spending per student in 1971-1972.

	Enrollment	Per Student
Episcopal	899	$5,754
Baptist, American	793	4,595
Presbyterian, US	616	4,436
Presbyterian, United	1,901	3,722
Methodist	3,641	3,346
Lutheran, American	1,166	3,251
United Church of Christ	1,170	3,137
Baptist, Southern	4,624	1,645
AATS Avg. (Accredited Schools)		3,043

This variance shows up in what can be paid professors. Methodists, for example with 983 fewer students, use 50 percent more teachers than Southern Baptists and average paying them 20 percent more. The problem becomes acute when seeking to enlist faculty members. At the time Graves gave his report, Golden Gate was seeking to employ a thirty-eight-year-old man who had earned his doctorate ten years earlier. The man was in a successful pastorate at a church with a $500,000 budget. He would have had to take at least a $5,000 annual cut in salary to come to the Golden Gate faculty.

Graves cited the response of men and women who were answering God's call to serve at home and overseas. In the past fifteen years, the major denominations had lost from 22 to 65 percent of their overseas staff of missionaries while Southern Baptists had been gaining 110 percent in theirs. God was blessing our efforts and he will continue to do so, but we must give diligence to do our part in providing for these who heed God's call.

The trustees promptly responded by adopting a resolution, calling for each trustee to give or seek to raise at least $3,000 to help endow the chair of evangelism. They also agreed to step up their efforts in telling the Golden Gate story to people in their own states. They approved the addition of the alumni president and the president of the student body to the long-range planning group.

The trustees took note of the retirement as of July 31, 1974 of Paul Mason, who had served Golden Gate for twenty-two years. He served first as business manager then as superintendent of buildings and grounds. The trustees also approved the concept of adding a director of admissions and student affairs. Max Lyall was elected assistant professor in music. Lyall, a native of Oklahoma and a graduate of OBU, was then serving at Belmont College. Work toward his doctorate from Peabody Conservatory in Baltimore was complete except for his dissertation.

A recommendation from the faculty calling for a correlation of diploma level work on campus with the SED was approved. After completing one year of work through the SED, the student could earn the diploma in an additional year on campus.

Commencement for the 1973-1974 year was held June 7. Dan Grant of Ouachita Baptist University in Arkansas delivered the address. Seventy-nine graduates received degrees or diplomas.

At the trustee meeting in Dallas on June 12, Nobel Brown was elected to the new position of director of admissions and student affairs. Brown, a native of Kentucky, was graduated from North Texas State, Golden Gate, and Southern Seminary (Doctor of Theology). He taught at the Nigerian Seminary for twelve years and more recently had served at the BSSB as an editor. He had served at two different times as visiting professor at Golden Gate. The trustees acknowledged the death of former professor L. A. Brown in Riverside, California, and voted to send a message of sympathy to Mrs. Brown. The financial picture for the SBC seemed to be improving as the year progressed and the advance funds could produce some added support for Golden Gate. In light of this, the trustees voted for their executive committee to consider in October the possibility of increasing faculty compensation.

Following the meetings in Dallas, Graves drove to Atlanta, Georgia, to attend the biennial meeting of the AATS. He was elected vice-president. Wednesday and Thursday, following the AATS gathering, were spent in a conference between SBC seminary faculties and the HMB personnel.

The BWA Youth Congress was held July 31-August 4, 1974 in Portland. Several congress participants visited the Golden Gate campus following that gathering. One of the most interesting groups came from Poland. They spent several days in the San Francisco Bay Area, staying in the homes of Tiburon Baptist Church members. One evening they were casually entertained at the Graves's home. The Ted Lindwalls were there also. Their two teenage sons brought their guitars and musical communication developed. Together, the young people sang familiar hymns in harmony, using Polish, Spanish, and English. God was praised, and hearts were warmed.

One of the most noticeable improvements in the fall program was in the area of church music. With the acceptance of candidates for the Master of Church Music degree, ten enrolled for degrees and seven for diplomas. Professor Johnson introduced a new singing group, "The Winds of Change," styled along popular lines of the day. It called for some rather sophisticated sound equipment, but that was arranged for, and Golden Gate student musicians were being prepared to reach young people through music.

When the trustee executive committee met in October, Graves reported a significant upturn in enrollment with a new record of 335. There were 126 new students aided materially by the Los Angeles center and a class in Seattle. Five students who enrolled at the L. A. center a year earlier had moved to the Mill Valley campus as full-time students. The work in Southern California had been enlarged, with classes in preaching being offered at both San Bernardino and San Diego. Graves, while encouraged with the progress of the center, reported efforts to cut expenses.

The trustees voted an additional 4 percent increase in the faculty salary scale, retroactive to August 1, 1974, due to the receipt of $58,000 in advance funds from the SBC. That meant a total of 10 percent increase in salaries for the year.

Robert L. Cate was elected as associate professor of Old Testament. The other trustees were polled by mail and approved the action. Cate had been pastor of the First Baptist Church, Aiken, South Carolina, for ten years. He graduated from Vanderbilt University and Southern Seminary, with his Doctor of Philosophy degree from the latter school. He accepted the call and began service January 1, 1975.

The trustees revised the long-range planning committee structure and clarified its purpose "to examine and restate the long- and short-range objectives and programs of Golden Gate Seminary in order to make the seminary as effective as possible in the future, including recommendations for action."

Founders' Day was held October 15, 1974 with Jack Manning as the speaker. His theme was "The Life Cycle of a Denomination, Updated." He made special reference to the growth of the Southern Baptist General Convention of California as it related to such a cycle.

October 22-25 was the time set for the Deere Lectures and George Beasley-Murray of Southern Seminary was the lecturer. A Britisher, he had long served as principal of Spurgeon's College in London before joining the faculty at Southern.

When the SBC seminary presidents met for their December, 1974 workshop in Florida, Landrum Leavell, president-elect of New Orleans Seminary, was present. The presidents agreed to again request 21 percent of the SBC operations budget goal to be distributed on the current percent to each seminary. Golden Gate would get 9.095 percent of that. Below 21 percent there was no agreement. The new formula suggestions from George Kaludis arrived and were discussed. There was general agreement that they had little value for solving the problem. They seemed more like aids in program budgeting, which SBC agencies do not do. It was a management document rather than a device for allocation and distribution of funds. Back to the drawing board!

The presidents met with the institutions' work group in Atlanta December 6 to discuss the Kaludis document. Though some favored it, there was general agreement that it had little value. In the February SBC Executive Committee action, Golden Gate was allocated $686,600 with a possibility of $57,300 in advance funds.

The winter quarter opened in January with Clayton Harrop bringing the convocation address. His topic was "A New Look at Mark 13." The world missions week was held in January with Sam Beene as the student chairman. The new musical group, "The Winds of Change," provided the special music.

Visiting speakers for the mission conference that followed were Jesse Fletcher, FMB, and Gene Garrison, pastor of First Baptist Church, Oklahoma City, who spoke to the conference theme, "To The Ends of the Earth." Bob Burroughs and a singing group from Samford University provided special music.

During the week of February 24, Dr. and Mrs. William Schweer were on campus to meet with the faculty. He was then pastor in Palatine, Illinois. Schweer, a graduate of the University of Missouri with the Bachelor of Divinity and Doctor of Theology degrees from Central Seminary, had spent fifteen years as a missionary in Indonesia. As a result of that week came a strong recommendation that Schweer be elected as professor of evangelism.

The third and final series of lectures on evangelism provided by the HMB was held in March. Delos Miles, director of evangelism for South Carolina Baptists, was the speaker. His theme was "Creative Evangelism." Lacking further outside financial support, the faculty voted to combine this emphasis with world missions week and to await leadership of the new evangelism professor for other efforts.

The ATS/WASC visiting team was on campus March 12-13, 1975. The ATS was primarily concerned with the Doctor of Ministry program. The WASC was doing its first rechecking after initial accreditation. The visit went well and accreditation was affirmed by both agencies. Harrop served as chairman of the self-study committee.

The convocation for the spring term was held April 1. Geil Davis spoke on "Perspectives on Change in Christian Education." When the enrollment figure was completed it had gone above 400. It was a thrill for Isma Martin to announce this in her final quarter at Golden Gate as the registrar. She had been with the seminary twenty-two years. The faculty gave her a departing dinner.

The trustees gathered for their annual meeting April 7-9, 1975. After reporting the record enrollment, Graves highlighted the state of the institution by listing the impending changes. In a brief three-year period (1975-1977), the trustees faced the prospect of addition or replacement of a dean, seven faculty members, and a president. The long-range planning committee was at work, and their evaluations would help determine directions. Many needs remained—

housing, the library, equipment, and so forth—all related to enrollment and support.

In speaking of the failure of a new effort at producing a formula to be used in allocating funds, Graves said:

> Obviously, the struggle in Nashville continues and a definitive program of support for Golden Gate is as illusive as ever. Our institutional efforts need to be redefined and supported as one means of improving the resource picture. . . .
>
> There is both an internal and an external need to develop and dramatize an image of Golden Gate that will excite and attract students while at the same time build tone and spirit in the seminary family. It is both a spiritual need and an academic one. . . .
>
> An analysis of what may be reflected in this need reveals several things, none of them bad in themselves, which could explain our plight. Our students are largely from small struggling churches. Survival and not optimistic growth is often the dominant theme. Many come from secular institutions where there is no thought of chapel so they do not associate school and worship. Other denominations are represented in large numbers and perhaps some never identify with us. Many are foreign students and both culturally and in worship patterns, they are confused. Add to this a number of Baptist college graduates who have been somewhat regimented in previous schools. It's a conglomerate that some would say presents an impossible situation.
>
> . . . I've often thought that a "Dean of the Chapel" to lead worship and counsel as a pastor might be the most valuable man to have on campus. President-dean-and-professors-each has his role that is demanding and somewhat clearly defined. This task for a pastor is being performed by all of us and yet perhaps by none of us. . . .
>
> Yes, this is a crisis time for Golden Gate—a time to take note of our place—our alternatives—and our need to choose well our course. We've much to build on. There are exciting needs and themes around which we can rally and

move ahead. I'm as excited about these possibilities as I ever was. Twenty-three years ago I pledged myself and the rest of my life to this institution. I remain committed to that task for these years I remain responsible and then on beyond to the degree that you and my successor may desire my service.

The full board of trustees was called into executive session to discuss the retirement of the president, only two years away. Out of that came several actions:

> That . . . retirement be in 1977 at the close of the school year at age 65 . . . and that the chairman appoint a Committee to recommend appropriate retirement arrangements . . . that the trustees use a system in searching for a new president for a PSC composed solely of trustees and an Advisory Committee composed of faculty, students, alumni, etc. . . . that the committees be appointed soon . . . that the PSC be composed of seven trustees.

Thus a plan was set in motion for an orderly transition from the administration of Graves to that of his successor in the summer of 1977.

Other trustee actions included changing Nobel Brown's title to "Dean of Students and Director of Admissions" and the chief academic officer's title to "Dean of the Faculty." William Schweer was elected associate professor of evangelism, effective May 15, 1975. The 1975-1976 budget was adopted, which included a 5 percent increase in salaries. Plans were authorized for twenty-four, one-bedroom apartments in village #5, with construction to begin when funds are available.

Joe Davis Heacock, retired dean of the School of Religious Education at Southwestern, was a visiting professor during the spring quarter.

Wayne Oates delivered the Hester Lectures April 22-25. His theme was "Preaching as Pastoral Care."

On April 10, the lecture/dialogue leader was Muriel James, who spoke on the use of transactional analysis in pastoral

counseling. Roman Catholic bishop, Joseph McGucken of
San Francisco was presented as the lecture/dialogue leader
on May 15.

The March/April *Gateway* announced that DuBose would
spend the summer in South America, Eakins at another dig
at Tell-el-Hesi, and that Chetti Devasahayam of Serampore
University, Calcutta, India, would be among the visiting
professors for the summer term.

William Hintze, president of Grand Canyon College,
spoke at the commencement exercises held June 6. There
were seventy-two graduates.

When the alumni met during the SBC sessions in Miami in
June, Stanton Nash announced that the drive to endow the
chair of evangelism had reached the half-way mark. Gordon
Robinson, missionary to Nigeria, and Steve Carleton, dean
of CBC, were chosen as the alumni of the year and received
awards. The Robinsons were the missionaries in residence
on the campus for the 1975-1976 year.

The 1975 September term recorded a major increase in the
enrollment of new students. When the fall quarter enrollment was completed in October, there were 146 new students, all but 23 on the Mill Valley campus.

Doctor of Ministry seminars were begun in Phoenix in
September with Professors Turner and Cate participating.
D. C. Martin of Grand Canyon College assisted Cate in Old
Testament.

The Deere Lectures were delivered by Eduard Schweizer,
professor of New Testament at the University of Zurich. His
subject was "From Text to Sermon."

The September/October, 1975 *Gateway* announced that
Dean Emeritus Carleton had suffered a heart attack on
September 29. J. E. Connally, Abilene, Texas, chairman of the
development council, had died August 23. It was also
reported that the presidential search committee (PSC) and
the advisory committee were beginning their labors.

The seminary trustees' executive committee met October
14, 1975. Graves had good news and bad news to report. The

good news was a record enrollment; the bad news, a record deficit. Actually, the deficit was just short of a record $51,000. Increased taxes, now at $31,000 annually, was a major item. With the SBC advance funds of $75,582 received in September, Golden Gate was now in the black. Total receipts for the 1974-1975 year were $766,182 for operations and $100,000 for capital. The music program enrollment had nearly doubled with twenty-six students. W. Morgan Patterson of the Southern Seminary faculty visited that week to be considered as dean of the faculty.

Graves reported on some excitement at the September meeting of the SBC Executive Committee concerning the possible campaign for endowment and capital needs for all six seminaries.

It all began with the reports in the opening session. We all reported a significant increase in new students—Golden Gate's the highest. This set the tone for an optimistic outlook for the denomination with its healthy and growing seminaries. Many felt that the Monday evening in Nashville was the greatest boost ever for the Cooperative Program. Mission boards had to talk about use of all these graduates. A healthy and positive attitude toward the seminaries was apparent for all the following hours of the meeting.

The finance committee of the SBC Executive Committee had before it a request from Southwestern Seminary for permission to launch a $8½ million campaign for Capital funds and endowment. When they recommended this to the full Executive Committee on Wednesday morning, Owen Cooper arose to support the motion as a part of a larger campaign of $60 million for all six seminaries. After about one and one-half hours' discussion the motion carried and a second motion carried to study, before February 1976, the possible enlargement of the campaign. Everyone was supportive.

Southern Seminary plans a campaign in Louisville ending in 1977. Southeastern is studying one. On and on it goes and divided it could be—the rich getting richer and the poor getting poorer. Together it can be done and there would be hope for Golden Gate which has no base to operate from like the other seminaries.

We have sought to gather all of our studies and plans since we moved to this campus for you to look at. We need projects and prices to present to the Executive Committee as our share. This gives me real hope for Capital funds and for endowment.

Graves closed his report by sounding a note of optimism concerning both the faculty and students:

For a long while we were able to secure few experienced men for the faculty. We got promising young men—most of whom have done well. But, coming to us young, they lacked pastoral and other church experience. Now we've seen a turn. In less than five years we have added four with experience from the firing line. These men come at great sacrifice but with deep conviction of God's leadership. And they are making a difference—Parrott, Schweer, Cate, Turner, all good men with years of experience and dedicated lives to serve here.

Now the students. Surely God has blessed Southern Baptists in the response of young people in our churches who are answering his call. Both the number and quality are outstanding this year . . . they are the finest, most responsive group we've had in many years. They came against great odds—shortage of housing, fears about work, etc., but on they came from all across the states and overseas. Housing facilities for families were gone in late July. Twenty-two were written after being approved, telling them that no campus housing was available. Still they came, found apartments, jobs, etc., and are glad to be here.

The trustee executive committee authorized a new study of fringe benefits for faculty and staff, along with the possibility of continuing life and health insurance coverage after retirement. The committee requested the SBC executive committee to reallocate $115,000 of capital funds to renovate executive offices and the president's residence to prepare for a new president and to supplement construction of village #5.

The November/December, 1975 *Gateway* reported actions on the long-range planning committee's plans: $14,000,000 in a capital needs campaign, the selection of a new president, and the immediate beginning of construction of more student housing. The *Gateway* also featured three profiles of students: Guillemo Kratzig from Argentina, a German, who could preach fluently in German, Spanish, and English; Amos Amoresemi of Nigeria, a CBC graduate, a man with a perpetual smile; and Tony Wood, a Colorado journeyman with a mission mind.

On December 5, the *Messiah* was presented by the Oratorio Chorus for the twenty-fifth consecutive year.

Turning again to actions of the SBC seminary presidents, they had continued to study the Kaludis report and its use for the allocation and distribution of funds. Albert McClellan suggested in the June, 1975 meeting of the presidents that they ask Oren Cornett to take the Kaludis material and produce a new formula. They agreed to invite Cornett to present some alternative plans for their consideration at their December meeting.

The Inter-Seminary Conference was held in September, following the meeting of the SBC Executive Committee. This conference was important to the operation of the seminaries but it had been difficult to fit it in with other gatherings in Nashville and have time for proper consideration of all matters. The conference, originally held during the February meetings in Nashville, was moved to January at the time the seminary presidents began presenting their budget requests. Now a time in September was being tried.

One of the issues before the seminaries at this time was the offering of Doctor of Ministry seminars in correlation with other off-campus efforts. At their June meeting, the presidents had voted to "ask our deans and other appropriate personnel to bring to the Inter-Seminary Conference a full statement of all such involvements, including locations, enrollments, supervision and other details."

The deans met at Midwestern Seminary on October 27, 1975. They agreed on the long-term aim of off-campus operations as being:

To provide theological education for men and women preparing for Christian ministry through study centers in strategic metropolitan areas of the SBC.

[The objectives of such efforts were:] To provide (1) components for D.Min. degree programs, (2) CTE programs such as workshops, conferences and seminars, (3) accredited theological studies in certain basic degree programs, and (4) theological studies in the diploma or certificate programs.

The deans expressed the belief that these objectives could be achieved through cooperative efforts. Their document was later refined and presented to the presidents, who never formally approved it. It remained as a suggested guideline for all off-campus efforts.

When the presidents met for their workshop in December, 1975, one session was set aside for Rigdon and consideration of the SED. Several sessions consisted of discussions led by Oren Cornett concerning alternative plans for a formula. It was decided to adopt one of his plans as the new formula. This was a scheme using certain ideas from several previous formulas but arranged in a different fashion. It continued the use of the average cost per student from non-Catholic, accredited seminaries of ATS and was based on enrollment. Benefits were reduced beyond the first 300 students at each school.

To assist in adjusting to the plan, New Orleans was to receive $100,000 off the top, to decrease one-third each year to zero. Golden Gate was given $35,000 to offset "certain unique expenses," with that amount decreasing $5,000 per year for seven years. The presidents then voted to ask the Executive Committee "to provide some procedure to match endowment funds raised by Golden Gate, up to $375,000, to provide funds for these unique expenses." It was envisioned that the resulting $750,000 in endowment would produce earnings to offset those "unique expenses" (taxes and excessive travel costs).

This was the first formula ever to consider Golden Gate's unique expenses because of location. It helped. When the formula was applied to the current ATS average of $3,308 per student, it was agreed to ask for 95 percent of that benchmark, or $3,142 as the base. The total request produced in this manner was $10,324,298, plus the $135,000 adjustment for New Orleans and Golden Gate. When the budget allocations were finally approved, Golden Gate was to receive $1,037,352. This almost matched their request.

The winter quarter opened at Golden Gate with Fred Fisher bringing the convocation address on January 7, 1976. The *Gateway* carried reports on progress in the endowment of the chair of evangelism—"Two Thirds Home." It also announced plans by the alumni to honor the three retiring professors on April 29.

On February 11, Golden Gate was host at a luncheon for directors of state conventions and editors of state papers and their wives. This was in connection with their annual meeting, held this year in San Francisco. It was a happy occasion, affording an opportunity for many of those SBC leaders to visit the campus for the first time. During the meetings of the editors, Graves spoke on the subject, "What I've Seen and What I See," reflecting on his nearly twenty-five years of service as president of Golden Gate.

The lecture/dialogue sessions during the spring of 1976 brought highly qualified and well-known leaders to the campus. Harry Hollis of the Christian Life Commission was the leader February 19. He presented "Christian Alternatives to Contemporary Violence." On March 4, Robert Schuller, pastor of the Garden Grove Community Church, was the speaker. W. D. Davies of England rounded out the series for that school year.

The spring quarter opened with the convocation address by G. Paul Hamm. Enrollment for the year set another record, up 10 percent from the previous session. California was now providing 221 students, up over 400 percent in twenty years. One third of these students were graduates of CBC.

The trustees gathered for their annual meeting April 26-28, 1976. Dean-elect Morgan Patterson was in attendance. The opening session featured the report of the president who began by recalling the peaks and valleys of the year past:

> Sometimes we're up and sometimes down. In the fall we were encouraged with the fine increase in new students, and then with the help of a large advance fund from the Cooperative Program. These came to pick us up from the report of a tremendous deficit for the year ended last July 31 and the apparent deadend in formula planning.
>
> Then just as the Executive Committee of our Board was meeting we were going through a period of re-assessing the Los Angeles Center, giving serious thought to closing it. Simultaneously, we were excited by the possible campaign to raise millions of dollars for capital and endowment. And so it's gone through the year with the months of 1976 continuing the cycle. Great news came in January with a breakthrough in Cooperative Program funds distribution that helps us see light for the first time in years. . . .
>
> Mingled with these concerns has been the on again off again faculty staffing problem. With the addition of Dean Patterson in the fall, we were on our way. We had long lists for every vacancy and real confidence that we would have a full slate by now. Well, we don't have, for there's been many a slip twixt the cup and the lip. . . .
>
> All in all, we feel good about what we bring to you by way of recommendations. These men are tops in every respect to fill the places of need. Others will be added. . . . We'll be ready for another fine entering class and the highest enrollment in our history for 1976-77. . . .
>
> Hopefully, I'll see that elusive 500 figure in the year ahead.

Continuing his report, he commented on the first three years of effort in the Los Angeles center. There had been a nonduplicating enrollment of 108 people for the three years. One who began there had already completed his work and

The 1976-1977 faculty included, top row from left, Max Lyall, Robert L. Cate, G. W. Schweer, Glenn Saul, James Patterson, A. L. Gillespie, Naymond Keathley, and Samuel Tang. Second row from left, Geil Davis, Paul Hamm, Paul Turner, Harold K. Graves, James L. Sullivan (SBC president), W. Morgan Patterson, Nobel Brown, Dan Boling, John Parrott, and Orine Suffern. Front row from left, J. Roger Skelton, Jack Manning, J. Lyn Elder, Clayton K. Harrop, Francis DuBose, J. E. Humphrey, J. Kenneth Eakins, and W. A. Carleton.

two more would graduate in June. Graves proposed that after retirement Fisher give part of his time to that effort in Southern California.

Graves wasn't too encouraged with cooperative efforts in a campaign for endowment and capital needs with the other SBC seminaries. He was pleased to announce a promise of $100,000 a year for five years for endowment from the BSSB. This was in addition to the $375,000 to be provided over seven years from the SBC if matched by seminary efforts.

Acting on various recommendations from their committees, the trustees approved resolutions concerning the imminent retirement of Professors Manning, Insko, and Fisher and voted to give each a parting sum of $50 for each year of service. They adopted a new salary structure that called for a 12½ percent increase in compensation. They confirmed the election (by mail ballot) of Morgan Patterson as dean of academic affairs. They also acknowledged the resignation of Richard Cunningham to join the faculty at Southern Seminary. They approved letters of commendation to him and to the faculty at Southern.

The trustees voted to change the name of the Los Angeles center to the Southern California Center of Golden Gate Baptist Theological Seminary. They approved the establishment of an advisory council for the center to be made up of trustees, area missionaries, and one representative each from the six associations involved. The purpose was to promote the development of the center through (1) publicity, (2) recruitment efforts, (3) providing information, (4) assisting in workshops, conferences, and so forth, (5) assistance in fund raising. Trustee Levi Price was asked to serve as chairman of the council.

Stanton Nash was given the title vice-president for development and Eugene England, vice-president for business affairs. The dean of academic affairs was designated as the one responsible in the absence of the president. Naymond Keathley of Palm Beach Atlantic College was elected as assistant professor of New Testament. A native of Memphis, Keathley held degrees from Baylor and Southern Seminary.

The long-range planning committee reported through chairman Glen Paden, assisted by Lewis Wingo of the Research Services Department of the BSSB. The partial report was received and an extension of two years voted for its work (1978). The trustees voted the continuation of health and life insurance coverage for the faculty and administrative staff after retirement.

They approved the initial report of the retirement arrangements committee concerning provisions for the president when he retired in 1977. Graves was designated as president emeritus and provisions were made for some financial assistance in housing. Retirement activities were to culminate with a luncheon in Kansas City at the SBC on June 15, 1977, honoring president and Mrs. Graves for their twenty-five years of service.

Charles Carter was elected chairman of trustees, succeeding Jack Flanders. Paden was elected as vice-chairman. The possibility of a full board meeting in October was left open due to a possible need to act on a PSC report.

The Hester lectures on preaching were delivered in April by David R. C. Reed, pastor of the Madison Avenue Presbyterian Church of New York City. His theme was, "Sweat, Tears, and Laughter—the Joyful Compulsion of the Pulpit." William Clark, director of the Chaplains Department of the HMB and Robert Hartsell of Southern Seminary led in the Chaplains' Conference.

During that week the alumni gathered in the student center for a dinner to honor the three retiring professors—Manning, Insko, and Fisher. It was a fun-filled evening with expressions of appreciation from those who had benefited most from the services of those faithful teachers.

May 27 was set as a holiday from classes as the seminary family paid respects to the three men. Students hosted a breakfast for them and their wives. A chapel service at ten o'clock was open to the public. Special luncheons were held, and there was an open house during the afternoon in each of their offices. The faculty honored them that evening with a dinner.

Commencement was held on June 5. Jack Flanders, professor of Bible at Baylor University and the retiring chairman of the Golden Gate trustees, was the speaker.

The alumni met in Norfolk, Virginia, June 16, during the sessions of the SBC. It was the first gathering of alumni to be attended by Dean-elect and Mrs. Morgan Patterson. Wayne Eurich was installed as alumni president. Following the Norfolk meetings, the Graveses and Patterson went to Boston for the biennial meeting of ATS. Graves, who had served as vice-president of ATS during the previous two years was program chairman and presided during some of the sessions.

As the summer advanced, anxiety began to build concerning an adequate faculty for the opening of school. James Patterson of Memphis was secured as an instructor in theology. Ronald Bostic did not arrive until August 22 from Fort Worth to serve as instructor in church music. Samuel Tang, president of Hong Kong Baptist Seminary, was visiting professor of Old Testament for the year. Manning continued as part-time teacher of church history.

On Saturday, August 28, word came of the death of E. H. Westmoreland, longtime chairman of the trustees of Golden Gate. His funeral was held in Houston on Monday afternoon with President Graves sharing in the service.

Final clearance came to begin construction of the student housing in village #5 as school was getting underway in the fall. Bids had been opened March 9, but the community leaders had been able to delay permits under new rules on limitation of building, adopted by the county. When the new council on allocation of permits met on September 30, Golden Gate's permits were cleared, but the delay called for a renegotiation with the low bidder and an additional cost of $28,000.

Enrollment figures continued to climb for the 1976 fall program. With 170 new students, including 26 at the Southern California Center, the total came to more than 400.

Morgan Patterson was installed as dean of academic affairs

on October 12, Founders' Day. He spoke on "Theological Education and the Baptist Experience."

The trustee executive committee gathered October 11 and remained for Founders' Day. In his report, Graves stressed the progress made in SBC support. The advance funds had provided $88,733 for Golden Gate in addition to the basic allocation of $686,600, a total of $775,333 for the 1975-1976 year. He spoke of an improvement in the enrollment picture in Southern California under the leadership of Fisher. There were thirty-eight enrolled besides the Doctor of Ministry students. The prospects for growth were the finest ever.

The enrollment of music students was of special interest in light of the resignation of John Johnson during the summer. Enrollment was the largest ever. Ron Bostic was doing a superb job, and morale was high.

The trustees voted a major adjustment in administrative salaries in light of the Oren Cornett report on a study of "A Plan for Compensation Administration at Southern Baptist Theological Seminaries." Golden Gate faculty salaries were above the average with only one other seminary being higher. Administrative salaries, however, according to Cornett, were sadly out of line. Trustee action made the changes retroactive to August 1 to match the faculty salary situation.

In light of rising housing costs, they also adjusted the previously voted annuity for housing for the president upon his retirement. That made it possible for the Graveses to purchase a house just sixteen miles from the campus with confidence that the monthly payments could be met.

Fred Fisher returned to the campus November 2-5 as the speaker for the Deere Lecture series. His theme was "The Holy Spirit and His Work."

Two musical programs were presented to help celebrate the Christmas season. The Concert Choir presented a variety program on December 7, consisting of six numbers from cantatas to hymn arrangements. The Messiah was given by the Oratorio Choir on December 10, the twenty-sixth annual performance of such a seminary group. Jeanne Kostelic, one of the featured soloists, was serving as a visiting instructor in voice.

The SBC seminary presidents had met at Norfolk during the SBC sessions in the summer to give further consideration to a possible cooperative campaign for endowment and capital funds. David Ketchum was present to report his ideas for a feasibility study. It was agreed to hold a one-day meeting in New Orleans on July 2 to discuss this with Ketchum. Trustee board chairmen and the presidents of the six seminaries, plus SBC Executive Committee representatives attended.

The July meeting opened with President Lolley of Southeastern reviewing activities leading up to that day. The Southwestern campaign was approved by the SBC Executive Committee but, in the approval, a unified campaign was proposed and a committee was appointed to study the matter. The presidents then agreed to enter the joint effort if feasible. The special group under the leadership of Owen Cooper met and decided to seek professional help, hence Ketchum. The Southern Seminary campaign was approved and then came the feasibility study for a united effort.

After noting all this, Ketchum commented that a unified campaign seemed impossible and suggested parallel campaigns. The group in New Orleans then agreed:

> That this subcommittee recommend to the SBC seminary campaign subcommittee that a national cooperative campaign be authorized in which the six seminaries conduct parallel campaigns with a national theme. To implement the campaigns, a committee of 15 members, including the six seminary presidents, be named by the SBC president. This committee will determine ground rules, secure necessary consultation, initiate and coordinate the campaign in keeping with Article VI of the Business and Financial Plan of the SBC. Expenses of the campaign will be shared by the six seminaries.

Graves left that meeting with a feeling that no real assistance would be given to assure success of efforts by Golden Gate. Lacking the volume of alumni that the older and larger schools had, located away from the main body of Southern Baptist churches, without some united effort toward raising funds for all schools, not much was likely to be secured for Golden Gate. The months following that July meeting revealed the validity of that judgment.

When the seminary presidents met in Nashville in September, shared information indicated that the three-year average enrollment totaled 6,534. Of these Golden Gate had the smallest average enrollment with 336. At the workshop in late November, they approved a strong resolution to the Executive Committee of the SBC, urging an additional capital needs portion of the Cooperative Program for the next five years. Some SBC agencies, not sharing in such a program, were questioning the need for its continuance. To eliminate it would free more money for operating budgets.

The presidents voted to look with favor on the proposal by Grady Cothen that the BSSB provide funds to add a religious education faculty member at each seminary. Ferguson announced plans for a dinner in Kansas City on Sunday evening, June 12, 1977 for the present seminary presidents and former presidents and their wives.

In considering the request for funds from the SBC, the presidents adopted a new format, produced by Naylor and based on the Cornett proposal, calling for 100 percent funding of the formula. The format was to be presented to the institutions' workgroup in January before using it in the request. When it was presented to them, they endorsed it enthusiastically. The formula application made the calculation of the request very simple. With 336 average enrollment, Golden Gate's request appeared like this for 1977-1978:

$$\text{ATS} \quad \text{Average } \$3,366, \text{ so,}$$
$$300 \times \$3,366 = \$1,009,800$$
$$\underline{36 \times 2,244 = 80,784}$$
$$\$1,090,584$$

When the program committee presented its report to the Executive Committee in February, it called for $1,120,000 for Golden Gate with a possible share in advance funds up to

$58,000. It was an exciting prospect for Graves to view as he contemplated retiring from his post before those funds began arriving at the institution he had served so long. Interestingly enough, this development came during meetings at the Hyatt Regency Hotel where the Executive Committee had to meet due to extreme cold weather in Nashville requiring both the BSSB and the SBC Building to be closed. It was cold outside but warm on the inside as Graves received the news.

The arrangement with the BSSB for the "BSSB Professor" on each campus was made in February with the blessing of the Executive Committee. It was viewed as "a purchased service arrangement" so that the funds could be transferred directly to each institution.

At a meeting of the presidents and the United Campaign Committee, it was agreed that the group should meet again in Atlanta in May. At that time there would be opportunity to consider detailed recommendations to be brought by a subcommittee appointed by Owen Cooper. McCall was asked by the presidents to write a tuition report as requested by the institutions' work group and to forward copies to each. The main thrust of his report was that a tuition charge was not the answer to financial problems at SBC seminaries.

As the winter quarter at Golden Gate began in January, 1977, another Golden Gate alumnus entered upon his duties as a faculty member. He was D. Glenn Saul (Master of Divinity, 1966), who completed his Doctor of Philosophy degree at Southern Seminary in the field of ethics. He had served pastorates in Colorado, California, Kentucky, and more recently at Southside Baptist Church, Tempe, Arizona. His wife, Martha, was also a Golden Gate graduate. She received her Master of Religious Education degree in 1965. Also sharing in the instructional program for two quarters was A. L. Gillespie, Japan.

DuBose brought the convocation address on January 5.

World mission week held January 25-28 had as its theme "Created: . . . to Love God; . . . to Become; . . . for Concern;

. . . and . . . to Touch" were the four individual daily emphases.

The mission conference following featured Charles Baker, pastor, University Baptist Church, Stillwater, Oklahoma, and Joe Ford of the HMB Evangelism Department as speakers and Forbes Woods of the North Phoenix Baptist Church in music. The theme for the conference was "Created for Conquest." A record 820 registered for the weekend, more than 600 of them from off campus. Forty-two students made commitments for careers in mission service and other church related vocations.

The lecture/dialogue speaker for February 3 was James L. Sullivan, president of the SBC. He stressed the opportunity and danger of the visibility of Southern Baptists with the inauguration of Southern Baptist Jimmy Carter as US president. "Communications is perhaps the greatest problem we face," he declared. He stated that we sometimes take our denomination for granted, suggesting that "if each generation does not surpass the one before, we've failed." He went on to say, "We are held together by a rope of sand, yet we're the most closely knit denomination in America. Rope of sand with strength of steel—it's quite a paradox, isn't it?"

Trustee chairman Charles Carter was on campus in early January, conferring with faculty and administration concerning the retirement of Graves and the selection of his successor. During that visit it was agreed that retirement would, indeed, be effective July 31 whether or not a new president had been chosen. The faculty retirement activity committee was to move ahead with specific plans.

The trustees held their annual meeting in April, 1977, the last one for President Graves. In his final report to them, he recounted some history and expressed appreciation for the opportunity afforded him these years, saying in part:

It is with mixed feelings that I bring you this 25th annual report of the President. I bring it with pride for the accomplishments of the year. As a final report from me it will in a sense be a resumé of 25 years of stewardship as your president. In many respects progress has seemed slow at times during these years, but when you look at the long term it is amazing what the Lord has done for us. In material assets alone the balance sheet of 1952 showed $266,000 in fixed assets for a total current assets of $347,000. The February 1, 1977 auditor's interim report shows $8,086,000 and that is at cost. Today's market would perhaps increase that by 75% to 100%. Nearly 4,000 students have enrolled at Golden Gate during this time.

The Seminary is accredited both by the Association of Theological Schools and the Western Association of Schools and Colleges, and we are accepted as full partners in the councils of both agencies. The faculty is recognized in an ever-widening circle. The student body is almost double and the quality represented in preparation for seminary study puts it in a different league from 25 years ago.

Community relations with respect to the business and professional leadership of the area is in good order. The institution is so well established that in many respects it is ready to move into a new phase, possibly including an effort to enlist support for further development.

Many things give me great hope for the future of the seminary. Financial support, while not adequate, is on a sound basis and so geared to the economy and growth that it should continue to assure minimum support. The possibility for improvement in the formula after next year gives hope that it can be even better.

After outlining the needs and prospects of the seminary, Graves proudly announced that enrollment for the year had reached 507:

As I close my report I desire to acknowledge my gratitude to many people who have made this quarter of a century so very significant to me and my family. I'm grateful to the trustees, you and all those who have gone before you. I think of the chairmen—Westmoreland, of sainted memory gone to his reward since last we met; Elwin Skiles, Ernest Guy, Jack Flanders, and now Charles Carter. I think of the

Building Committee—Westmoreland, Rutland, Golden, Raley and Kennedy. I think of the other chairmen of standing committees and I'm grateful to them all. God has been good in providing such a wonderful group of men, preachers and laymen, who have been our official family these years.

I'm grateful for the faculty. Aulick, Deere, Hyatt and Brown have gone to their reward. Some have retired, like Royal, Carleton, Bennett, Pearce, Insko, Manning and Fisher. Staff members too have been real yokefellows. There was Gray, Mason, Beasley, Halvarson and Isma Martin. There remain Nash, England, Patterson and Brown, and a wonderful crew of faculty and staff who contribute to make Golden Gate the institution it is.

. . . I've not felt adequate for the demands often made on me for leadership; yet, somehow God has seen us through and I rejoice. I've never felt better about the future of Golden Gate. God grant that we all may be equal to the challenge of the future.

The faculty-trustee dinner held that evening honored president and Mrs. Graves. Jack Craemer, editor and co-publisher of the *Independent-Journal,* spoke on "Community Salute to President Graves"; Levi Price's topic was "Trustee Commendation to Harold and Frieda Graves"; and Jesse Fletcher's speech was "The Challenging Future."

An oil portrait of Graves, made in 1969, was presented to the Graveses by Guy Rutland. Wayne Barnes presented a diamond Golden Gate ring. Among other guests present was Edward Landels, attorney for the seminary since 1952.

As the trustees met in plenary session the next morning, the PSC could only make a progress report. They approved a change in the constitution and by-laws, replacing the SBC doctrinal statement of 1925 with that adopted by the SBC in 1963 as the guiding instrument for Golden Gate administration and faculty. They voted to name village #5 the I. T. Tichenor Village and the three halls after three other HMB executive secretaries, namely, B. D. Gray, J. B. Lawrence, and Courts Redford.

They elected Ronald Bostic as assistant professor of church

music and advanced several faculty members in rank. They authorized the beginning of seminary level courses to be offered at Grand Canyon College in Phoenix. Approval was also given to the plan for the BSSB to provide funds for an additional professor in religious education. Concern was expressed for faculty housing needs by authorizing a study of ways to give more assistance in this regard.

A challenge gift of $50,000 for the Chair of Evangelism was announced, with the provision that an additional $50,000 be secured and that the chair be named for E. H. Westmoreland. The challenge was accepted and plans made to step up campaign efforts. Cooperation in the joint seminary fund raising campaign was approved. Future details were to be presented at the June 15 meeting in Kansas City.

Recommendations from the retirement and recognition activities committee were approved: to name the administration building the "Harold K. Graves Administration Building"; to give the 1976 automobile being driven by the president to him upon his retirement; and to allow the Graveses to take with them any furnishings in their present home or office they desire to use in their new home. The move was to be cared for by the seminary.

Current trustee officers were reelected and adjournment was voted, to reconvene in Kansas City on June 15 for the purpose of electing a new president for GGBTS.

The following week Clyde Fant brought the H. I. Hester Lectures on Preaching. Fant—former professor at Southwestern, then pastor at Richardson, Texas—spoke on "The Pulpit: The Message Looks for a Medium"; "Post-Reformation: Comets in the Gutenberg Galaxy"; "The American Pulpit: Another Victim of Recent Bad History"; and "The Pulpit Today: Voices in the Wilderness and Echoes."

Retirement plans and activities occupied much of the time and thoughts of administration, students, and faculty throughout May. A Silver Jubilee Celebration was held on campus May 24. It was a holiday from classes and began with a breakfast for the Graveses hosted by the student association. At the ten o'clock chapel service, a representative of each of the twenty-five graduating classes spoke in tribute to President Graves. The faculty established an annual award for outstanding service to the seminary, naming it the Harold K. Graves Award, and gave him a plaque as the first recipient of the award.

The alumni association held a luncheon in the student center, at which time the Graveses were presented a silver tray and made permanent members of the association. That evening the faculty hosted a dinner for President and Mrs. Graves and presented them with an engraved silver tray along with silver goblets to commemorate their years of service.

Commencement exercises were moved to the Veterans Memorial Auditorium at the Marin Civic Center for Saturday June 4. This move had been contemplated for several years since the crowd had necessitated admission by ticket. The faculty requested Graves to bring the principal address for this final graduation of his administration. A large congregation gathered in honor of the ninety graduates. The senior breakfast had been held earlier that morning where Mrs. Graves presented the "Put Hubby Through" certificates to wives of graduates for the final time.

In the commencement address Graves said:

Dean Patterson, colleagues and fellow graduates; I've got my '77 ring, too. Forty years ago, almost to the day, when I sat where most of you in this graduating class sit to receive the first basic degree from the seminary, it was a difficult time in our American history. The "Depression" was still on. The church of which I was the pastor had been running about 180 in Sunday School attendance and raised for all purposes that year $2,456.90. It was the end of the "Dust Bowl" days. In the Southwest they had sent all of their dust back East where I was living and all their people West to California. It was three years later that 13 little congregations in California organized the Southern Baptist Convention of California.

Since that time there has come World War II, the Korean conflict, and Vietnam. In that span of time, man was able to harness the energy in the breaking up of the atom and we have known the atomic bomb and the power that is available for good from the use of atomic energy. Jet airplanes have come. There has developed in that period of time television and radios that are so small that you can wear them in your ear.

There have developed also a great many needs. In contrast to just a few brief years ago when people were telling us there is enough energy in reserves of petroleum in the earth for the foreseeable future for all mankind, now we're being told that unless we are willing to pay the price of conservation we could literally run out of energy in our lifetime. In that brief period of time, we have seen power tools and power equipment developed so that a handful of people can do what thousands were doing just a few brief years ago. . . . Communications have developed so that one laser beam the size of a lead pencil can carry literally millions of simultaneous TV pictures and sound without confusion.

. . . Along with this we have developed the power to literally destroy the civilization that we know in one, or two, or a half dozen atomic blasts. It's into this kind of world that you have been born and for which you have been trained. I've recounted these changes simply to remind you that similar changes, if they keep the pace of the past, will be even more significant in the next 40 years. And it's into this kind of world that you have been called to minister.

What kind of ministry is yours to be? Well, we know it's not going to be a ministry by the book, and I do not mean the Bible, for, hopefully, it will be that kind of ministry. But it's not going to be operating in the kind of world that functions with a set of predigested rules with very clearly drawn guidelines. The simple kind of life, with all of the cultural and community standards clearly drawn so that men can know exactly what they should do under all circumstances, is gone. . . . But the wonderful thing about it is that the principles you have learned, those your father and my father before knew, given by the Lord Jesus Christ, these principles will guide you in the counsel that you give.

The knowledge you've gained in the classroom. . . . and the skills that you have developed in the seminary, will be more important than ever. But these are not enough. They have never been enough for I am quite confident we have been mistaken in equating the spiritual over against the technical skills and knowledge that we have. It's as though somewhere along the way everything is going to be all right if we say the right words, utter the right pious phrases and praise the Lord at the proper time, everything is going to work out. There is no such guarantee. There never has been.

I believe that God is calling you and me to do the very best that we can with the mind and the abilities that we have. We're to act as though all that would be achieved is depend-ent on what we know and what we can do. We acknowledge that, beyond that, the plus is what God can do. It's not an either or; it's not one over against the other; it's not setting up in contrast that if you're spiritual enough all is well. I've heard that across the generations in which I have ministered and it's never spiritual, it's "spurtual." There's something in that inflection that has a particularly pious ring. Well, I am quite sure that the presence of the Holy Spirit is vital in the practice of your faith. . . . He means for us to use all the resources that are about us. Knowledge and skills have never been more important or will they ever be more significant than they are for the practice of your ministry now.

It's not to these, however, that you must ultimately look for success in your ministry. You must rather look to the person that you are, to the spiritual being that you are, to that unique person that you are in terms of your call. . . . If you do not have the sense of call, if you do not have the sense of direction, if you cannot put down a post, lay a foundation and say I am sure I met God here, you cannot survive. You must feel without any searching or reasoning . . . that God was in this place at this time directing you to do this thing.

When I felt God's call to the ministry, I had already finished college. I was a pre-med student with majors in zoology and chemistry and minors in mathematics and physics. I was a thousand miles from home in an audience of five or six thousand people—and I hardly knew a half-dozen of them—when, for the first time, I felt the sense of God saying to me, "I would have you do this for me." I could not believe it. Who was I? How could it possibly be? I couldn't get up before a crowd and speak. I had been singing almost since I could talk, but I couldn't get up and preach. Yet there came this clear sense of what God would have me do. . . .

Now in the some 44 years since that happening there have been a lot of times when I have had to go back to that place. Either God was saying, "You are to preach the gospel," or he had never said anything to me. It was that clear. I couldn't have been more amazed nearly 20 years later when I walked into a room thinking I was meeting a committee but to discover the whole room full of Golden Gate Seminary trustees, and hear their president say, "You've been elected president of Golden Gate Seminary." They hadn't even talked to me about it.

In the days that followed, with conviction I left that pastorate where I suppose we would still be had we not had to come here. That was an experience of God's leadership. Men who had never seen me before got up and said, "Surely God was in this." Here was an institution that needed leadership to accomplish what California Baptists and all Southern Baptists thought it ought to do. Somehow again here was a foundation on which I could stand. Time and time again I had to go back to the foundation that God had called me to this task. As the years rolled by, year by year a group like this would go out. I would go to Japan and there would be graduates, and to Hong Kong and there would be graduates or anywhere in America and there would be graduates. I began to sense that more important than the buildings we were able to build, more important than all the outward physical things that have to be are these.

The monument of the efforts of the faculties across these years and the contributions of Southern Baptists that make possible our campus, our library, and this excellent faculty— the monument to these is the class that sits here today and the some 1,500 or so who have gone before and who even today are scattered all over the earth. They are what make these years worthwhile. You join a great crowd. You're part of a great heritage. It's a heritage made possible by your families that got you here and by this institution and denomination. You're here through the support of the faculty and the trustees. You're a monument to the kind of prayer and financial support that has gone in to make Golden Gate Seminary possible.

I could not possibly be more proud than I am today to stand before you and to say God speed you in your way. May the choicest blessings that are possible be yours as you render the kind of service that would honor the God who called you.

The March/April issue of *Gateway* had featured in pictures and outline story the Graves's years at Golden Gate. Faye Brown wrote several articles concerning the Graveses that appeared in various publications, including a special brochure with many pictures and articles from other authors as well.

The climax of the Silver Jubilee celebration and retirement came at the alumni/trustee sponsored luncheon on June 15. It was held in the grand ballroom of the Radisson/Muehlebach Hotel in Kansas City. The head table was graced with SBC President and Mrs. James L. Sullivan, Dr. and Mrs. Porter Routh, Dr. and Mrs. Grady Cothen, Mr. and Mrs. Owen Cooper, Mr. and Mrs. Guy Rutland, Dr. and Mrs. Floyd Golden, Dr. and Mrs. Millard Berquist, and alumni president and Mrs. Wayne Eurich, Jesse Fletcher, Glen Paden and trustee chairman, Charles Carter, who presided. Each of the men and Allen Graves made comments or presentations.

Seated at a table of honor were the Graveses' kin: Mrs. Homer (Nancy) McLaughlin, their daughter (their son, Harold K., Jr., was unable to attend), Dr. and Mrs. Allen W. Graves, Dr. James H. Graves, Dr. Rachel Graves Brake, William Arnold Jr., brother-in-law, and his daughter, Mrs. Bart (Judy) Huemmer. In attendance also were those representing SBC agencies, state conventions, colleges, the faculty, trustees, students, hundreds of alumni, and many other friends. It was a happy affair, celebrating the accomplishments of twenty-five years of joint efforts to build an effective institution for theological education in California.

Immediately following the luncheon, the trustees met as agreed. It had been planned as another happy occasion when action could be taken to place a new president in charge at Golden Gate. Such was not the case, however. PSC chairman Jack Pollard had to announce that they had hoped to present the name of William M. Pinson, Jr., but could not. Pinson had called the night before to say that he could not accept a call to go to Golden Gate at this time. Pollard "assured the board that the PSC would continue to work diligently to find the best possible president."

The trustees voted to elect David Roberts as assistant professor of church history. They also approved an agreement with Graves to write a history of the seminary. After words of appreciation were spoken commending Nash and England for their efforts in preparing for the Silver Jubilee luncheon and some words from retiring President Graves, the meeting adjourned, subject to call—hopefully soon, to elect a new president.

Following the Kansas City meetings, many felt that Pinson was just the man for the post and were not willing to let the matter rest. Among these was Glen Paden who did something about it. He wrote a letter to Pinson, indicating that the door was still open. Pinson responded to this letter by indicating a growing interest. Out of this exchange came further contacts by members of the PSC and ultimate agreement to reissue the invitation and Pinson's affirmative response.

Chairman Carter called for a special trustee meeting at the San Francisco Airport Hilton Hotel July 25 at two PM. Even on such short notice, twenty-three trustees were able to attend. Also present were Dr. and Mrs. Pinson and their daughter, Meredith, President Graves, Dean Patterson, Vice-Presidents Nash and England, and Dean Brown.

PSC Chairman Pollard presented William M. Pinson, Jr., pastor, First Baptist Church, Wichita Falls, Texas, former professor at Southwestern Seminary, as the committee's nominee for the presidency of Golden Gate Baptist Theological Seminary. Pinson was asked to share with the trustees his pilgrimage in coming to this moment. Pinson took several minutes to describe the struggle through which he had gone in recent weeks. Following his remarks the trustees were invited to ask questions, and several did. When all had been asked and answered, the trustees, in executive session, acted: "Les Arvin moved that Dr. Pinson be called to be president of GGBTS upon the retirement of Dr. Harold K. Graves on July 31, 1977, in accordance with and on the conditions set forth in the report of the PSC." The motion was seconded by Carl Scott and carried unanimously.

The minutes further record: "Later in the evening Dr. Pinson accepted the Trustees' call at a dinner meeting with Trustees and members of the faculty and administrative staff, including Dr. and Mrs. Graves, after which the meeting adjourned."

The following Sunday was July 31, the final day of President Graves's official connection with Golden Gate Seminary. He spent it as a supply pastor at the First Southern Baptist Church of South San Francisco. Following the evening service, he and Mrs. Graves drove to Santa Rosa to spend the waning hours of the day with their daughter and her family. It had been a truly eventful period, these twenty-five years, two months and eighteen days, since, in far away Miami, Florida, they had been charged with charting the course of Golden Gate Seminary. Mistakes and misjudgments forgotten, there remained the joy, pride, and sense of satisfaction with what God had wrought.

We had occupied our new home on July 22. We were happy in the midst of making it truly ours by refurbishing it to our tastes. After thirty-six years of life in parsonages and official presidential residences, we had our own home for the first time.

President Pinson assumed responsibility for Golden Gate Seminary on August 15 and soon had his family and furnishings in the president's home.

Epilogue

Thus the first one third of a century for Golden Gate Baptist Theological Seminary came to a close and she entered the second third under the dynamic leadership of a new president, William M. Pinson, Jr. His service was to last for only five years, however. Though few in number, these years have been very significant in the life of the seminary. Growth is the most descriptive word to be used in characterizing them. It has been growth in enrollment, in support, in facilities, in programs, and in outreach.

From an enrollment of just over 500 during the 1976-1977 year, a peak of 929 has been reached. This increase has come both on the Mill Valley campus and in the satellite centers— the one in Southern California and new ones in Portland, Oregon, and Salt Lake City, Utah.

The endowment of the seminary has more than doubled. This, along with a marked increase in denominational support through the Cooperative Program has enabled the institution to expand its programs and enlarge the faculty and staff. Additional financial support has made possible expanded and refurbished facilities.

New programs have included family enrichment, a continuing education emphasis, a counseling center, intercessory prayer ministry, an expanded Church Growth Institute, L.I.F.E. revival teams, and a multiethnic theological training program (in cooperation with the HMB). A new Doctor of Philosophy degree program has been accredited by the Western Association of Schools and Colleges to begin in the fall of 1982. The Doctor of Ministry program has been restructured to make it more suited to contemporary ministry situations.

The major addition to the physical plant came with the dedication of the new $4.5 million library in October, 1981. With more than 100,000 volumes in its holdings, along with auxiliary materials, and with room and facilities for use by students and faculty, the library is the answer to a long-held dream and an inspiration just to visit. Adequate space has been provided and preparations made for expansion for multimedia production and use. Direct connections with other libraries will in the future make possible the recovery of almost any information available anywhere in the world.

With the moving of the library materials into the new building, space was released for the development of an excellent faculty center with support services. Other administration and service facilities are also being refurbished and enlarged. These include additional classrooms, an enlarged post office, more book store space, additional practice rooms for music and quarters for the counseling center and prayer ministry.

Student family housing has been improved with the purchase of a thirty-two-unit apartment complex near the seminary campus. Further development in this area and in faculty support will be provided through an expanded master plan for the campus which provides for some land use that would produce supplemental income.

President Pinson left the Seminary in July to assume his new role as executive director of the Texas Baptist Convention. In departing he said, "The future of the seminary is bright. . . . I believe God will not only provide just the right person for president but also for the other needs of the seminary. I look forward to the continued progress of Golden Gate and will pray for those involved."

In a called meeting of seminary trustees on February 8, 1983, Franklin D. Pollard, pastor of First Baptist Church of San Antonio, Texas, was elected president of Golden Gate Baptist Theological Seminary. Frank Pollard has served as host and Bible teacher for "At Home with the Bible" since this popular television program began in 1978 and as preacher for the worldwide "Baptist Hour" radio program since 1976. Pollard was selected by *Time* magazine in 1979 as one of the seven most outstanding Protestant preachers in America.

Concerning his election, Pollard commented, "I am a mystic about following God's will. I genuinely feel this is God's place of ministry for me." He continued, "I am thrilled about the prospect of helping other ministers prepare for ministry. The seminary is much more than a graduate school of theology. Our primary function is the practical preparation of men and women for ministry."

The future of Golden Gate continues to be promising. With gratitude to God for his guidance to this point, the seminary family looks ahead with trust in his leadership for challenges to grow, learn, minister, and serve. May God grant the sensitivity to recognize the opportunities as they occur and the necessary strength to match each challenge.

Appendix A:
Trustees

Appendix B:
Faculty

Teachers from 1945 to 1952 sometimes designated Instructor or Professor

Adams, Louis R.
Averett, W. M.
Brown, L. A.
Brown, Mrs. L. A.
Dawes, J. V.
Deere, D. W.
Faulkner, G. Dallas
Garrett, Clyde J.
Garrett, Dorothy D.
Hanna, Louis V.
Harper, Landon
Hodges, Isam
Ibsen, H. P.
Johnson, Perry
Kincannon, J. B.
Langford, Lila Fae
Langford, W. E.
Maxwell, Mrs. C. B.
Nichols, J. B.
Powell, F. M.
Sanders, Leslie E.
Stagg, H. H.
Walker, James
Aulick, A. L.
Bronson, B. B.
Browne, Miriam
Childress, Mrs. E. Hardy
Daugherty, E. K.
Dodson, F. G.
Gerbracht, NeVoy A.
Hall, Darlene
Halvarson, Carl
Halvarson, Ruth
Herring, B. O.
Hyatt, A. J.
Insko, C. A.

Kendall, George
Kinlaw, Howard M.
Manning, Jack
Martin, Wilbur
McClain, Joseph
Posey, S. G.
Royal, Claudia
Royal, R. F.
Townsend, Edward

Those chosen by trustees elected by the SBC 1950 and following:

Appleby, David—1956-60
Aulick, A. L.—1948-53
Bennett, Carlyle—1953-72
Bennett, Elma (Ins. 1953-72)
Boling, Daniel—1973-
Bostic, Ronald D.—1976-78
Bradley, J. C.—1959-61
Brown, L. A.—1950-67
Brown, Mrs. L. A. (Ins. 1950-51)
Brown, Nobel—1974-79
Carleton, W. A.—1953-70
Cate, Robert L.—1975-
Cunningham, Richard—1967-76
Davis, Geil—1957-78
Deere, D. W.—1950-68
Dobbins, G. S.—1956-66
Dodson, F. G.—1949-52
DuBose, Francis—1966-
Eakins, J. Kenneth—1970-
Elder, J. Lyn—1954-
Fisher, Fred L.—1952-76
Gray, Elmer L.—1959-67; 1970-74
Green, Gordon—1970-72
Hamm, Paul—1967-79
Hancock, Charles (Ins. 1967-74)
Harrop, Clayton K.—1955-

Humphrey, Edward—1967-
Hyatt, A. J.—1950-51; 1954-67
Insko, C. Arthur—1950-76
Johnson, John—1972-76
Keathley, Naymond H.—1976-
Kincannon, J. B.—1947-53
Lyall, Max D.—1974-
Manning, Jack W.—1950-76
Martin, Wilbur—1949-56
McClain, Joseph T.—1950-52
McClendon, James—1954-66
Moore, LeRoy (Ins. 1964-66)
Nichols, J. B.—1951-71
Parrott, John—1973-79
Patterson, James (Ins. 1976-77)

Patterson, W. Morgan—1976-
Pearce, J. Winston—1961-70
Peterson, Wayne—1969-74
Powell, F. M.—1949-52
Royal, Claudia—1950-57
Royal, R. F.—1946-68
Schweer, William—1975-
Skelton, J. Roger—1967-
Suffern, Orine (Ins. 1956-   )
Tilden, Philip N. (Ins. 1956-61)
Townsend, R. Edward—1950-51
Turner, Paul—1972-
Walker, James—1951-52
Yates, Kyle Jr.—1953-69

Appendix C:
Development Council

Arvin, Lester
Baker, John J.
Bascom, Clifford C.
Bayless, O. L.
Coffey, Charles C.
Connally, J. E.
Connally, Mrs. J. E. (Virginia)
Dayvault, Bernard
Flanders, H. J.
Green, Charles
Gregory, James
Golden, Floyd D.
Guy, Ernest P.
Haldeman, John H.
Harwell, C. F.
Hewitt, Purser
Hooper, Herbert
Horn, H. B.

Hudgins, W. Douglas
Johnston, Preston
Johnstone, Carl
Jones, Reginald
Koonce, John
Maddox, Dan
Mitchell, George
Moore, J. Carey
Morgan, Royce C.
Pitts, Frank
Roberts, M. V.
Rutland, Guy Sr.
Rutland, Guy Jr.
Sanders, E. N.
Westmoreland, E. H.
Wheat, Jerry
Wood, Cecil
York, Don

Appendix D:
Community Advisory Council

Andresen, Robert H.
Arntz, Eugene S.
Barron, Roy L.
Berry, Lowell
Bianchi, Albert
Bucknum, Jack E.
Castro, Walter R. Jr.
Chapman, Irving
Collins, Mrs. Jane
Craemer, Jack
Crowell, Mrs. Marilyn
Egger, J. E.
Fogarty, Frank T.
Hollis, Virgil
Hoyt, Lawrence E.

Leininger, C. Ray
MacDonald, D. Ken Jr.
MacPhee, Chester R.
Mauzy, Byron
Murray, William Jr.
Myers, Wallace S.
Neal, Charles E.
Overstreet, Robert K.
Peck, Leonard
Quilici, Al
Schultz, Mrs. Barbara
Seymour, Kent O.
Silvernale, Rex T.
Walker, Carroll

Index